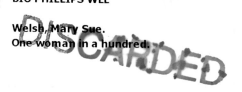

# ONE WOMAN
## IN A HUNDRED

MUSIC IN AMERICAN LIFE

*A list of books in the series appears
at the end of this book.*

# ONE WOMAN
# IN A HUNDRED

# EDNA PHILLIPS
## AND THE PHILADELPHIA ORCHESTRA

## MARY SUE WELSH

UNIVERSITY OF ILLINOIS PRESS

URBANA, CHICAGO, AND SPRINGFIELD

Frontispiece: *The Harpist*, portrait
of Edna Phillips by Arthur B. Carles.
(Courtesy of Mr. and Mrs. James J. Maguire).

Library of Congress Cataloging-in-Publication Data
Welsh, Mary Sue.
One woman in a hundred : Edna Phillips
and the Philadelphia Orchestra / Mary Sue Welsh.
p.   cm. — (Music in American life)
Includes bibliographical references and index.
ISBN 978-0-252-03736-8 (cloth : alk. paper)
ISBN 978-0-252-09454-5 (e-book)
1. Phillips, Edna, 1907–2003. 2. Philadelphia Orchestra—History.
3. Harpists—United States—Biography.
I. Title.
ML419.P486W45     2013
787.9'5092—dc23 [B]     2012023403

*For Richard*
*with unending*
*love and gratitude*

"Miss Edna Phillips, first harpist of the Philadelphia Orchestra, is one woman in a hundred—or at least she is when the serried ranks of Stokowski's men are drawn up before the public's gaze on the stage of the Academy of Music."

—*Philadelphia Record,* February 26, 1933

———•———

I do not like to see women in orchestras. As an orchestra member once said to me, "If she's attractive, I can't play with her. If she's not, I won't."

—Sir Thomas Beecham, 1879–1961

When I think of women as I see them in the musical world, I realize what a splendid power we are letting go waste.

—Leopold Stokowski, 1882–1977

# CONTENTS

*Illustrations follow page 140*

# FOREWORD

"The men," was the term symphony orchestra administrators used well into the last quarter of the twentieth century to describe their players. The term came from a crystallized cultural tradition that made men musicians and women teachers and amateurs. Breaking that mold fell to harpist Edna Phillips, a small-town girl with steely nerves, just out of the Curtis Institute of Music, who became the first woman principal player in a major U.S. orchestra.

She was the choice of Leopold Stokowski, the Philadelphia Orchestra's music director, a conductor who liked to jar his audiences. Even Stokowski, the brash iconoclast, was ambivalent about what he had done. He seated Phillips proudly on the stage apron for all to see, but also couldn't resist poking fun at her in rehearsal with sexist comments.

Newspapers, at the time, called her "plucky," a term both admiring but subtly deprecating. She faced them all down to open the world of symphonic music to women. Her life in music was like no other, for her achievements were both artistic and personal, musical and intensely practical. Her legacy is celebrated in every orchestra whose members are no longer called "the men."

*Daniel Webster*

# PREFACE AND ACKNOWLEDGMENTS

"Today girls' eyes glaze over when they hear about my being the first woman in the Philadelphia Orchestra, but they wouldn't be so blasé if they knew what it was *really* like," Edna Phillips said with a wry laugh in 1990, when she asked me to work with her on the writing of her memoir. By that time, I had known Edna for ten years, first in my role as executive director of the Basically Bach Festival of Philadelphia (now known as the Bach Festival of Philadelphia), where she chaired the board of directors, and then as a friend. Long fascinated by the vivid stories Edna told of her tenure in the orchestra, I happily agreed to help her with the project, not realizing how long-term my commitment would become.

As we settled into a routine of weekly interviews that lasted over a year, I soon discovered that Edna didn't intend to confine her memoir to her experience as a female pioneer in an exclusively male world. Yes, she wanted to talk about the obstacles she faced and explain the strategies she developed to overcome them, but she also had another story she wanted to tell—that of the Philadelphia Orchestra she knew as a member from 1930 to 1946 and the conductor she credited with making it so extraordinary, Leopold Stokowski.

"I was born in 1907," she told me, "and when I was young, everybody talked about the great opera singers. The tenors and sopranos of the Met were the reigning deities of the day." But as the twentieth century advanced into its teens and beyond, she explained, that began to change, and the major U.S. orchestras rose to worldwide prominence under the leadership of a handful of extraordinary conductors. Then it was the conductors who began to attract widespread attention and adulation.

"This is not a sentimental reminiscence," she insisted. "These conductors were the builders of the orchestras they presided over. The great American orchestras grew in their images, and they became the new stars in the firmament."

Among the conductors Edna included in her pantheon of musical giants were Serge Koussevitzky and Arturo Toscanini for developing the Boston Symphony and the New York Philharmonic into the splendid modern orchestras each became under their respective leaderships. But, of course, the maestro Edna knew best, the one she watched and learned from for eleven years was Leopold Stokowski. Her regard for him was immense, just as it was among her colleagues. "There was something magical about his conducting and his command of the orchestra," she said. She wanted her book to speak of the joy she felt at being part of the glorious music the orchestra made under Stokowski and to show what was so compelling and effective about his leadership.

Of course, not every moment Edna remembered was joyous. As much as she honored the maestro, she wasn't shy about pointing out instances when he tormented his players with his relentless, even ruthless, search for perfection, his impetuous demands, and his tendency to use his players as fodder for his humor. She often referred to the general tension the players felt in the highly charged atmosphere of a world-class orchestra that was expected to perform at the highest level at all times. She also wanted to acknowledge her colleagues, many of whom were extraordinary virtuosos, and convey a sense of what it was like to go forward with them as Eugene Ormandy, a fine conductor but of a different caliber than Stokowski, took over the reins of the orchestra.

Holding her own in the Philadelphia Orchestra as its first woman and as a young player straight out of the conservatory presented huge challenges for Edna, but she was blessed with abundant musical talent and a quick wit, which helped her survive and thrive in the face of the complexities that confronted her. Fascinated by everything that surrounded her in the orchestra, she loved to talk about what she observed, frankly noting the triumphs of the musicians she worked with as well as their peccadilloes and near disasters. It was great fun to interview her. She also sent me out to interview former colleagues and recommended that I visit the Salzedo Harp Colony in Camden, Maine, to talk to her good friend Alice Chalifoux, a visit I thoroughly enjoyed. Then, sadly, before I finished writing the memoir she envisioned, Edna had several strokes and was not able to continue work on the project. At that point, I put it aside, thinking I should not write her memoir without her active oversight.

But her stories kept tugging at me. They were too important not to be told. Finally, I decided to take up the project again, this time as biographer, instead of cowriter. Using the information Edna had given me in our interviews as the core of this book, I did extensive research into the world Edna had laid out for me. My research confirmed what I had known all along: Not only was Edna a gifted musician with a spirit strong enough to overcome great challenges, she was also a perceptive and accurate chronicler of an important era in the history of orchestral music.

Edna was a vivid talker. She was charming, frank, funny, emphatic, and often irreverent. Not wanting to lose the vitality of her speech, I've used her expressions throughout the book in direct quotations and in running text to convey the flavor of her lively personality. Since it would interrupt the flow of the narrative to attach an attribution to each of those phrases, I've let many of them stand alone in quotation marks, so the reader should understand any unattributed quotations to be her words. All of the episodes in the book that are told from Edna's point of view are taken from the interviews we recorded and the many discussions we had over the years. In fact, the entire book represents Edna's point of view as closely as I could ascertain it. It is her book, and I have tried throughout not to insert my opinion. My job was to listen to her remembrances, check their accuracy through research, and assemble them in a narrative that I hope does justice to the great value of her life and her achievements.

When Edna spoke of her fellow musicians, she invariably called them by their surnames, and that is what I have done for her in this book. Just as she referred to her colleagues as "Tabuteau" or "Kincaid" or "Salzedo," she is called "Phillips" when she is spoken of in a professional sense. Finally, Edna lived from 1907 until 2003, but she wanted the focus of her memoir to be on her life in the Philadelphia Orchestra, and that's where the focus of this biography lies.

———•———

So many people provided support throughout the long gestation of this project that I may not be able to acknowledge them all, but I am deeply grateful for all the help I received. Foremost among those I wish to thank are Edna's children, Joan Rosenbaum Solaun and David Hugh Rosenbaum, who wanted very much to have their mother's story told. They've been tireless in offering suggestions, locating information, and sharing photographs that have added immeasurably to the book. Rowena Rosenbaum, Hugh's wife, helped with copyediting early on, and

Joan's daughter, Emma Solaun, provided legal advice. Rosamond Bernier, Edna's stepdaughter, and Rosamond's stepson, Olivier Bernier, were also helpful in the early stages of the project.

My special gratitude goes to those who read the manuscript and commented on it. Their suggestions and corrections have proved invaluable. Two of those readers carried their support even further by contributing sections to the book. Daniel Webster, retired music critic for the *Philadelphia Inquirer*, wrote a foreword that sums up in a few excellently chosen words what I took a whole book to convey, and Clinton Nieweg, retired chief librarian of the Philadelphia Orchestra, compiled the appendix, which lists the compositions for the harp commissioned by Edna Phillips and her husband Sam Rosenbaum. Others who kindly offered important advice and support were Laila Storch, Marc Mostovoy, Harold I. Gullan, Naomi Graffman, Diana Burgwyn, Robert Capanna, Barrie Trimingham, Linda Baldwin, Daniel Dannenbaum and Kate Hall, Nathan Sivin, Phyllis White Rodriguez-Peralta, Debra Lew Harder, Kathleen A. Lynch, George and Joan Forde, Franny Maguire, Jerry and Penny Martindale, Angela Archer, and Carol Fitzgerald.

Edna's fellow harpists supported her book from the beginning. The current principal harpist of the Philadelphia Orchestra, Elizabeth Hainen, has been unflaggingly helpful, as have Ann Hobson Pilot, retired principal harp of the Boston Symphony, and Judy Loman, retired principal harp of the Toronto Symphony. One of Edna's devoted students, Hulda Kreiss, stepped up immediately to offer a grant for the project, and for that I am most grateful. Mary Coppa, Ruth Papalia, and Patricia Pence-Sokoloff also spoke glowingly about their former teacher. Alison Simpson, as president the Philadelphia chapter of the American Harp Society, tried hard to find a home for the project. Jane B. Weidensaul, former editor of the *American Harp Journal*, shared important information with me when I worked with her on "A Tribute to Edna Phillips" for her magazine in 1996, and current editor Elizabeth Huntley also helped me find facts and articles that I needed.

Unfortunately, many of Edna's colleagues from the orchestra and other of her associates who shared their memories with me have since passed away. I am thankful that I was able to talk to Marilyn Costello, Lynne Wainwright, Sol Schoenbach, David Madison, Alice Chalifoux, Boyd Barnard, Ray Green, Irene and Billy Wolf, Vera Bruestle, and John Francis Marion, for they gave me many insights into Edna as a person and a musician.

Without the happy chance of Oxford University Press executive editor Nancy Toff hearing me talk about my manuscript at a harp conference and taking the trouble to mention it to Laurie Matheson, University of Illinois Press acquisitions editor, *One Woman in a Hundred* might never have found such an appropriate publisher. I am deeply grateful to both editors for seeing the possibilities in the book, and, of course, I am grateful to Saul Davis Slatkovski, artistic and executive director of the Philadelphia Harp Conference, for creating the opportunity for this to happen and for his longtime interest in the book. Copyeditor Deborah Oliver's sharp eye and valuable suggestions saved me from many a faux pas, for which I'm most appreciative.

I received wonderful assistance from archivists and librarians in researching the book and wish to express my gratitude to them. They include James Ramos, Radio City Music Hall Productions; Edward Heilakka, curator of the Leopold Stokowski Collection when it was still at the Curtis Institute of Music; Elizabeth Walker, head librarian at Curtis, and Curtis archivists Joanne Seitter, Susannah Thurlow, and Helene van Rossum; JoAnne Barry, the excellent archivist for the Philadelphia Orchestra before the archives were shut down; Darrin Britting, associate director for communications for the Philadelphia Orchestra; Aurora Deshauteurs, curator for the Print and Picture Collection of the Free Library of Philadelphia; Marjorie Hassen, who curated the University of Pennsylvania Otto E. Albrecht Music Library special collections that include the Ormandy Music and Media Center and the Leopold Stokowski Collection; John Pollack and the very helpful staff of the University of Pennsylvania Rare Book and Manuscript Library; Patricia Manley of the Settlement Music School, and David Day of the International Harp Archives, Brigham Young University.

My deepest gratitude goes to my beloved husband Richard, who supported my work on this project for so many years. My family—sons Brian and Tracy, grandsons Harry and Frederick, Peggy Hunt, Celia Creskoff, and Catherine Welsh—as well as many wonderful friends provided the inspiration I needed to keep going. I'm deeply grateful to all of them.

# ONE WOMAN IN A HUNDRED

## CHAPTER 1

# In the Lions' Den

Leopold Stokowski wasted no time on idle words in his rehearsals with the Philadelphia Orchestra. By the fall of 1930, he was forty-eight years old. He had taken over the orchestra in 1912, when he was thirty, and within a few years transformed what had been a stiff, undistinguished ensemble into one that enraptured audiences in Philadelphia and beyond with its striking virtuosity and rich, vibrant sound. Tall and slender and very much in command, he engineered this transformation with remarkable vision and determination.

Knowing exactly what he wanted to accomplish in rehearsals, he drove his players forward with relentless intensity to achieve it. He spoke little. Instead, he communicated his wishes to his players with his riveting blue eyes and expressive hands so masterfully that they were able to respond to the nuances of his direction instantly, almost as if they could read his mind. He expected total concentration, and he got it.

Nothing interrupted the progress of a rehearsal—no unnecessary pleasantries from the maestro, no comments from the players, no excuses, nothing—except for the rare occasions when Stokowski chose to break into the rigorous routine he had established with a comment that might stray somewhat from the serious music making at hand. Those interruptions were much appreciated by the musicians. They usually introduced a bit of humor into the proceedings and lightened the intensity of a session for the moment, even though the humor could, and frequently did, come at the expense of one or the other of them. That's what happened during a rehearsal early in the orchestra's 1930–31 season when Stokowski said something that might have amused the orchestra as a whole but that caused sharp discomfort for a particular player, who remembered the incident vividly and told it to me sixty years later.

It began when Stokowski signaled a halt to the playing during a rehearsal one morning in mid-October. "Violas," he said in the immediate silence that followed, "you make me think of the Parable in the Bible about the Foolish Virgins." Then he stopped and glanced to his right, where a new member of his orchestra, a young woman of twenty-three, sat in accordance with his seating plan, which called for the harps to be placed in front of the orchestra, parallel with and not far to the right of the podium. Smiling a sly smile, he looked back at the men of the orchestra seated before him on the stage of Philadelphia's Academy of Music with a question.

"But then, aren't *all* virgins foolish?"

After allowing a few seconds for the import of his comment to sink in, he appeared to catch himself and turned to face the young woman full on, clasping his hands to his chest in an extravagant show of remorse. "Oh, I beg your pardon," he said, hanging his head in mock contrition as all eyes turned toward her.

The mortified young woman, grasping for a way to hide her dismay, kept her head close to her harp's soundboard and pretended to be intent on adjusting the tuning, which was something she had to do often, sitting as she did at the front of the stage where strong drafts from the wings swept across the instrument and played havoc with its tuning. If ever she needed a moment to think, now was the time. The last thing she wanted was to let the maestro and the men of the orchestra see how embarrassed and vulnerable she felt, but what was she to do?

"Some instinct told me to deflate that balloon as quickly as possible," she would later say, and an idea came to her. Following its dictates, she focused on her harp's strings, pretending to be busy tuning them for as long as she dared. Then she raised her eyes to meet Stokowski's with an inquiring look, as if she wondered why he seemed to be beseeching her so plaintively. After all, she had been concentrating on her tuning while he dealt with the viola players and hadn't been listening to what he said. At least that's what she hoped he would think.

Stokowski held his contrite pose a moment longer, waiting for the blushing, girlish reaction he expected. Then, realizing that the young woman wasn't going to fall into his trap, he drew up to his full height once again and snapped back into his usual role of fiercely focused leader, returning the full force of his attention to the viola section. When the problem there was resolved—if there ever was one—he drove the rehearsal forward at his usual rigorous pace with no further mention of foolish virgins, and the young woman breathed a long sigh of relief.

————•————

Edna Phillips was the player Stokowski put on the spot that day. Just two weeks earlier, she had entered the Philadelphia Orchestra as its only woman. She was young and very much alone among her male colleagues, but that didn't mean she was without resources. As a member of the Roxy Theatre Orchestra three years before, she had learned what troubles could stalk her if she let down her guard, and this time she was prepared to be vigilant. If she could help it, there would be no missteps on her part that might send the wrong signals to the men who surrounded her. The last thing she needed was to have any of them think of her as an object of interest. What she desperately wanted at that point was to be allowed to find her way in the strange new world of a major orchestra with as little notice as possible. She knew that her position as a newcomer in such a prestigious organization was precarious enough without the added pressure of undue attention being focused on her because she was a woman.

But avoiding attention had been difficult from the day the Philadelphia Orchestra announced her appointment. At a time when orchestras all across the country barred their doors to women, the news that such an august ensemble had hired one intrigued the press, and a rash of stories soon broke out, turning a spotlight on her that added greatly to her anxiety. An article in the *Philadelphia Evening Bulletin* topped the lot. "Miss Phillips," it said, "looks more like an illustration on a magazine cover than a member of an orchestra. She might be the typical American girl with plenty of light, golden curly hair, shining brown eyes, the peaches and cream complexion of sixteen, and full red lips."[1]

That was not the kind of attention an untested player entering one of the world's finest orchestras needed. Nor was it helpful to a woman stepping into an organization that in its entire history had never allowed a member of her sex to play in the orchestra in an official capacity. Ever since 1903, when the various U.S. musicians unions were incorporated into the American Federation of Musicians under the American Federation of Labor, qualified female as well as male instrumentalists who were members of the AFM were eligible to play in professional symphony orchestras, but that fact had little effect on orchestral hiring. "It would be like oil and water to put men and women in the same organization," one irate music director complained at the time. "Women musicians alone might be alright, but they don't belong with men."[2] That attitude had prevailed in the orchestral world for decades. Little had changed by 1930.

According to Christine Ammer in her book, *Unsung: A History of Women in American Music*, the foremost reason for the exclusion of women from traditional orchestras was economic. Hiring women threatened the jobs of men, but there was more to it than that, Ammer explained. Women had been excluded from performing in public for centuries, and they were not encouraged, and often not allowed, to play instruments other than those considered suitable for the home, such as the piano or harp, until late in the nineteenth century. The idea of including women in symphony orchestras was anathema. Many musicians and much of the public thought women lacked the talent and musical training to hold their own in an orchestra, let alone not having the stamina, power, and reliability to do so.[3]

With so many perceived problems, a woman's chances of being hired by a professional orchestra were slim, so slim that no woman other than Phillips held a principal position in any of the major U.S. orchestras in 1930. Below the major orchestra level, which was then inhabited by the New York Philharmonic, the Boston Symphony, the Chicago Symphony, and the Philadelphia Orchestra, a scattering of less prominent orchestras such as the San Francisco Symphony and the relatively new Cleveland Orchestra included a small number of women in their overwhelmingly male rosters, and surprisingly, the New York Philharmonic employed one woman, Stephanie Goldner, as second harpist, but those appointments were true rarities. In most cases, the best way for a woman to be hired by an orchestra on a professional basis was to join an all-female ensemble. "In the first half of the twentieth century, especially during the 1930s and early 1940s, women's orchestras in the United States offered skilled female players and conductors experience and employment in the symphonic world. Women created their own opportunities because they could not obtain positions in all-male ("standard") orchestras," J. Michele Edwards writes in *Women and Music: A History*.[4]

Thus Phillips was a true novelty in the traditional orchestral world, especially at the major orchestra level. Having chosen the harp, an instrument that women played in drawing rooms in the Victorian era and one that was associated with ethereal, feminine attributes (wrongly, Phillips and her teacher at the Curtis Institute of Music, the brilliant French-born harpist Carlos Salzedo, would insist), she was more easily accepted into an orchestra than a player of another instrument might have been, but that did not mean her colleagues or the orchestra's audiences accepted and welcomed her arrival. As a woman invading a male bastion, she was just that, an invader, a pioneer in uncharted territory, and her arrival was met with curiosity at best and hostility at worst.

Phillips understood that her life in an all-male orchestra would be full of challenges, but that was not her primary concern when she entered the Philadelphia Orchestra. Her biggest fear was that she wouldn't be able to hold her own as a musician among the orchestra's superb players, not because she was a woman, but because her training had been cut short. In a move that shocked and surprised both Phillips and her teacher, Stokowski had appointed her to the first-chair position in his orchestra rather than choosing her for the second harp position she thought she was auditioning for. The added responsibilities and exposure that came with the first chair, or principal, position gave her no time to continue her studies with Carlos Salzedo at the Curtis Institute and forced her to go forward in the professional world as a novice in a key position among giants.

Whether or not she could survive in such a competitive arena was very much in question, and Stokowski hadn't made her situation any easier with his sardonic comment about foolish virgins. But then, the maestro wasn't much concerned about making things easier for his players, be they male or female.

When Salzedo, first suggested that Phillips audition for the Philadelphia Orchestra in December of 1929, she declined in unequivocal terms. "I'd feel like a ewe lamb in a lion's den," she told him, and she knew what she was talking about.

In 1927, when she was just twenty years old, Phillips had joined the orchestra of the Roxy Theatre in Manhattan as second harpist under the auspices of her teacher at the time, Florence Wightman, a talented young woman from Philadelphia who had become the Roxy's principal harpist. The Roxy was New York's newest movie palace. Its symphony orchestra, an important component of the era's larger movie palaces, contained many fine players, but as the times ordained, no women. Dire predictions about the likelihood of women ruining orchestras or orchestras ruining women abounded, and it took courage for Wightman and Phillips to challenge those prejudices.

One person who might have kept Phillips from making such a daring decision was her mother. The prospect of having a daughter join an orchestra, especially one along Manhattan's Great White Way, might have daunted a less determined woman, but Anna Phillips had great faith in her daughter's talent and dreamed she would have an important career in music someday. Not one to be intimidated by the raised eyebrows of her neighbors in Wyomissing, a small borough sixty miles northwest of Philadelphia near the city of Reading, she saw that her daughter's appointment was announced in the *Reading Times* in glowing terms. "Edna Phillips, Reading's distinguished harpist and musician, has been selected as harpist of Roxy's great orchestra of 110 artists, New York city [sic], and will begin her duties next week," the story began. It went on to heap copious, and as yet unearned, praise on both the Roxy orchestra and its fledgling second harpist.[5]

Unfortunately, it didn't take long before Phillips began to rue the naive enthusiasm with which she and her mother had embraced her new position, for the haute vaudeville world of the Roxy Theatre proved to be far more perilous and complicated than they had imagined.

Built by noted radio and theater impresario Samuel L. Rothafel, aka Roxy, with the backing of a Hollywood film producer who almost went bankrupt in the process and had to be rescued at the last minute by William Fox of the Fox Theater chain, the Roxy Theatre was located on the corner of Seventh Avenue and Fiftieth Street just off Broadway.[6] It opened with much fanfare on March 11, 1927, and was widely touted as the grandest of the movie palaces built during the Roaring Twenties.[7] At a cost of twelve million mid-1920s dollars and with the help of a leading theater architect of the day, Walter W. Ahlschlager, and a famous decorator, Harold W. Rambusch, Roxy created a lavish Spanish Baroque palace inspired "inside and out . . . by an exuberant grafting of Renaissance details on Gothic forms with fanciful Moorish overtones."[8]

*Exuberant* also describes the entertainment Roxy offered in his palace. At the top of Roxy's roster of performers stood the Roxy Theatre Orchestra, billed as "the largest symphony orchestra in existence." It was followed by a chorus of one hundred singers; a ballet corps of fifty dancers; three organists who played a massive pipe organ with three consoles; a sensational high-kicking dance group called the Roxyettes (which five years later moved on to Radio City and enduring fame as the Rockettes), and an assortment of individual performers. To top off this bulging bill of fare, Roxy installed an impressive set of cathedral chimes and called his creation the "Cathedral of the Motion Picture." The pièce de résistance—a motion picture straight from Hollywood featuring Roxy's friend Gloria Swanson or other stars of equal magnitude—completed the bill.

Apparently, Roxy had gauged the tastes of his audiences correctly, for day after day, show after show, four times a day, seven days a week, people lined up, often around the block, to fill his theater's six thousand seats. He had created a marvel of flamboyance in a flamboyant time.

When Phillips arrived at the Roxy, she found it to be just as glamorous as she expected it to be, but she quickly discovered that her dreams of an exciting life as a member of the Roxy orchestra were much inflated. While audiences luxuriated in the theatre's plush seats under a glowing bronze dome, surrounded by rich paintings, profusions of gold leaf and elaborately festooned velvet draperies, Phillips and the rafts of other performers on the docket spent their days assigned to different levels of the theater's basement in what felt like the inside of a battleship or, better yet, a submarine beneath the sea.

Other than a few hasty forays into the Roxy's marble and gold rotunda (never to be called a mere lobby) to catch a glimpse of the famed changing of the usher ceremony that was staged in full military style on the grand staircase each evening, Phillips found herself confined in a subbasement, three levels below the stage. There she and the other members of the orchestra rehearsed between performances or whiled away their time waiting for the next show.

When it was time for a performance, the players would take their places on a huge platform that was then propelled upward three levels by a giant hydraulic lift into the darkened auditorium above, where they would materialize as if by magic before the waiting audience. After performing a program of light classical music, sometimes in conjunction with famous singers like Nelson Eddy ensconced in pulpits above the stage, they would slowly disappear from view as mysteriously as they had appeared, descending on their magical platform deep into the bowels of the theater and leaving behind a mesmerized audience to be further dazzled by the rest of Roxy's extravaganza.

The subterranean space that Phillips and her colleagues inhabited between shows consisted of various rehearsal rooms and a bewildering maze of battleship-gray corridors. At the time, a joke about the enormity of the Roxy stage made the rounds among the performers: "never be caught onstage without bread and water." But the stage was nothing compared to the vast area beneath it, as far as Phillips was concerned. Her level alone was so big and confusing, someone had painted red lines on the floors to help performers negotiate their way through the warren of corridors and passages confronting them. But the red lines didn't help much. Bewildered and overwhelmed, Phillips felt lost most of the time.

It was in those mystifying, labyrinthine corridors that her troubles began. That was where the Lotharios in the orchestra came out to prey. And who better to prey on than the two attractive young women in their ranks?

To Phillips these men were a slick, unappealing bunch. Although they didn't represent the majority of the orchestra's members, there were enough of them to make her life miserable. She was used to the attentions of young men when she was growing up on the outskirts of Reading and at nearby Mt. Gretna, where her family spent the summers, but she soon discovered that the easygoing friendships and flirtations she had enjoyed with the boys at home didn't work with this cohort. In fact, the slightest smile or comment seemed to provoke an unwanted overture from within the group, and it quickly became obvious that these men had more serious business on their minds than did her hometown boyfriends.

At first, she thought to turn for support to the teacher who had brought her there. A lively, intelligent woman as well as a gifted musician, Florence Wightman was very much of the times. She wore her dark hair bobbed in the latest fashion and had a sharp, no-nonsense way about her. At twenty-four, Florence appeared worldly-wise indeed to her twenty-year-old student, and having grown up in Philadelphia, she exuded an air of sophistication that made Edna feel more than a bit rural by comparison. Surely, Edna thought, Florence would know what to do.

But it turned out that Florence was otherwise occupied. As the Roxy's principal harpist, her responsibilities were greater than Edna's. In charge of the harp section, she was often called upon to play solos that she had to work out and rehearse, requiring much of her attention and time. Edna's responsibilities were lighter. Florence would show her what she was to play in the different pieces on the program, and Edna was then able to practice and perform what she was told to do without much trouble, leaving her with little to occupy her mind as she passed the days in the confines of the Roxy's subbasement.

Initially, she assumed that Florence's many responsibilities were what was keeping her from noticing the troublesome wolves who were harassing her second, but then she realized with a shock that the worst of the lot, "a bad egg" as far as Edna was concerned, had turned his charms on Florence full force. And what was worse—he seemed to have won her over. Edna couldn't understand the attraction at all. The fellow reeked of the predator to her, but Florence didn't see him that way. Edna tried dropping comments about how slick and untrustworthy he appeared to be, but they only annoyed Florence, and Edna found herself more and more isolated in the Roxy's vast underworld.

Then the same brigand started making passes at her! As she made her way through the maze of underground corridors, distracted by the ugly sounds of loud machinery that seemed to be always clanging away, she would suddenly find him beside her, having emerged stealthily from one dark corner or another. Then he would give her "a lot of blather" about how pretty she was and try to edge her into an isolated corner or an empty room. His friends were no better. They were just as sneaky and aggressive.

Trapped in the confusing underworld of the Roxy Theatre with those wolves lurking about, Edna grew increasingly frightened that one of them would suddenly step out from the shadows and trap her. She was finding it harder and harder to get away from them, but what could she do? She couldn't turn to Florence. Obviously smitten with the two-timing rogue at the head of the pack, she was no help.

Making matters worse, Edna found she wasn't able to work effectively on improving her playing. Although she wasn't immune to the excitement and glamour she expected to find at the Roxy, she was essentially a serious musician. She cared deeply about becoming an accomplished harpist. Florence was the teacher who had introduced her to the instrument and helped her learn to love it, and she had promised to continue their lessons between performances at the Roxy. But Edna quickly discovered that there was precious little time among the Roxy's multitudinous attractions and distractions for serious harp study.

What made it so important to Edna to concentrate on learning to play the harp well was that she had begun studying the instrument barely three years before. She had loved making music all her life and had studied the piano from an early age seriously and even passionately with a local teacher, who made the appealing youngster with her shiny curls and happy smile the darling of the Reading recital scene. But when the young girl moved on in her piano training to a teacher in Philadelphia, Mauritz Leefson, she got a rude awakening. Leefson determined that the technique she had learned from her hometown teacher was faulty and proceeded to drive her relentlessly in an effort to wipe out the bad habits she had picked up.

Years of scales and exercises and more scales and more exercises under orders from her gruff teacher followed. Nothing Edna did seemed to please him. In the end, she became exhausted, overwrought, and thoroughly disillusioned with the piano. Her mother, seeing what was happening and worrying that her daughter might abandon music altogether, cast about for a way to keep her musical imagination alive. Having spotted a harp in the window of a Reading music store, she gave it to Edna for her eighteenth birthday, hoping that it would relax her to play such a beautiful instrument. At first, Edna wasn't much interested. She didn't consider the harp a serious enough instrument to merit her attention. Its reputation as a drawing-room instrument put her off, but her experience with playing it eventually led to a real love for the instrument, and now she was anxious to make up for lost time by working as hard and fast as possible to improve her harp technique and become a first-rate harpist.

However, it was becoming increasingly clear that she was in exactly the wrong place for that at the Roxy. There she was a tiny cog in a huge performance machine, and even though she had been able to elude her pursuers so far, she knew she could be trapped by one of them any day. There seemed to be no way out unless she chose to "take the rosy path," and that she didn't want to do. Not with these fellows, anyway.

Thus, just six weeks after she arrived in New York, Edna said goodbye to Florence and the Roxy, moved out of the Manger Hotel (renamed the Taft Hotel in 1931), where she had been living, and headed back to Reading, determined never again to set foot inside an all-male orchestra.

———

That didn't mean she intended to give up pursuing a career as a harpist. She still wanted to follow that path, but in chamber or solo settings rather than in an orchestra. Then she encountered a problem she hadn't considered. Once she returned home, she couldn't find an independent teacher with enough expertise to help her progress. Classically trained harpists were hard to find at that time. Most harpists focused on light music for the drawing room, the kind of "by-the-fountain music" Edna thought was silly, rather than the more-fulfilling classical music and rigorous training she was looking for.

At that time, the only place in Philadelphia where she knew she could find the kind of advanced instruction she sought was at the Curtis Institute of Music. Though Curtis, which had been founded in 1924, was only three years old, it was already a highly esteemed music conservatory, "the closest American equivalent to the conservatories of Moscow and St. Petersburg."[9] Phillips knew it had an excellent harp department. During the time she studied with Florence before they departed for the Roxy, she had had an unofficial introduction to that department and its brilliant leader, Carlos Salzedo. As Salzedo's assistant at Curtis, Florence had managed to sneak Edna in "through the back door" to observe classes.

Still, even though Edna had sat in on those classes and had played for six weeks in the Roxy orchestra, she knew she wasn't prepared to meet the rigorous standards of the prestigious conservatory, which accepted only the most superior students. The actual time she had been playing the harp was just too limited to raise her technique to a high enough level. But what other choice did she have?

She played two auditions for Curtis, one on the harp, and one on the piano. Those who heard her piano audition recognized her musical gifts immediately, and she was accepted to study with a distinguished member of the piano faculty, Abram Chasins. As much as the fearsome Leefson had intimidated her, it appears, he had also rescued her from being dragged down by the faulty technique she had picked up from her beloved hometown teacher.

The harp was a different story. Although she had indicated it was to be her primary instrument, harpist extraordinaire Carlos Salzedo decided that she was too elementary a student to study with him and decreed that she would have to complete a program of study with his current assistant before he would take her on. Luckily for Edna, that assistant, Lucile Lawrence, turned out to be an excellent harpist and a rigorous teacher. Lucile worked with Edna diligently and effectively to improve her skills, and after six months, Cher Maître, "Dear Master," as Salzedo preferred his students to address him, deigned her ready to study with him.

———•———

Edna envisioned a long period of study after that, but Salzedo changed that plan. Less than two years later, in late fall of 1929, Leopold Stokowski asked him to recommend a harpist for his orchestra for the next season. For reasons that puzzled Edna, Salzedo chose her. She knew that a request from a figure as famous and powerful as Stokowski was not to be taken lightly by someone in Salzedo's position, but what could he be thinking to choose her as his candidate?

In the early part of the twentieth century, conductors often relied on esteemed teachers and principal players to recommend candidates for positions in their orchestras without going through the elaborate process of publicizing openings, forming committees, and auditioning large numbers of players that evolved as the century wore on. Salzedo, a man whose ambitions were as large as his talents were prodigious, was proud to answer the call of Leopold Stokowski, who was an inspirational figure at Curtis and who often engaged the brilliant harpist as a soloist with the Philadelphia Orchestra. The two also worked together on important avant-garde music projects in New York City and had many highly regarded musician friends in common. Edna could understand Salzedo's desire to please Stokowski, but why had he chosen her from all his students, past and present, to audition? And why, at a time when symphony orchestras excluded women from their ranks so thoroughly that people called orchestra members "the men" rather than "the players," was he so determined to talk her into auditioning?

She first learned of Salzedo's plan for her on a chilly afternoon in early December. Prepared for a normal lesson, the tall young woman with "a classic profile and mass of bronze-gold hair" had climbed the stairs to Salzedo's studio on the third floor of the gracious limestone mansion that housed the Curtis Institute, expecting to get right to work, but when she entered the studio, she found her usually dynamic teacher in a contemplative mood, standing with his back to her at the window across the room.[10] Rather than greeting her in his usual brisk manner, he remained at the window gazing down on Rittenhouse Square, a beautiful park directly across the street from Curtis at the center of Philadelphia's most fashionable residential neighborhood, one of the five original open-space squares designated by William Penn when he laid out the city grid in 1683. Now that its many trees had shed their leaves, the elegant square's diagonal walkways were visible from above, and people could be seen scurrying along with their heads down against the early winter wind.

After surveying the scene outside for several minutes while Phillips waited, Salzedo turned from the window and walked solemnly to a nearby chair, looking as if he had something of great import on his mind. A small man with extremely erect posture, he wore his dark hair pomaded straight back in the continental manner and peppered his speech with French phrases in a way that often made Edna smile. When she was with him, she couldn't help thinking of Agatha Christie's peacockish detective, Hercule Poirot. Salzedo looked and acted just the way she imagined Poirot would, "but without the mustache."

That afternoon, rather than having his pupil settle herself at the harp as usual, Salzedo indicated that she should take the chair across from him. Then he announced with pride that Maestro Stokowski had asked him to find a new harpist for the Philadelphia Orchestra.

Whom had he chosen to audition for the position?

"You, my child."

For a moment, Edna sat speechless before him. She had always been wary of Salzedo, sensing a certain air of cunning in him that put her on guard. What was he up to this time? He had never given her the impression that she was a favored student. In fact, he had often been annoyed at her for not accepting his every word as gospel the way his other students did. Now what did he have up his sleeve? Why would he choose her to audition when he had other students to call on who had studied the harp much longer than she had?

Surely she could talk him out of it, she thought. She had to. But however hard she tried, Salzedo seemed to have an answer for all her objections, even when she reminded him of her troubles with the lecherous Roxy players.

"Ed-naa," Salzedo replied on that point, drawing out the last syllable of her name as he always did as if to point out that it didn't fall trippingly off his Gallic tongue. "You cannot compare the men of the Philadelphia Orchestra with those Roxy Romeos."

Edna had to admit to herself that Salzedo might have a point there. The Philadelphia players did appear to be a "different breed of pups" from the Roxy gang. Maybe she didn't need to worry about them accosting her in a dark corner of the Academy of Music, but how could she know?

Besides, it wasn't just the "Romeos" who had bothered her in the Roxy orchestra. She had also felt a strong sense of disapproval emanating from many of the other men toward the two women in their midst. They obviously viewed the presence of women as an invasion of their exclusive territory and possibly a threat to its strength, and their displeasure showed. Their cold stares had made Edna feel uneasy. She imagined that the Philadelphia players might display a similar disdain toward her. It would be better than having them chase her down dark halls, she guessed, but it wouldn't be pleasant to endure.

That disdainful attitude was another reason she didn't want to join an all-male orchestra, but it was too complicated to explain that afternoon. Salzedo might not understand what she was talking about; she didn't quite understand it herself. Besides, she could tell he was growing impatient with her. Cher Maître wasn't used to challenges from his students, most of whom idolized him and met his pronouncements with doe-eyed acceptance. She knew he had been annoyed with her skepticism in the past, but still she pressed on.

The next tack she tried was to point out that it would be fruitless for her to audition. A conductor of a major orchestra like the Philadelphia would never give a woman a place on his roster of players, she told him, especially in conservative Philadelphia. Everyone knew that. She couldn't believe a wily man like Salzedo didn't know it.

"There's no use for me to take up the maestro's time," she told him. "He would never hire a woman. It just isn't done."

"What is this bourgeois notion 'it isn't done'?" Salzedo asked huffily. "Maestro Stokowski does not carry such thoughts in his head. You know that."

With that, he reminded her of the many innovations Stokowski had brought to the Philadelphia Orchestra—his fervent devotion to new music, for example, which regularly ruffled the feathers of his audiences and the orchestra's board of directors, and his bold experiments with the technologies that were then emerging in the recording and broadcasting industries. Most conductors of the day treated the new technologies dismissively. They were only peripherally interested in the new-fangled devices that Stokowski concerned himself with. In their view, producing fine music in the concert hall was all that counted, but Stokowski wanted to take music beyond concert halls to people on the outside, and he spent many hours experimenting with new technologies to reach his goal.

Salzedo's arguments stopped Edna for a moment. She had to admit to herself that Stokowski didn't seem to be the type to be hemmed in by convention. He was always experimenting with something new, like making the world's first electrical recording with an orchestra, and over the years he had shaken conservative Philadelphia audiences to the core by championing the cause of modern music—some of it pretty shocking, like the revolutionary *Amériques* by Salzedo's friend and compatriot Edgard Varèse with its loud sirens, roars, and other clanging and banging that sparked a near-riot at its premiere.[11] A man who programmed music like that, Edna had to admit, must not be afraid of breaking the bonds of accepted custom. Perhaps such a man would challenge the traditional prejudices that kept symphony orchestras from adding women to their rosters. If anyone ever did, she supposed, it would have to be someone like him, and so she switched to another point.

"But, Cher Maître, I'm too much of a novice for the Philadelphia Orchestra," she told him. "You know how much I have to learn."

On that point, Salzedo made no objection, conceding it with more alacrity than Edna might have wished.

However much it stung to have him agree with her so quickly, Edna knew that was the truth. Even though music was practically the first language she spoke, she was a long way from taking her harp technique to the highest levels. It's almost impossible for any musician to excel in the classical world on an instrument taken up as late in life as eighteen, when Edna began playing the harp. At that advanced age, it's hard to achieve true mastery because the technique required to play complicated classical works takes years to acquire. The harp is especially tricky in that regard. A simple tune can sound lovely once one learns the basics, especially if one is as musically gifted as Edna, but when one gets into more difficult music, the physical technique required to play the harp is quite challenging to master. Knowledge of the piano is helpful in an overall musical sense in learning to play the harp, but the two instruments require vastly different physical techniques.

None of that seemed to worry Salzedo, however. Stokowski had previously talked to him about wanting to replace his second harpist, and he assumed that that was what the maestro wanted to do now. Edna was the right candidate for that position, he decided. She hadn't had time to develop her technique to its highest potential, he knew, but she was naturally gifted, and as second harpist, she would have Vincent Fanelli, the orchestra's principal harpist at her side to help her. An excellent player, Fanelli had been Philadelphia's principal harpist since 1913.

Fanelli could introduce Phillips to the orchestra's routine and show her what to do, and since she wouldn't be overburdened in the second harp position, she could continue her studies at Curtis. What more could she want? Salzedo asked. She could keep on studying and at the same time have the experience of playing in a magnificent orchestra.

Then with a conspiratorial glint in his dark eyes, Salzedo lowered his voice and beckoned Edna to lean closer so that he could tell her how much Stokowski liked the method for playing the harp that he had developed.

"Don't you see, Ed-naa?" he asked. "When my students take positions in great orchestras like the Philadelphia, more and more people will learn about the Salzedo Method. They will see how important it is."

As skeptical as she was, Edna did agree that Salzedo deserved to have his work and his ideas recognized. She had no argument with him on that. She believed that the new method he had developed for playing the harp, which he claimed would bring the ancient instrument out of the Dark Ages and into the twentieth century, deserved attention. He wanted to bring the harp forward as a vibrant solo instrument, instead of having it relegated to an accompanying role, and his new method was designed to do that. In explaining his friend's major achievement, Edgard Varèse later said, "Carlos is an innovator, an adventurer. He has succeeded in changing the sex of the harp—minimizing its golden aura of Victorian femininity; he has discovered and explored its virility."[12]

In his quest for a stronger sound, Salzedo concentrated on finding ways for a harpist to play loud and fast at the same time, which is hard to do on the harp without the right technique. He focused on the tone his players produced, urging them to strive for a strong, rich, rounded sound. He also wanted harpists to play first-rate classical music, rather than the lighter fare then associated with the harp. To that end he transcribed many classical pieces for the instrument and composed numerous important and innovative works for it.

"No other musical instrument, except the pipe organ, offers such a wealth and variety of musical color and effect,"[13] Salzedo asserted in the preface to his *Method for the Harp*. To prove his point, he created a series of thirty-seven "harpistic signs" (written symbols) to depict different sonorous effects that can be achieved on the harp, including his own innovations such as *Striking Anvil*, *Rolling Surf*, and *Rocket Ascending*.[14]

To emphasize the aesthetics of playing such a beautiful instrument, he worked with the legendary ballet dancer and choreographer Vaslav Nijinsky to create a system of gestures that required harpists to keep their elbows elevated and hands rounded while playing and to close their hands and raise their arms gracefully at the end of a phrase before lowering them to the soundboard. No more dropping them straight down as had been the traditional practice. These ballet-like gestures developed by Nijinsky and Salzedo were meant as an elegant expression of the music that would relax a player and help produce a better sound.

However, those gestures met with ridicule from Edna's nonharpist friends at Curtis, who "just about rolled in the aisles" when the harp students kept raising and lowering their arms in recitals. They called the whole idea "balderdash." Edna herself agreed with that point of view early on in her training, which put her on the wrong side of Salzedo the first time she appeared in a recital at Curtis as part of an ensemble of harpists. Throughout the performance, all the harpists raised and lowered their arms as Salzedo had instructed them to do. All, that is, except Edna.

"What difference does it make?" she asked when Salzedo reprimanded her afterwards. "It still sounds the same if I just put my hands down when I'm finished."

*Mon Dieu*, how could she say such a thing? Her impertinence caused a minor scandal in the harp department and did not endear her to Cher Maître. He had never quite forgiven her for it, although she eventually came to recognize the value of the Salzedo Method and used it with excellent effect to improve her playing. Now, although she had come to appreciate Salzedo's genius, she still didn't agree with him on everything, especially on the subject of her auditioning for the Philadelphia Orchestra, and she tried once again to deflect him.

"Why don't you get one of your more advanced students to audition?" she asked.

"Ed-naa," Salzedo answered, irritation clearly sounding in his tone. "I told you, it is for the second harp position. That's just right for you at this stage." Then he reminded her that the principal harpist was in charge of the harp section. He played the solos. He had all the responsibility, not the second harpist.

"But why me?" she tried one last time.

"Your *musicalité*," Salzedo answered, rising from his seat. That was what Stokowski looked for in his players, he told her. The maestro cared about technique, of course, but according to Salzedo, what was even more important to Stokowski was *musicalité*. He wanted players who had a special feeling for music and who were flexible enough to grasp quickly what he wanted them to do. Edna had those qualities, and under Stokowski's leadership, Salzedo was sure she would develop into a fine orchestral harpist.

"You must have faith in me, my child," he concluded with his head held high. "I would not recommend you for a position that is beyond you."

———•———

As Edna left Salzedo's studio and wound her way down the richly carved staircase of the elegant mansion built by George Childs Drexel that had been converted for use by the Curtis Institute, she looked at her handsome surroundings with renewed appreciation. She loved the slightly worn elegance of the building that contrasted sharply with the grandiosity of the Roxy. Even though her studies were extremely demanding, she had felt comfortable and happy there, blossoming in the stimulating conservatory atmosphere and forming many friendships with people who lived in the world of music as she did. Along with all the hard work, she had great fun keeping up with the intrigues in Salzedo's harp department and enjoying herself by "playing straight man," as she said, to one of Cher Maître's most brilliant students, Casper Reardon, who later became the first great jazz harpist. He played with Paul Whiteman and on his own in Manhattan clubs before his tragic death at the young age of thirty-four. At Curtis, while Edna played the music as it was written in their informal performances, Reardon riffed around her, and their duets delighted their fellow students.

When she reached the first floor of the Curtis Institute that afternoon, Edna stood for a moment in the Common Room, a large foyer that served as a meeting place for students and faculty as well as the entrance to the school. Used for the teas that the founder and great benefactor of the school, Mary Louise Curtis Bok, held for students and faculty every Wednesday afternoon, the Common Room was one of Edna's favorite places, a happy meeting ground for all. Two stories high and paneled in the same richly carved dark wood as the staircase, it invited gatherings with its comfortable benches and chairs, oriental rugs, and its splendid limestone fireplace almost big enough to walk into, all lit by an expanse of stunning leaded glass windows along one wall.

Why, she asked herself, would she want to disturb the rich life she had at Curtis when she still had so much to learn? As she pulled open the heavy door onto Locust Street, she was firm in her conviction that her final answer to Salzedo's proposition would be no, even though his arguments had been persuasive. Her resolve was strong as she walked across Rittenhouse Square through the afternoon chill toward the room she was renting as a Curtis student in a home a few blocks away at 2028 Pine Street. The whole idea of auditioning for the Philadelphia Orchestra was impossible, she told herself. It would never work.

But as the afternoon faded into evening, her mind began to change. A few hours earlier, she had been convinced that auditioning for the Philadelphia Orchestra would be absolutely the wrong thing to do. Now her reasons began to seem less distinct. She was no longer so sure about them. As wary as she was of Salzedo and his wily ways, she wasn't immune to his arguments. She knew she had musical gifts, and she had her own share of ambition. Before that afternoon, she had seen herself becoming a recitalist or a member of a chamber group, and perhaps—after years of preparation, of course—a soloist like Salzedo, who performed alone and in chamber groups with other prominent musicians and as a soloist with symphony orchestras. She had no doubt that she wanted to make a life for herself in music and make that life as significant as possible, but whatever her dreams for her future, they did not include becoming a member of an all-male orchestra, even one that played as beautifully as the Philadelphia. That, she had been sure, was a course she would never take.

Still, as the evening wore on, the impediments to that course, which had loomed so large earlier in the day, began to recede in Edna's mind.

Her fears about lurking Lotharios lying in wait to accost her, her conviction that a woman would never be allowed into the Philadelphia Orchestra, and even her doubts about her own readiness to become a member of such a prestigious organization—all began to diminish when she weighed them against Salzedo's persuasive arguments. Slowly, in place of her old doubts, a surprising sense of resolve began to emerge in her, and within a few days she had made a new decision, one she never thought she would make, but one that would soon become as firm and strong in its way as her old resistance to the idea of joining an orchestra had been. Why, she ultimately concluded, should she deny herself an opportunity that might open so many doors for her? If she could perform well enough to be chosen for the Philadelphia Orchestra, then that was where she belonged. And nobody—including herself—could tell her she didn't.

## CHAPTER 2

# A Formidable Arena

Of course, playing well enough to be chosen for the Philadelphia Orchestra would be a tall order even with all of Salzedo's talk about Edna's *musicalité*. This wasn't just a major orchestra. This was one of the greatest orchestras in the world. Critics, audiences, and musicians raved about its virtuoso players and the magnificent music they made under Leopold Stokowski.

Early in 1929, Sergei Rachmaninoff, in an Associated Press interview from Paris, discussed the growing importance of the United States in the classical music world after the destruction that war and revolution had brought to Europe. "At present New York is undoubtedly the musical center of the world," he said. "It has taken the place that Berlin occupied before the war, but it is more brilliant than Berlin ever was. And Philadelphia! Philadelphia has the finest orchestra I have ever heard at any time or any place in my whole life. I don't know that I would be exaggerating if I said that it is the finest orchestra the world has ever heard."[1]

There was no doubt about it. People everywhere testified to the excellence of the Philadelphia Orchestra. It took people's breath away.

So, by the way, did its maestro. Stokowski radiated a kind of magnetism on the podium that electrified audiences and musicians alike. Not conventionally handsome (he had a rather prominent, hawklike nose), there was something about his bearing that commanded attention wherever he went. He had the grace of a natural athlete, and with his intensely blue eyes, oft-described halo of blond hair, lithe figure, and exquisitely tailored wardrobe, he presented such a glamorous figure that certain observers, especially those with traditionalist tendencies, wondered aloud and in print whether this matinee idol could also be a great artist. Or was he, as some claimed, just a charlatan after all?

*Time* magazine weighed in on both sides of the debate in its cover story on the maestro on April 18, 1930. "Stokowski has permitted himself to develop prima donna tendencies, but the public at large continues to encourage them—perhaps because, like a shrewd prima donna, he has stayed picturesque. . . . But no amount of posing could have built and maintained for Stokowski the sound prestige which he has everywhere . . . few have denied his tremendous musical genius."[2]

In 1930, the final word on Stokowski's greatness as an artist could not be declared. It still remains a topic of discussion, but there was and is no denying that he presided over a magnificent orchestra. For even the finest, most experienced of orchestral instrumentalists to think of playing in that orchestra under that conductor would be a distant dream. For the young Edna Phillips, such a feat would appear to be impossible.

———•———

Founded in 1900, the Philadelphia Orchestra was led during its early years by two German-speaking conductors, Fritz Scheel (1900–1907) and Carl Pohlig (1907–12). Maestro Scheel made a good start on developing an organization of distinction, but he succumbed to an untimely illness in 1907. Unfortunately, the man who followed him to the podium deflated many of his predecessor's gains, and Philadelphia's orchestra became a competent but stiff ensemble that inspired strained admiration from its own audiences and little respect from other cities. Critical reaction in New York had been especially humiliating. After the orchestra appeared in Carnegie Hall on November 5, 1907, the *New York Sun* review snidely noted that Maestro Pohlig was "employed in the pleasant city of Phila-delphia where he conducts the local orchestra. Its work was so rough as to cause wonder that the organization should have been brought all the way across the State of New Jersey." After similar reviews from the *New York Times*, the *Tribune*, and the *World* (which labeled the orchestra "provincial"), Philadelphians tried gamely to support their new conduc-tor, but eventually Pohlig disenchanted even his most loyal supporters in the city.[3] "As of 1912," Joseph Horowitz wrote in *Classical Music in America*, "[the Philadelphia Orchestra] and its conductor, Karl Pohlig, were a disappointment to wealthy Main Liners, who sought a cultural adornment to rival the orchestras of Boston, Chicago, and New York."[4]

Happily for Philadelphia, its place in the world of music underwent a dramatic change when the thirty-year-old Leopold Stokowski became the orchestra's leader at the beginning of the 1912–13 season. The young conductor immediately set out to replace the orchestra's less-effective members with the finest players he could find and began to move away from the orchestra's rigid Germanic tradition. "He took over a demoralized ensemble and infused it with new players and strict discipline. . . . Within three years, Stokowski had created an orchestra that was the envy of nearby New York."[5] And of every other major orchestra.

In the process, he "introduced a new kind of personalized, broad, sweeping, boldly romantic conducting to the United States, setting a style that prevailed for many years, and Philadelphia responded to it with delight."[6]

The dramatic transformation that Stokowski wrought upon the Philadelphia Orchestra became apparent to the wider world in 1916, when the young conductor used his considerable powers of persuasion to talk the orchestra's board of directors into providing the funds for the U.S. premiere of Gustav Mahler's Eighth Symphony, the *Symphony of a Thousand*. It was a staggering undertaking that called for 950 choral performers, an augmented orchestra of 110, and eight soloists—all this at a time when the work was only six years old and considered much too new and forbidding for U.S. audiences.

In the face of naysayers who predicted the cast would be bigger than the audience, Stokowski staged an event that turned out to be a spectacular success as a musical performance—and as a public relations coup. With a strong instinct for creating effective publicity, he managed the release of news about the upcoming production so skillfully that by the time the concert took place, thousands of music aficionados made the trip to Philadelphia for opening night or for later performances. Scalpers got an astonishing $100 for a ticket, and news of the event spread quickly throughout the country. It was "the most sensational American premiere of a musical work the country had ever witnessed."[7]

The day after the first performance in Philadelphia, Samuel Lacier exclaimed in the *Philadelphia Public Ledger*, "Every one of the thousands in the great building was standing, whistling, cheering and applauding, when Leopold Stokowski, his collar wilted, his right arm weary, but smiling his boyish smile, finally turned to the audience in the Academy of Music last night. He had scored, so famous musicians agreed, the greatest triumph of his career, the greatest triumph the Philadelphia Orchestra has known in its sixteen years of life and he had done it on a stupendous scale."[8]

"Vast Throng Hears Mahler Symphony," read the headline of the *New York Times* story about the presentation in New York's Metropolitan Opera House on April 9. "The performance of this enormous and exacting work, which lasts just less than two hours, was little short of magnificent," the article went on. "The chorus made up of the Philadelphia Orchestra chorus of 400, the Philadelphia Chorale Society, Mendelssohn Club and the Fortnightly Club of 400, and a children's choir of 150, was trained to a remarkable degree of precision and flexibility. Its tone was magnificently full and rich, its enunciation clear. The orchestral portion of the work was played with entire mastery. Mr. Stokowski gave evidence of his high abilities as a conductor by his preparation of such a performance and his firm command of all forces under his baton."[9]

Referring to Stokowski's awesome ability to marshal so many forces within the city of Philadelphia, author John Mueller wrote, "Never before, and probably never since has a permanent symphony orchestra and its activity been so thoroughly integrated with the life of a city. Never before had there been such a genius for publicity who extended the functional boundaries of a concert so far into nonmusical realms. It was a civic enterprise in which one thousand citizens cooperated in the actual performance, in which commercial and cultural interest were well mobilized, and in which, still more miraculously, each interest was completely gratified with the results."[10]

With this triumph, Philadelphia civic pride began to swell. Finally, its orchestra was on the map as one of the leading musical institutions in the United States. It could now be ranked alongside the country's foremost orchestras at that time—the Boston Symphony, the New York Symphony, the New York Philharmonic, and the Chicago Symphony. And at the same time, these orchestras were beginning to surge ahead of the best orchestras that Europe had to offer. With so many excellent and highly trained European players coming to the United States to find work, the major orchestras were growing into astonishing powerhouses that combined the best players in ensembles that had a much wider array of talent than those in Europe, where orchestras were organized along national lines, each country drawing its players from among its native sons. In the years that followed, U.S. orchestras only grew in stature.

By the early 1920s, the Philadelphia Orchestra under Stokowski's dynamic leadership had risen to the top of the nation's major orchestras. The Boston Symphony, which had long been the premier U.S. orchestra, was caught up in a patriotic frenzy over the reputed German sympathies of its conductor Karl Muck, and music was the loser in that argument. Of New York's two orchestras, the Symphony under Walter Damrosch was considered the better of the two, while the Philharmonic under Josef Stransky was in a weakened state.[11] Although the Chicago Symphony under Frederick Stock was a fine orchestra, it didn't have the exceptional quality it would have in later years. That left the field open for Stokowski and the Philadelphia Orchestra to shine as the foremost conductor and orchestra in the nation and the world, and shine they did. According to biographer Abram Chasins, "Stokowski had taken Philadelphia to the summit."[12]

Soon rumors began to fly that the golden boy among maestros would leave Philadelphia to take over the uneven New York Philharmonic or move on to some other prestigious position. But, against all predictions, he chose not to leave. He remained in the Quaker City and devoted himself to cultivating its orchestra to make it fit his musical paradigm. But it was not an easy ride. Stokowski's visionary plans, his experiments and innovations, his much-rumored womanizing, and especially his insistence on playing the music of his time raised the eyebrows of the conservative denizens of Philadelphia, while their stodginess, which Stokowski attributed to a lack of imagination, provoked irritated responses from him. Still, in spite of vexations on both sides, Stokowski continued to lavish immense attention and energy on his orchestra, and Philadelphia audiences continued to respond to his efforts with intense and sustained loyalty.

Stokowski had become "a Philadelphia fixture."[13] Whether by nature or plan, he had the elegant, aloof manner of a European aristocrat, albeit one of mysterious lineage, and he spoke with an intriguing accent, also of mysterious lineage, that enhanced his stature among Americans who looked to Europeans as their cultural superiors.

"America [in the early twentieth century] had a stifling feeling of inferiority where music was concerned," explains David Ewen, a mid-twentieth-century music chronicler. Thus a musician "was compelled to acquire European prestige . . . before he dared to court American favor."[14] Stokowski, although his background might not have been impressive—he was born in the Marylebone section of London to a father of Polish descent and a mother with Irish roots—had learned that lesson well. The mysterious accent and aristocratic persona he adopted helped him secure the backing of wealthy Philadelphians for the development of his orchestra as well as abundant attention from the press. "He was just the way a musician should be, beautiful, temperamental, scandalous, colorful. And, of course, a good musician," Nathaniel Burt writes in *The Perennial Philadelphians*.[15]

Those attributes coupled with the magnificent music Stokowski drew from his orchestra attracted the ardent devotion of scores of Philadelphians who learned to appreciate and love classical music under his tutelage. They gobbled up tickets so voraciously that the orchestra played to sold-out houses throughout the 1920s.

Stokowski had a habit of keeping audiences a little off balance, unsure of what he would do next, that intrigued them and kept them coming back to the Academy of Music. Was he going to present a work in total darkness, with only the shadow of his graceful hands dancing in a spotlight on the ceiling, or premiere a piece as raucous as Varèse's *Hyperprism*, which reminded critic Olin Downes "of election night, a menagerie or two and a catastrophe in a boiler factory"?[16] Or would he lead a concert in which the music was so profoundly realized that an audience would be completely lost in its beauty? Nothing was routine with Stoki (the sobriquet given to him by Curtis students). His unpredictability fascinated his audiences and made them susceptible to the allure of the music he presented. In fact, according to music critic Harold Schonberg, "There was a kind of alertness, of dynamism and imagination that made Stokowski in his prime one of the greatest conductors in history."[17]

Not all critics sang Stokowski's praises, however. His intensely personal style of conducting, his radical technical experiments, and the temerity he displayed in premiering the works of contemporary composers curled the lips of some, as did his transcriptions of works by Bach and other old masters for modern orchestra. Musical purists scoffed at him for taking liberties with scores, but even the purists had to admit that although Stokowski might have emphasized drama and showmanship in his performances, he never played down to his audiences or demeaned the music. In fact, he did just the opposite. He insisted on pushing audiences forward in their understanding of music, no matter how sophisticated or unsophisticated they were, by designing programs featuring old and new music that made unusual connections and raised important questions.

His proselytizing for new music caused the most trouble. Stokowski believed it was essential for audiences to hear the music of their own time. He insisted that there were only two kinds of music, and they weren't old and new. They were good and bad. Whether a work was a well-known favorite or a brand-new offering didn't matter. The question for Stoki was: Was it good music? That's what counted. To make his point, he would often program a new work more than once even if audiences hated it the first time they heard it. He wanted to give them a chance to grow to understand it.

So intent was Stokowski on giving new compositions a chance to be heard, he presented the world or U.S. premieres of more than a hundred compositions while he was at the helm of the Philadelphia Orchestra, including works by Stravinsky, Rachmaninoff, Schoenberg, Falla, Sibelius, Varèse, Villa-Lobos, Richard Strauss, Shostakovich, Scriabin, Webern, Prokofiev, Hindemith, Enesco, and Mahler, which are now considered key works in the twentieth-century canon.[18]

His premieres often elicited not-so-subtle objections from the more outspoken members of his Philadelphia audiences. When they couldn't stomach an especially modern-sounding piece, they would let the maestro know just how they felt by hissing loudly, and if they were really provoked, they would march up the aisles and out the doors. But that didn't stop them from coming back for the next concert. And, in spite of their general conservatism, the vast majority of Stoki's Philadelphia audiences supported him and his orchestra with genuine enthusiasm.

A unique aspect of Stokowski's relationship with his Philadelphia audiences was the lively give-and-take between audience and conductor. Just as the audience sometimes let him know their feelings about modern music by hissing or walking out, he communicated with them by giving short lectures from the podium on their behavior. In an ongoing effort to teach the supposedly proper Philadelphians their concert manners, he urged them to listen with respect. Annoyed by what he considered rude conduct—too much coughing and rustling about, clapping at inappropriate times, inattention, late arrivals, and early departures—he would try to set the transgressors straight with stern lectures on keeping quiet while the music was being played and on carrying cough drops with them to stop their coughs. Those podium speeches were delivered in the maestro's best "orchestrese" (another word invented by Curtis students).

The Friday afternoon audience, made up largely of women who came into Center City from outlying locales like Germantown and Chestnut Hill and the suburbs of the Main Line and New Jersey to shop, have lunch, and attend the concert, was a particular target of Stokowski's lectures. Many of the ladies made a habit of hurrying into concerts at the last minute with their arms full of bundles, which they noisily stashed under their seats as they settled into their places. Some with larger bundles even dashed forward and parked them at the foot of the stage as the concert was beginning. That was bad enough, but then the same ladies would create more disturbances by gathering up their bundles and heading for the door to catch an early train home just when the maestro was bringing the music to a meaningful ending.

Their lack of respect drove Stoki wild. Believing that music was a spiritual activity that deserved everyone's full attention, he would give the ladies a talking-to whenever their behavior proved too disruptive to bear. One such occasion occurred on November 18, 1921, at an all-Wagner program when some members of the audience began heading up the aisle to catch their trains as the penultimate piece on the program reached its climax. Stokowski turned on them and delivered, no doubt in his best "orchestrese," a fiery podium speech reprinted verbatim in *Those Fabulous Philadelphians*:

> Try as hard as we can, we cannot make a divine music amid so much untranquility. There is constant walking in and out. You know you cannot live in the material life alone. You must have something else. All the rest of the week you are immersed in worldly affairs. On Friday you come here. Will you not say to yourselves: "I will give to the other side of life the two hours or less that the music requires"? You will gain enormously and so shall we. Even at four o'clock I see old ladies rushing out at the side doors with packages in their hands. Cannot you make the music the all-important thing? Give me the two hours with no noise and no moving about. I only speak this to those who are the moving ones. For the sake at least of musical good manners to each other, let us have that atmosphere of tranquility in which alone the best musical results are obtainable.[19]

Then he turned back to the orchestra and led a "rhapsodic" performance of his transcription of the *Liebestod* from *Tristan und Isolde*.

Five years later the maestro felt his podium speeches still hadn't put enough of a dent in the late comings and early goings of the ladies, so he tried another tactic. To get their attention, he devised a ploy that is famous in orchestra lore. On April 23, 1926, the Friday afternoon women noticed as they settled in for the concert that only two players were on stage—the first violinist and the first cellist. The rest of the chairs were empty. At two thirty sharp, Stoki made his usual dramatic entrance, striding to the podium like a lion tamer full of authority and power. After sweeping his eyes over the breadth of the orchestra as he always did before each performance, he gave the downbeat for the first work on the program, *Fantaisie Contrapuntique* by Guillaume Lekeu, and the two players onstage forged ahead as the music prescribed. Then other players began to straggle in, settling themselves rather noisily into their chairs just before their turn to play. Some were so late they had to begin playing as they hurried to their places.

Audience members exchanged glances with one another. What was this?

The next two works on the program proceeded more or less normally after still more breathless musicians rushed to their seats just in time to play. Then came the final work, Haydn's *Farewell Symphony*, which gave Stokowski the perfect opportunity to reverse the procedure of the opening selection. As the different members of the orchestra finished their parts, they got up and left the stage, again as the music dictated, but, as Stokowski slyly planned, not before ostentatiously checking their watches, gathering their belongings from around their chairs, and making little fusses over folding their music. Finally, the last violinist played his way to the exit and left the stage empty except for Stokowski, who signaled the phantom orchestra to rise before he turned to the audience. Then he bowed his usual formal bow in complete seriousness and strode off the stage to a chorus of laughter and applause as well as a spattering of hisses and walk-outs from indignant concertgoers who did not appreciate the lesson of the day.

The next Monday, *Time* magazine reported the incident. "Philadelphians were dumbfounded by Stokowski's satire. Some applauded. Some hissed. Forty odd first-row patrons walked out. At last a conductor had had the courage to give a Philadelphia audience a few hints on behavior."[20]

Stokowski's involvement in Philadelphia reached all the way to its children. In 1921, he established a series of children's concerts that became so popular that rules had to be implemented to limit the number of adults allowed in. After several grown-up couples were caught trying to sneak in, the men wearing short pants and the women patent leather Mary Janes, it was ruled that all adults had to be accompanied by children. The concerts brought out the showman in Stokowski, and he made liberal use of stunts in the service of introducing children to music. But underneath the stunts, his message was deeply serious and intended to enlarge the understanding of his audience, however young its members might be.

Of course, that did not preclude having some fun. Just as a concert featuring the *Carnival of the Animals* by Saint-Saëns was about to begin, Stokowski and the players suddenly put on an impressive show of fear. A whole caravan of animals was trying to get onto the stage, Stoki exclaimed to his youthful audience, acting very afraid.

"Oh, you don't believe me?" he asked when the children laughed in response. With that, three young elephants, three ponies, a donkey, and a camel rambled onto the stage to the children's delight.

For Prokofiev's *Peter and the Wolf*, Stoki tried to find a real wolf to do the honors, but he had to settle for a large German shepherd. Another time he found within the orchestra's ranks an excellent Charlie Chaplin impersonator in cellist Adrian Siegel and created an afternoon of slapstick fun for the children. And he scored a big hit when a policeman in helmet and goggles rode his motorcycle across the stage to the podium to give the maestro a ticket for breaking the speed limit in the Overture from Mozart's *Marriage of Figaro*.[21]

Setting enormous store on youth, the maestro always treated the children in his audiences with gentle respect. They, after all, were the audiences of the future. But one day, a little girl named Viola, who was sitting in the front row with a big white bow in her hair, made a mortifying mistake.

"Do you know what instrument this is?" Stokowski asked the audience, holding up a viola. "Oh yes, Mr. Sto*KOW*ski," the little girl shouted, jumping up, thrilled with her special knowledge, "its a vi—"

"*Sit down*, young lady!" the maestro ordered in a stern voice before she could go any further. "There is no *COW* in Stokowski."

Never again would that little girl or anyone else in the audience that afternoon forget that the "w" in the maestro's name was pronounced as a "v." It was Sto*KOV*ski, not Sto*KOW*ski.[22]

———•———

In the mid-1920s, two other conductors of exceptional stature arrived on the U.S. orchestral scene and began to garner attention. Serge Koussevitsky took over the reins of the Boston Symphony in 1924 and began to lavish on it the kind of extravagant attention that Stokowski had given to the Philadelphia Orchestra. As had Stokowski, Koussevitsky revamped and reenergized his orchestra and within a few years propelled it back to the top rung of the country's major orchestras. Soon Boston became Philadelphia's greatest rival—until 1928, when Arturo Toscanini assumed the leadership of the New York Philharmonic, which that year had merged with the New York Symphony, to create an orchestra of higher quality than either ensemble separately.

Now the New York Philharmonic began to attract the musical press, inviting comparisons with the orchestras that had previously been considered superior to it—Boston and Philadelphia. And Toscanini, a giant who countenanced no rivals—particularly Stokowski—quickly attracted the spotlight. There were now three major orchestras in the United States vying for attention—and three superb maestros, as well as the Chicago Symphony, also a contender in the major orchestra category. In addition, orchestras in many other cities were gaining in respect and support from their citizenry.

As Rachmaninoff had noted in his Paris interview, the pendulum of orchestral preeminence was swinging heavily in favor of the United States. By 1930, it was time for French music critic Henry Prunières to visit the United States to evaluate the leading orchestras for the *New York Times*. "The Germans excel on brass instruments and the clarinets. The French possess incomparable woodwinds, and the Italians are distinguished by their mastery of wind instrument playing in general, while the Russians, Poles, Czechs and Hungarians surpass in the string sections," he wrote. "[But] the great American orchestras are essentially cosmopolitan in character. They bring to their midst the best musicians of the world and employ instruments of the highest quality." Summing up his observations, he wrote, "I am quite sure that if the Berlin Philharmonic Orchestra, which is the best in Europe, in my opinion, were to visit America, it would be adjudged as being in the fifth or sixth rank, certainly below that of the Chicago Symphony Orchestra, which seems to me to be inferior to those in Boston, Philadelphia, and New York."[23]

Without a doubt, the United States was in the midst of a glorious era in orchestral history when Edna Phillips decided to audition. Although the stock market had crashed that fall, and the Great Depression would inevitably dim some of the glory that surrounded these splendid orchestras, the Philadelphia Orchestra was a formidable arena to think about entering, especially for a young woman with so much to learn.

———·———

Salzedo had won Edna over to the idea of auditioning in December 1929, a few weeks before the Curtis Institute emptied for Christmas vacation. That vacation turned out to be one of the happiest Christmas holidays the Phillips family had enjoyed in a long time. Mrs. Phillips was so taken by the idea that her daughter might become a member of the Philadelphia Orchestra that she was moved to abandon the grim attitude she had displayed toward Christmas ever since her husband's death eleven years before. Actually, Mrs. Phillips had not had much to celebrate for a long time. Even before her husband died in the influenza epidemic of 1918, she had lost four of her eight children, most in infancy. The death of Edna's brother Albert in 1915 was especially hard to bear. The sixteen-year-old had broken a tooth while tobogganing and developed bacterial endocarditis. When Albert died, the grieving had been so terrible that Edna, who was eight at the time, didn't think any of them could endure it, especially her mother.

Albert had shared with Edna something their mother seemed to prize more than anything else in her children—a natural gift for music. Born in Stuttgart, Anna Louise Caroline Wascher was brought to the United States when she was young. After she married John Davies Phillips, of Welsh lineage, and had all those children, she didn't pursue the musical education she had had in Germany, other than playing on a big square piano in the evenings with her husband and children gathered about, a common entertainment at the time. But Anna Phillips never lost her deep love of music. When she realized that two of her children were musically gifted, she did everything within her power to ensure that they made the most of their talents. By the time Albert died at sixteen, he was a fine violinist who might have had a notable career.

When Mrs. Phillips heard that Salzedo wanted her daughter to audition for the Philadelphia Orchestra, she had no reservations at all. She didn't worry that Edna would suffer the fate of a lamb in a lions' den or be over her head musically in such a prestigious orchestra. She had full faith in her daughter. This was the best news she had heard in years.

"Shh-h-h, don't disturb Edna. She's practicing for Stokowski," she would say as Edna's younger sister Margaret, whom they called Peggy, opened the front door to let in a beau, or her brother Arthur, recently graduated from Bucknell College, clomped down the hall, or her older sister Caroline stopped in for a visit. Having restored quiet, Mrs. Phillips would bustle back to her Christmas preparations, humming to herself in a way the family hadn't heard in a long, long time.

---

Finally, the day of the audition dawned. It was January 7, 1930, Edna's twenty-third birthday. That morning she put on her best brown silk dress and took the train from Reading to New York. She was to play for Stokowski that afternoon at Salzedo's apartment on Riverside Drive.

Today, union rules wouldn't allow such an audition. Now auditions are announced publicly well in advance and held under rigorous supervision to overcome possible biases against female or minority players, or others who might not be favored by those with the power to choose. Blind auditions, where players perform behind a screen, were instituted in the 1970s. Such auditions ensure that applicants are heard on their merits alone without reference to their gender, race, or connections. Before that, women had little chance of breaking through the intertwined network of conductors, teachers, and performers that supported the all-male makeup of orchestras.[24]

But, there was Edna Phillips in 1930—a woman granted a special opportunity at breaking through the gender barrier. It was a rare chance indeed, and it had to be kept absolutely quiet, Salzedo told her, because the second harpist couldn't know he was to be replaced until the end of the season.

Salzedo's apartment, where he lived with Lucile Lawrence, who had become his second wife by then, had a clear view across the Hudson River to the New Jersey Palisades, but the view made far less of an impression on Edna that afternoon than the apartment itself. It was the most *moderne* thing she had ever seen. Salzedo had a good friend, Jules Bouy, a furniture and lighting designer from France who was in New York as manager of Ferrobrandt, a famous Art Deco ironwork plant that produced metal lamps and furniture. Bouy was also a sought-after interior designer, and he had given Salzedo's apartment in Edna's words, "a complete Art Deco do."

He had stripped it down to the bare essentials and designed built-in furniture that contrasted vividly with the overstuffed Victorian chairs and sofas Edna was used to. Everything in the apartment was spare, simple, and dramatic. No distractions, like ornate carvings on table legs or extra pillows on chairs and sofas, were allowed to spoil the look of a piece. Everything was strikingly simple. The walls were a rich walnut brown, the color that dominated the room, broken only by dramatic splashes of vermilion. The effect was stunning, but a little sophisticated and stark for the young woman from Reading.

A harp unlike any Edna had ever seen stood in the living room next to the grand piano. Streamlined and sleek, it was completely free of the ornate, gold-leaf decoration that adorned the harps she usually played. Salzedo had worked out a simplified design with the well-known artist and *New Yorker* illustrator Witold Gordon, which featured layers of beautifully polished white maple wood aligned in the rectangular, stepped-back skyscraper motif so popular with Art Deco designers. It was the first Salzedo Model Harp built by Lyon and Healy Harp Company in 1928, and it was like his apartment—spare, simple, and dramatic.

Edna had only a brief time to acquaint herself with this impressive harp before the doorbell rang. Soon she heard Salzedo's Scottish housekeeper, Janet, a holdover from Cher Maître's previous marriage to a socially well-connected heiress, bustle out of the kitchen to answer the door. Immediately, Salzedo jumped up and headed to the foyer to greet his important guest. Phillips heard "*mon ami*s all over the place" as the diminutive Frenchman welcomed into his home the man whose friendship added so much to his own standing.

His head held high, Salzedo walked into the living room with Leopold Stokowski, who looked every bit as glamorous in person as he did on the podium—just as tall, just as slim, just as flaxen-haired. Salzedo, whose impeccable wardrobe and dark good looks usually made him a person who stood out in any setting, looked like a fidgety little sparrow next to the maestro, who somehow made everything around him appear slightly insignificant by comparison.

Salzedo had arranged for them to have tea before Phillips played, and so Lucile, who was just Edna's age, busied herself with the tea service brought in by the housekeeper. In spite of her nervousness, Edna was fascinated to see how engaged Stokowski was in the process of making tea. He seemed as interested in discussing with Lucile, who came from a cultured and wealthy New Orleans family, which tea leaves to use, what kind of water, whether it should boil or just come to a boil, and how hot the teapot should be, as he was in hearing Phillips play.

The conversation bumped along pleasantly, but Edna was so stiff with fright that she couldn't contribute much to it. "What the devil am I doing here?" That's all she could think. It felt so strange, and she was so far out of her element. She had been nervous before recitals in the past, but this was so much more than that.

Then someone made a light comment that made everyone laugh, even Edna. At that second, the maestro swept his arm toward the harp.

"If you please," he said, nodding in her direction.

Salzedo had had her work up four pieces that he knew would appeal to Stokowski. First, she was to play Debussy's *Danses sacrée et profane*, which she had been studying that year, with Salzedo taking the orchestra's part on the piano. And so the audition began.

When they finished the *Danses*, the maestro nodded his head politely, but that was all. His face showed neither approval nor disapproval. It was strangely impassive. Edna couldn't tell what he was thinking. Lucile seemed to want to acknowledge the performance, but her polite gesture soon petered out in the face of Stokowski's muted response.

Next Edna played a solo piece called *Introspection* that Salzedo had written. It was a complicated, atmospheric piece, very quiet. "A player really had to delve into it to make it mean something. It had to be built and deepened all along the way," she explained, and she strove to give it a certain quiet intensity to allow its beauty to come through. She loved the piece and had often played it, working always to bring out its meditative quality.

Again after she finished playing, stillness filled the room. Then Stokowski stood and started toward the door.

"But, *mon ami*, Mademoiselle Phillips is prepared to play more . . ." Salzedo sputtered.

"No, it is enough," Stokowski said as he left the room, thanking Phillips for her playing and Lawrence for her hospitality, but speaking in a quiet, distracted way almost as if he was talking to himself. She thought she heard him say, "That is what I like." But she couldn't be sure.

## CHAPTER 3

# The Little Goat

Phillips didn't hear another word about her audition for over a month. Then, toward the end of February 1930, she got a call from the office of Arthur Judson, manager of the Philadelphia Orchestra, telling her to report to his office immediately after her Curtis Symphony Orchestra rehearsal.

Sitting through rehearsal was almost impossible for Phillips that afternoon. It seemed to her that they had been plodding through César Franck's *Symphony in D minor* forever. Emil Mlynarski, conductor of the Curtis student orchestra, had started rehearsing it with the students in October and had subjected it to section-by-section, note-by-note scrutiny for so long that Phillips had almost lost her love for the wonderful work. Now that she had an important appointment to keep, she found Mlynarski's painstaking approach especially excruciating. Still, in spite of her impatience, she couldn't help relishing the rousing job her fellow students did on the final march that day. The joyousness of their playing made her feel ready to take on the world.

Rehearsal ended at 3:30, and as quickly as she could, Edna flew out the door of the practice hall at Twenty-first and Spruce Streets, shoving her arms into her raccoon coat and pulling her woolen hat over her ears as she went. The quickest way to get to the orchestra's business offices, which the caller had told her were in the Packard Building at Fifteenth and Chestnut Streets, was to cut through Rittenhouse Square. As she sped through the square, she passed a small bronze statue of a goat titled *Billy* by its creator Albert Laessle. It was a favorite of the children whose mothers and nursemaids brought them to the park. Prancing there in the clear winter sunshine, Billy looked as happy as Edna felt, but she didn't stop to watch the cluster of children playing around the statue as she had so often in the past. She had to hurry.

Continuing through the square, she reached the exit at Locust and Eighteenth Streets across from the Curtis Institute corner. But instead of proceeding straight down Locust for four blocks to the Academy of Music at Broad Street, a route she had taken countless times to attend orchestra concerts with her Curtis friends, she turned left at Sixteenth, heading north toward Chestnut Street. Before long, she said, she began to feel confused. She had gone only a few blocks, but the buildings she passed seemed somehow grayer than the ones she was used to and much taller. Compared to the gracious mansions surrounding Rittenhouse Square, these buildings loomed above her, grim and uninviting. It was hard to tell one from another. Where was the Packard Building anyway? she wondered with a panicky feeling. Did the caller say Sixteenth Street? No, it was Fifteenth, she remembered and headed east one block. Now, which of these stern towers was it? What if she didn't find the correct building in time?

A moment before she had felt invincible. Now she felt very small and out of place. This wasn't the world she was used to—the familiar world of practice studios, aspiring music students, and inspiring teachers. This was the world of commerce. This was business.

Finally, Phillips found the Packard Building and rode the elevator to the orchestra's offices, where she was immediately shown into the office of Arthur Judson, who didn't seem at all pleased to see her. Frowning, the imposing impresario motioned for her to step forward from where she had paused just inside the door of his office to catch her breath. Barely greeting her, he pointed to a contract on his desk.

"Sign here," he commanded. "You're taking Vincent Fanelli's place."

*Vincent Fanelli!* The principal harpist? It couldn't be Fanelli, Edna told herself. There must be some mistake. Salzedo had promised her that Fanelli would be there to guide her if she became second harpist. Frank Nicoletta was the second harpist. This couldn't be right.

From the way Judson was scowling, she could tell he wasn't happy about her appointment, either. Her own confusion and dismay at being told she was to take the principal harp position didn't prevent her from sensing Judson's disapproval. He was obviously an important man, the kind of man who was used to having things go the way he wanted them to, and it didn't appear that he liked the way things were going in her case one bit. She didn't fully grasp the reason for his disapproval at the time, but she felt it strongly. Later she would understand those reasons. Judson had been the orchestra's manager since 1915 and had had to deal with hostile reactions to many of Stokowski's experiments and innovations over the years. Now the maestro had done it again. Another groundbreaker. This time he had brought a woman into the exclusive men's club of the Philadelphia Orchestra, and he had put her in a first chair position—all this at a time when women were thought to be unsuitable as orchestral players in any position. It was a lot for Judson to take, especially when the woman Stokowski had chosen was standing in front of him with her raccoon coat half off her shoulders, looking like a college girl.

To say that Judson was an important man in the business side of classical music is an understatement. *Omnipotent* would be a better word. Judson ruled a musical empire.[1] Not only was he manager of the Philadelphia Orchestra, he also managed the New York Philharmonic. On top of that, he managed the careers of many of the leading conductors and musicians of the day through Columbia Concerts Corporation, the artist management firm he had founded. In addition, he had established the Judson Radio Program Corporation to secure jobs for his artists. That radio corporation eventually grew into the Columbia Radio Network and then, under William Paley, the Columbia Broadcasting System, better known today as CBS.[2]

Whatever this very busy mogul-manager may have thought about Phillips's appointment, he didn't have time for pleasantries with a young recruit. That was clear.

"Well? What are you waiting for?" he said, pushing the contract forward for her to sign.

Maybe he has the names mixed up, Phillips thought in a fit of wishful reasoning. He has so many men under contract. So many orchestras. So many Italian names. So many French and German and Hungarian and Russian names. How can he keep them all straight? That must be it, she told herself. He's confused.

Judson was too daunting for her to dare to speak her thoughts. He looked enormous behind his big desk. Not easily intimidated into silence (except by her former piano teacher), she held her tongue this time. Without reading a line of the contract or saying a word about which position she had auditioned for, she signed her name and rushed back along the streets she had just traversed, hoping to find Salzedo at the Curtis Institute.

"Cher Maître, I've just been to Arthur Judson's office," she gasped after bounding up the stairs and bursting into Salzedo's studio unannounced. "I signed the contract! I'm in the orchestra!"

Salzedo, who was not accustomed to students entering his studio so precipitously, paused a moment to remind her of her faux pas before he replied.

"So, my child, the maestro did see the possibilities in you."

"But it was strange," she plunged ahead, too excited to observe proprieties. "When Mr. Judson gave me the contract to sign, he said I'd be replacing Fanelli. I'm replacing Nicoletta, aren't I?"

With that Salzedo blanched. "Really, Ed-naa? Are you sure Monsieur Judson said *Fanelli*?"

"Yes. *Vincent Fanelli*. But he must have the names mixed up," she said, still persisting in her innocence about Judson, who, she soon came to realize, knew perfectly well the name of every musician in both of his orchestras and then some. "He must have meant to say *Nicoletta*. It would be impossible for me to replace Fanelli."

"This is very strange," Salzedo said, looking perplexed. He got up and walked to the window, where he stood with his back to her for several minutes. Finally, he said, "I will call *mon ami*. I will find out. Tonight I will tell you."

That evening Edna joined a group of Salzedo's students for a harp ensemble rehearsal in the basement of Knapp Hall at Curtis. None of the students knew about her appointment (none of them even knew she had auditioned), and the evening began as all their gatherings did, with seven or eight young men and women sitting here and there about the room, tuning their harps and chatting quietly as they waited for the entrance of Cher Maître.

As soon as Salzedo entered the room, he strode over to Edna's chair and laid a heavy hand on her shoulder. "It is for first," he whispered.

This time Edna was the one who turned white.

"I can't . . . I won't do it," she gasped.

Salzedo silenced her with a severe look and continued on to the front of the class. Somehow she got through the rehearsal and waited for her chance to talk to him alone.

"I will not do this," she protested when the moment finally came. "It's too much too soon. I'll fall straight down from the top to the bottom before my career even has a chance to begin. I'll be a laughingstock. You told me the audition was for second harp, not first."

Salzedo let her wind down.

"Ed-naa, a chance to play with such a great orchestra—you cannot pass up such an opportunity."

"But didn't you tell the maestro that we thought the audition was for second harp? Didn't you tell him I began studying the harp not even five years ago . . . that I have so much more to learn?"

"Shh, shh," Salzedo answered. "Don't you know how musical you are? If we cut your wrists, you would bleed music, not blood. You must not let a chance like this one slip away."

"But didn't you tell the maestro—"

Full of dramatic dignity, Salzedo rose and stood before her, his shoulders pulled back and his head held high. "I cannot be disloyal to your future," he said. "You must do this."

Later, as Phillips walked back across a darkened Rittenhouse Square toward her lodgings, the bright February moon shone through the bare branches of the trees, making the little bronze goat she had passed earlier that day glisten so brightly that she stopped for a moment beside it, hoping for the feeling of pleasure it often brought her. But this time the goat's frolicking stance didn't look so joyful, and she began to wonder if the sculptor had not portrayed it in a prancing, carefree gambol after all. Maybe that little goat was struggling to get away from something. In the cold moonlight, it began to look frightened to her, not playful.

Just then, the real meaning of what Salzedo said struck her. Cher Maître wasn't being loyal to *her* future. He was being loyal to *his* future. She was young, but not too young to understand Salzedo's dilemma. For the sake of *his* career, he needed to stay in the good graces of Stokowski. He couldn't afford to offend a world-famous conductor by telling him that a mistake had been made. He couldn't suggest that perhaps the maestro had misread the candidate's capabilities or explain that while this young woman might have some of the attributes the maestro liked to see in his players, she didn't have enough seasoning to handle a principal's position. One did not embarrass the conductor. How could someone in Salzedo's position tell such a luminary that he had chosen the wrong candidate? No, Cher Maître couldn't bring himself to do that. *His* career was at stake. *His* future lay on the line. *Her* future? That was her problem, Edna realized as she looked at the little bronze goat.

"I cannot be disloyal to your future."

"Applesauce," she said out loud, using a popular cussword of the day as she looked at the statue glistening there in the moonlight. What kind of future did she have now? Whether that little goat was about to be sacrificed or not, she felt sure she was. She would never be able to survive as the principal harpist of the Philadelphia Orchestra. She was sure to fail miserably and face public humiliation.

———•———

Back in her room on Pine Street, Edna said, she faced what she feared to be her fate. Her career in music, a career for which she had lately begun to have such high hopes, seemed already doomed to fail, publicly and finally, before it ever got under way. The only thing left for her to do now, she realized, to save herself from utter humiliation was to work as hard as she could for the next seven months before the season opened in October. In the short time she had until then, she had to become the best possible harpist she could be.

Music had always been important to her. But now it became her whole life. She spent twelve, fourteen, sixteen hours a day, day after day, at her harp, struggling to master its intricacies. She needed time, and time was what Stokowski's unexpected appointment did not give her. Somehow, before the next season opened, she needed to make her still-unwieldy harp her friend, her best and most intimate friend.

Although he would never admit to such a thing, Salzedo did seem slightly penitent about the role he had played in getting Edna into her predicament. Whether he felt sympathy for her or concern about his own reputation as a teacher, he lavished extra attention on her over the next few months, doing his best to whip her into shape and prepare her for the rigors of life in the Philadelphia Orchestra. In coaching session after coaching session, he prodded her toward stronger mastery of harp technique, trying to pour as much understanding of the instrument into her as possible in the short time that was available.

He also did what he could to get her ready to take on her role as a first-chair player, a role he knew would be difficult for any greenhorn— and especially a female greenhorn who would have no first-chair player and no female allies to show her how things worked inside the arcane orchestral world she was about to enter. His first piece of advice was to tell Edna to go back to Judson's office and ask him to specify in her contract that she was to be the principal harpist. Her original contract had just said *harpist*, failing to specify that she was to be principal harpist, something that she had been too green to notice. But not Salzedo. He was an artist, but he was also practical. Edna would be a principal player, and he wanted to make sure she would be recognized and paid appropriately. Facing Judson again was the last thing she wanted to do, but following Salzedo's instructions, she forced herself to make an appointment to see him.

When she again faced the imposing impresario across his big desk, she asked, in what she was sure was a quavering voice, "Since I am to be the principal harpist, wouldn't the word *principal* have to be in the contract?"

"Well, give it to me. I'll write it in," Judson said, getting rid of her as fast as he could.

After making sure her contract was in order, Salzedo next turned his attention to Edna's wardrobe. What was a young woman to wear among all those men on the stage of the Academy of Music? What would be appropriate? One day he surprised her by taking her on an impromptu shopping trip to Bonwit Teller, a fashionable women's store, to look for suitable gowns to wear among the white ties and tails worn by the men of the orchestra. Unfazed by the raised eyebrows of the women in Bonwit's eveningwear department at the sight of a middle-aged man shopping for clothes with a younger woman, the quintessential Frenchman quickly dispatched a saleswoman to search for appropriate gowns.

In the end, two dresses were chosen. The first, to be worn for the Friday afternoon concerts, was a simple black crepe de chine gown, three-quarter-length, with a full skirt, long sleeves, and a little white ruching at the neck. The other, chosen for the evening concerts, was of black peau de soie. An elegant full-length gown, it was sleeveless with a decorous, slightly V-shaped neckline in front and back. Once again it had a full, flowing skirt that would gracefully hide Edna's feet as she operated the harp pedals.

After her dresses were chosen, Salzedo took it upon himself to advise Edna about her behavior, which was something he often did with his students, whom he strove to cultivate as impressive performers as well as proficient harpists. Always interested in ferreting out just what a student needed to work on to make his or her playing appeal to an audience, Cher Maître had what Edna called X-ray vision about his students.

Going beyond their grasp of the music, he focused his attention on their performance style and gave them important advice on: how they dressed; how they sat; how they were to behave if something went wrong in a concert ("Never look behind you even if a bomb goes off!" he told them); how they were to acknowledge applause, and many other non-musical matters that might enhance the effect of a performance. One of his students used to let his mouth hang open when he played, Edna said. Salzedo thought he "looked like a hayseed" doing that and made him practice with a pencil clenched between his teeth to remind him to keep his mouth closed.

That spring Cher Maître, at his most paternal, zeroed in on a special area of concern for Edna—how she was to behave as one woman among one hundred men.

"Ed-naa," he cautioned her with great gravity. "You will arrive at the orchestra like a little queen. Remember you must *stay* that way."

He made his pronouncement with such a serious air that Edna had to suppress a giggle. She knew that Salzedo had a reputation for being quite the roué. In spite of his short stature—"my tragedy," he called it—he had much success with women. There were many stories of his romantic conquests, almost as many as there were about Maestro Stokowski. Both had robust reputations for their amorous exploits.

At that time, Salzedo was in his midforties, and even after his recent second marriage, there were rumors of dalliances. Like Stokowski, Salzedo eventually married and divorced three times. In fact, Edna was slightly offended that her teacher never made a pass at her when he had done so with many others. Not that she would have wanted him to, she insisted, but one has one's pride after all. Perhaps she was too independent for him or too tall, she speculated. Whatever the reason, she said, "there just wasn't any chemistry" between them. But she knew one thing for sure—when Salzedo warned her to avoid the pitfalls that might follow a romantic entanglement, she was getting advice from an expert on the matter.

"Do not let yourself get involved with . . . ahem . . . any of these men in the orchestra, or you will one day find yourself thrown away like an old shoe," he warned her one day with an air of the highest sanctity.

Of course, they both knew that the most dangerous ladies' man of all, the "ahem" Salzedo was really alluding to, was the maestro himself. Stokowski radiated a kind of glamour, magnetism, and power that drew women to him. Talk of his amorous exploits buzzed around the Curtis Institute, Philadelphia, New York, and would eventually spread to Hollywood. Everyone knew, or thought they knew, about Stoki and his romantic adventures.

"There are many stories about the maestro, Ed-naa," Salzedo told her another day with a serious, reflective look in his eyes, as if he were speaking from high ground indeed. "But, do not worry, my child. They can't all be true. He must have *some* time to study his scores."

At that point, Edna didn't have time to worry about Stokowski's philandering. She had often heard about the young ladies who plotted chance meetings with him, lining up outside the Academy of Music and his apartment in hopes of encountering the glamorous maestro. With such easy prey available, he would have little inclination to bother with her, she decided. Other than chuckling at Salzedo's air of personal innocence on the subject—when she knew he was anything but innocent in these matters—she didn't give much thought to his warnings.

She couldn't. She was too worried about the possibility that she would be judged a failure as principal harpist to fret about the chance that she might become a target of the maestro's attentions. Every concert she heard that spring sent her deeper into despair. How could she keep up with those master players—many of whom she also admired as awe-inspiring teachers at Curtis? Their virtuosity overwhelmed her. How could she presume to perform alongside them? She would have found it hugely demanding to play in the same orchestra with them in the second harp position, but as first harp—the thought was agonizing.

That April, Stokowski presented the first fully staged U.S. performance of *The Rite of Spring*. It had been rechoreographed by Léonide Massine and mounted with wondrous panache. The revolutionary harmonies and jagged rhythms of Stravinsky's score fascinated Phillips, but watching Martha Graham dance to her death as the Chosen One who is sacrificed to placate the powers of the earth made a sharper impression on her, reminding her a little too vividly of her own precarious situation.

Driven by her fear of failure among the stars of the orchestra, Phillips practiced relentlessly to improve her technique, knowing that she needed all the time she could get to prepare herself. Still, she sometimes wished that the time would pass more quickly so that her ultimate humiliation would be over and done with.

As if trying to increase her angst, various newspapers and magazines picked up on the news of her appointment as the first woman in a major orchestra when it was announced in May, after the season ended, speculating on it with a kind of juicy relish that stirred up old worries about ewe lambs and lions' dens in Phillips.

"Ah, Ed-naa, you're so fortunate," Salzedo sighed at one point. "I would have to pay a fortune for that kind of publicity. You get it all for free."

But it was not the kind of spotlight Phillips wanted focused on her when she felt so unready. With all the pressure she was feeling, she knew one thing for sure: she would never have to face anything so frightening in her entire life as her entrance into the Philadelphia Orchestra. In her single-minded struggle, she could imagine nothing that would ever be so full of danger. Certainly nothing so insignificant as her own throat.

Then in June, she developed a high fever and raging sore throat that made it difficult to swallow. One morning she awoke and found that she couldn't open her jaw at all. Floating in and out of consciousness in the days that followed, she was aware of doctors, nurses, her mother being called to Philadelphia, being taken back to Reading, and operations being discussed. Finally it was determined that she had quinsy, which in the days before antibiotics was a dangerous illness. It causes the uvula to swell along with the glands in the throat. If it's not stopped, quinsy impedes breathing and swallowing and can be fatal.

Two operations followed and then weeks of gargling and being propped up all the time so she wouldn't choke to death. Practicing was out of the question. Even Edna realized that her physical survival had to take precedence over her musical survival at that point.

She didn't begin to recover her strength until the middle of August. There stood her harp untouched for two months, the precious months she had meant to spend strengthening her muscles, and working, working, working to get ready for the orchestra. All she could think as she began to recover was that she had to get back to work. Not understanding how much her bout with quinsy had sapped her energy, she gathered as many scores from the Curtis library as she could handle and somehow got herself onto a train and up to Seal Harbor, Maine, where Salzedo was holding a summer training session for a group of his students and where she hoped to be able to prepare herself for the coming season with the orchestra.

To her dismay, she soon discovered that she was too weak to make much progress. Salzedo and Lucile clucked around her, looking worried and telling her how pale and thin she was, and everyone in town, it seemed, had a special potion to help her regain her strength. A few offered suggestions that were even more important to her: ideas for helping her get her fingertips toughened up quickly. While she had been ill, the skin on her fingers had softened, and now practicing was so painful on her tender fingertips that it was difficult for her to concentrate. Her harp strings dug into her fingers and left blisters that oozed and formed painful sores that made her reluctant to play even though she desperately wanted to. Sticking the blisters with pins didn't make the blisters go away. Salves didn't work. Nothing seemed to work until someone suggested that she soak her fingers in her own urine. Desperate enough to try anything, Phillips did it. Whether that did the trick or not, the tips of her fingers finally toughened up. At least she wouldn't have to worry about blisters hampering her practicing anymore.

"Cher Maître, look at all the music I brought up," she sighed in frustration one day, telling Salzedo that she had hoped he would help her learn some of the important parts she might have to play with the orchestra, the ones she had never worked on.

"My child, that wouldn't help you," Salzedo answered huffily. "I teach you to play. The rest is up to you." Then he told her that it wouldn't help her to know the big parts until she knew where they belonged and reminded her that playing in an orchestra is not the same as playing alone. "You must hear how a part fits into a work," he said. "Playing your part alone is not enough. You need to have the whole picture."

The whole picture? Although he meant to comfort her with that remark, it struck terror in Phillips's heart. She knew that her orchestral training had been much more limited than her solo training, which was brief enough. Her days at the Roxy were a blur and had provided no real background for her, and the training at Curtis at that time was more focused on fostering the solo talents of its students rather than on developing the student orchestra. Orchestra rehearsals weren't governed by the same sense of mission back then that individual lessons were. But those rehearsals still showed Phillips that in many ways it was more difficult to play in an orchestra than it was to play alone. Coming in at just the right time, blending into the ensemble, creating the effect that was needed—she knew she hadn't had a chance to develop that kind of flexibility. She had played in the Curtis orchestra for only one year, and during that time they had concentrated on a few works like the Franck Symphony. There were so many important compositions out there that she had never played.

On top of that, Phillips was by no means the principal harpist in the Curtis orchestra—she wasn't considered advanced enough for that position—so she hadn't felt the sense of responsibility for understanding the whole process that she might have felt otherwise. She realized now that she had spent much of her time in rehearsals, especially during those long rests a harpist has, enjoying the byplay as Maestro Mlynarski struggled to impose a sense of ensemble on Curtis's individualistic young talents.

Instead of concentrating on learning the complexities of orchestral playing, she feared she had wasted too much time on the fun of it all rather than trying to understand the nuances that Mlynarski was trying to make the students see. She hadn't thought enough about the special colors that the harp adds to the texture of the different orchestral works. More often than not, if things were going well, she allowed herself to be swept away by the beauty and power of the orchestral sound that enveloped her without analyzing what effect the harp was having on the whole.

Salzedo's remark reminded Edna of everything she didn't know. She barely felt comfortable with her own playing. What did she know about the whole picture? How could she fit in among one hundred players who were artists and virtuosos? She felt like a raw recruit in wartime about to be thrown into battle without the proper training. Like that recruit, she would have to learn to perform under fire or she would not survive. But unlike the recruit, she couldn't do it as a rank private. She had to do it as a principal, an officer. The difficulties of her situation exploded before her, and every time she thought about them her nerves grew more jangled.

"Don't worry, my child," Salzedo said as she prepared to leave Seal Harbor for Philadelphia. "Just be calm."

Phillips had heard that before. It was what he always said to his harp students as they waited backstage at Curtis before their recitals. The minute he said it, they would go to pieces and have to be put back together again, but she couldn't allow herself that luxury now. Her first battle was upon her.

## CHAPTER 4

# Keeping Up with
# the Speed Kings

Back in Reading, Phillips's mother had decided that her daughter wasn't up to facing her entrance into the Philadelphia Orchestra on her own. Anna had lost too many loved ones to the scourge of illness to take lightly Edna's bout with quinsy. Moreover, Edna was embarking on the career of her mother's dreams. She wanted to be right there in Philadelphia to prop her daughter up with eggnogs and other home remedies, and so she rented a small townhouse at 1910 Panama Street for the two of them and her youngest daughter, Peggy, who was attending Beaver College (known today as Arcadia University), just northwest of Philadelphia in the suburb of Glenside. A cheerful, fun-loving person, Peggy was happy to live with her mother and sister and use the new roadster she was so proud of to run back and forth to classes.

The house Mrs. Phillips found was an easy walk from the Academy of Music on Broad Street. Edna had only to head west on Locust four blocks to Rittenhouse Square, angle through the square—passing her friend the little goat each time—and head south on 19th Street a few short blocks to the house on Panama, a tiny street, barely wide enough for an automobile to pass through, wedged between Delancey and Pine Streets. Leafy ginkgo trees, old-fashioned streetlamps, and townhouses lined its brick-paved sidewalks and made it feel more like a quiet village lane than a street in the midst of a big industrial city. As the year went forward, that little street and the home her mother had rented became a refuge for Edna, a place of retreat from the hectic field of battle on the stage of the Academy of Music.

But she didn't have much time to enjoy her refuge now. As soon as she moved in, she hurried over to the Academy to pick up her music for the first concert of the season and immediately began "to perspire all over the place trying to figure out what to do." It was to be an all-Russian program, and two of the works, Stravinsky's *Firebird Suite* and Scriabin's *Prometheus*, were totally new to Phillips. Their strangeness and complexity perplexed her, leaving her wondering how the different sections fit together and what they sounded like. *Prometheus* worried her with its mystical, mysterious undercurrents, but the *Firebird* terrified her. "It's as familiar as 'My Country 'Tis of Thee' now," she explained, "but back then it had me completely baffled with all those dissonances and changing rhythms. I wasn't used to that kind of thing at all."

Today if a player wants to hear how a work sounds, she can easily find a way to do it. But in 1930 one didn't have that luxury. The days of easy access to recorded classical music were still to come. In fact, the Philadelphia Orchestra under Stokowski was busy building a body of recorded works that others could listen to in the future. Few recordings were then available, certainly none of works as new and strange as *Prometheus* and *Firebird*. It was up to Phillips to unravel their complexities without hearing what they sounded like. How was she ever going "to get in and out at all the right places?" she worried. If only Salzedo were back in town, he could help her figure out these mysterious compositions. But Cher Maître—who had promised her he would be there to help her whenever she needed him—wasn't back from Maine yet.

At least, she noted with relief, she didn't have to worry about the other work that Stokowski had chosen for the program, Tchaikovsky's Fifth Symphony. There wasn't anything for the harp in that.

As the first rehearsal drew near, she spent almost every waking hour at her harp. One day as she practiced with the window in her bedroom open, she began to hear the sound of a trumpet coming from an apartment building down the block at the corner of Panama and 19th Streets. The virtuoso playing delighted her. It was so expressive. The beautiful sounds floating through her window soothed her worried soul—until she realized with a shock that those notes were from *The Firebird* and the player must be Saul Caston, the orchestra's first trumpet, a member of the elite corps she was about to join. Her tight nerves came back with a vengeance. There was no question about it, she said, "I did not belong in the same ranks with such a master."

With the opening of the new season at hand, the press started up again on the novelty of a young woman entering the august Philadelphia

Orchestra. Phillips thought she had gotten those stories behind her in the spring when her appointment was announced, but now they began anew. "Solo Harpist to be First Girl in Philadelphia Orchestra," the *Philadelphia Public Ledger* proclaimed, and other papers followed suit.[1] At least the *Record* used the word *woman* instead of *girl*. The other new players (there were fourteen in all), some of whom were friends from Curtis, were also announced, but Phillips got the headlines.

Salzedo might have envied her all that free publicity, but even he understood that what Phillips wanted and needed was to slip in among the ranks of players as inconspicuously as possible. She wasn't ready for the spotlight, and both of them knew it. Every time someone showed her one of the articles that mentioned her, she would imagine an audience lying in wait for her first mistake, ready to pounce on her as an invader, an upstart female who didn't belong up there among the men of the orchestra in the first place. If she made one wrong move, she feared that her mistake would be the talk of the town.

Actually, Philadelphians would have had to have a strong interest in music to pay much attention to the articles about Phillips in the midst of the excitement that was then building over Connie Mack's Philadelphia Athletics. The team had just clinched the American League championship. While Phillips was dreading October 3, the opening day of the orchestra's season, as the most momentous date in history, sure that the whole city, maybe even the whole world, was waiting to see whether she would survive her first performance, most of Philadelphia was focused on the prospects of the Philadelphia Athletics in the 1930 World Series, which was going on at that time, and rooting for the Athletics to beat the St. Louis Cardinals. A music writer once noted, "During the heyday of the Philadelphia Orchestra under Stokowski, leading players in the orchestra became as famous in musical circles as star baseball players in the sports field."[2] But that wouldn't be true during the World Series. Then even the orchestra's most beloved players didn't stand a chance of attracting as much attention as the Athletics players did.

If she hadn't been so preoccupied with her own pressures, Phillips might have been more aware of the series herself, because her sister Peggy's new beau was Christy Mathewson Jr., son of the venerated New York Giants pitcher, Christy Mathewson Sr. A friend of their brother Arthur, the young Mathewson often visited Peggy, and when he did the house was full of baseball talk. But Edna's attention was so fixated on her precarious position she barely registered anything beyond the range of her harp—not the Athletics, not Connie Mack, not even her old boyfriends who "still came trotting down from Reading." The only thing she focused on was her harp. Practice, practice, practice—it was all she had time for and all she cared about.

When September 29 dawned, the day of the orchestra's first rehearsal, Phillips walked to the Academy of Music with trepidation. She pushed open the stage door on Locust Street early in the morning, more than an hour before the rehearsal was to begin. No one was in the green room, which was just inside the door, except a burly fellow with a shiny bald pate and the shoulders of a stevedore. He was Marshall Betz, the orchestra librarian, perhaps the only stagehand ever to attain such an erudite position. He had signed on with the orchestra in 1912 when the young Leopold Stokowski took over the podium. Stokowski picked him out as a particularly reliable worker among the stagehands and gradually gave him more responsibilities until he ended up with the librarian's job, which meant that Marshall was in charge of all the orchestra's music, the scores, the individual parts, everything—in spite of the fact that he couldn't read a note of music.[3]

Phillips didn't know anything about Marshall's history, but his gruff, kindly manner seemed to lighten the load of fear she was carrying. "Call me Marshall. Everyone does," he told her as he walked with her through the green room toward the stage, drew back the dusty red velvet curtain that stood in for a stage door, and pointed to her harp.

The brief sense of comfort Marshall offered quickly fell away. There stood her harp at the very front of the stage almost touching the foot-lights, in front of all the other music stands and chairs. She walked to it and stood a moment, looking out at the famously beautiful Academy of Music in front of her. A grand opera house modeled after Milan's La Scala, it spread before her in dizzying glory with rows and rows of scarlet seats marching toward her. Three levels of cream and gold tiers containing still more scarlet seats encircled the first level and climbed upward toward the gorgeously painted ceiling with an immense crystal chandelier hanging from it. The sight made Phillips feel faint for a moment, but she mustered all her resources to put a stop to that. She had no time for weak-kneed reactions now. Her harp had to be tuned. That was the job at hand. She sat down, got out her tuning fork, and leaned her ear close to the sounding board to begin the arduous task of listening to the pitch of each of the harp's forty-seven strings so that she could adjust each one until the instrument was tuned exactly as it should be. That required concentration, so that at first she didn't notice the other members of the orchestra gradually taking their places onstage.

At one point she heard the sound of footsteps nearby and raised her eyes to look around. The first eyes that met hers, those of a cellist taking his seat not far from her, startled her with their hostility. She knew she might face resistance from some of the men of the orchestra, but the wave of hostility that came at her from that cellist and from others around him shocked her. It was so palpable it felt like a slap.

Later she discovered that the men were angry about more than just the fact that a woman had invaded their private domain. They were also upset that Vincent Fanelli had been replaced so precipitously. An excellent harpist, he was a cherished colleague who had worked with them for many years. Apparently, he had developed a problem in his right hand, and the players thought Maestro Stokowski had moved too rapidly to replace him after the hand problem had worsened during the past season. That made Phillips a usurper in their eyes, and it certainly didn't win her favor with the second harpist, who seemed to think he should have been promoted to the first chair. His attitude toward her was hostile from the start. There would be no help coming from that quarter. She could see that.

Once again her anxiety rose, but she had so many other things to think about she managed to suppress it. First, she had to finish tuning. When that was done, she sorted through the music that Marshall had put on her stand to make sure everything was there. It was, but there was also something puzzling in the pile. Behind the folder that held the music for *Prometheus* and *The Firebird* was another folder containing a batch of music she had never seen before, much of it in manuscript form. What was that doing on her stand? It must be a mistake, she surmised. She would tell that nice Marshall about it when she got the chance.

Just then the acting concertmaster (Stokowski was experimenting with rotating concertmasters at the time)[4] nodded to the principal oboist, Marcel Tabuteau. Instantly, the cacophony of different instruments warming up and orchestra members greeting one another ceased. A ripple of tension fanned through the orchestra. Tabuteau sounded the A. The winds tuned. The brass tuned. The strings tuned. Phillips rechecked her harp, which she was soon to learn would be devilishly hard to keep in tune when wind gusts billowed through the curtains at the side of the stage.

A moment of silence followed. All sat at attention. At ten-thirty sharp, Stokowski brushed through the curtains and strode briskly onto the stage, wearing a well-tailored suit and looking more like a businessman about to chair an important meeting than the dramatic maestro Phillips had watched in concert. He stepped immediately onto the podium, said "Good morning," with a slight bow of his head, and paused for a brief moment to cast his eyes over the whole orchestra. Then he announced, "The Scriabin, please," and allowing only seconds for the players to pick the piece out of the music on their stands, gave the downbeat for *Prometheus*.

That was all—no opening speech to the orchestra after the summer break, no welcome to the new members, and no special words for the noted pianist Harold Bauer, who was seated at the piano, waiting to play. Nothing. Just a sweeping look that took in everyone, followed by the downbeat.

In a flash, Phillips found herself swimming around in the murky waters of Scriabin's tone poem while "the speed kings of the Philadelphia Orchestra" played with perfect confidence. They didn't seem in the least intimidated by the work's strangeness. To Phillips, they sounded as if they were playing a Saturday night concert, except that the maestro didn't have them play through the whole work. Instead he jumped from one section to another, addressing only the briefest of comments in a quiet but authoritative voice to different players along the way. Everything went so fast and the maestro said so little that Phillips was hard-pressed to keep up. Afraid she might get lost in Scriabin's "strange dream that just goes washing over you," she fought "to keep [her] chin above water" as the harp part wove in and out through the work.

Where was the painstaking step-by-step preparation she was used to in the Curtis Symphony Orchestra? Emil Mlynarski had talked the students through what seemed like every note. Wasn't that the way orchestra rehearsals were supposed to work? Why didn't they play the whole work through? Wouldn't the players want to hear the whole thing to feel assured about what they were doing? Stokowski kept jumping from place to place. Obviously he had totally mastered the score, knew exactly what he wanted, and wasn't wasting any time on the easy parts. Those the players could handle on their own. Too bad if the player was a neophyte who wanted to hear how the parts fit into the whole. He—or she—would just have to figure it out.

"The Tchaikovsky, please," the maestro announced when he decided they had done enough with *Prometheus*, speaking in a quiet, firm voice in a tone that Phillips said reminded her of a dog trainer. He kept his voice low, but it was full of unmistakable authority. Instantly, the other players rearranged the music on their stands and readied their instruments to play. Since Tchaikovsky's Fifth had no part for the harp, Phillips stood up and headed offstage toward the green room, relieved that she didn't have to face the terrors of *The Firebird* just yet. She wanted to talk to

Marshall about the extra folder of music on her stand and had taken three or four steps when Stokowski spoke to her.

"Harp"—he had a habit of calling his players by the names of their instruments—"I want you to play G-sharp octaves at the end of the first movement."

Phillips quickly returned to her seat, and Stoki directed the orchestra to play a portion of the first movement so she could hear where she was to play. After that, he had the men play the section again, directing her to fit in the octaves where he indicated. That was it. Phillips had no music, and he gave her no more instruction. It was up to her to "stick those blasted octaves in" where the maestro wanted them.

Satisfied that Phillips understood what he meant, Stokowski continued, "Now I want you to imitate the cellos just before the horn solo in the second movement." Again he had the orchestra play the section for her.

Luckily for Phillips, she was blessed with absolute, or perfect, pitch. "It saved my life because I could hear what the cellos were playing and duplicate it on my harp even though it was complex. The trick was, they were playing pizzicato, plucking the strings, and that was complicated to match. But once I heard what and where I was to play, I was able to pick up the markers and stick my part in."

That was Phillips's introduction to the way Stokowski ran things. Out of the blue, with no warning, he had given her an assignment to carry out with no preparation and no music to follow. She had to count 265 measures and play. That was it. She had never heard of such a thing! He just assumed she could do it and made no fuss about it. Was this what life under Stokowski would be like?

Totally engrossed with counting her way through Tchaikovsky, she didn't have time to worry about her big dread of the day, the fearsome *Firebird*. She also forgot about the second folder on her stand with all that strange handwritten music in it. Then once again, suddenly, just as with *Prometheus*, Stokowski called a halt to work on the Tchaikovsky. A brief break flew by. Then *The Firebird*. Without wasting a second, the maestro plunged ahead. Every ounce of Phillips's concentration was required to follow his direction. Eerie, haunting, spooky music rose up around her. She was intrigued by it, but she had to resist its spell and keep her mind on what she had to do in the midst of its complexity. *The Firebird* is filled with abruptly changing, complex rhythms and sudden silences. At times delicate, sometimes glittering and melodious, some-times shattering and dissonant, all of the piece was foreign to Phillips's ears. With the harp having to play "in all sorts of unexpected spots," she feared that she would become confused and miss an entrance or get out of step with the ragged rhythms.

Stokowski continued through the work, picking out areas that needed attention and giving different players quiet directives about what he wanted done. "Harp," he said at one point, stopping her in the midst of playing, "I want you to make your harmonics walk out of your instrument the way a note walks out of a horn."

It was a puzzling instruction similar to the little word-picture instructions she had heard him give other players, telling them to think of luscious, round, purple grapes when playing a passage, or some such thing. But it was also enlightening in a strange way. It would require some thinking for her to do what he wanted. Harmonics are high, bell-like tones that result when the lower part of a string is briefly held while the string is being plucked. Producing a harmonic is almost a percussive act on the harp, and that can get in the way of making a clear sound like that of a horn. It would take practice for Phillips to be able to produce the sound Stokowski wanted, but she was intrigued by his suggestion.

He also "shushed" her several times, motioning for her to play softer and steal in so that she would blend in with the flow of the ensemble. It made her feel somewhat reprimanded, but she knew she had much to learn about playing in an orchestra. Once again she hoped Stokowski would go over the entire *Firebird* so she could get a better grip on it, but after one stop-and-start run-through, the maestro turned and nodded at a man sitting out in the empty auditorium. Then he stepped down from the podium and walked off the stage. What was this? So much remained to be done on the *Firebird*. How could the orchestra stop working now?

The man who had been sitting in the auditorium, Alexander Smallens, the orchestra's assistant conductor, walked onto the stage and stepped up to the podium. Out of the corner of Phillips's eye, she saw Stokowski take a seat in the auditorium. All around her she heard a shuffling sound as the men fiddled with the music on their stands. Oh no, Phillips realized, they were putting *The Firebird* away and opening the other folder—the one she had meant to ask Marshall about, the one with the collection of music in manuscript.

Suddenly, Phillips realized that they were going to have to sight-read those works. Stokowski was apparently planning to sit out in the auditorium and listen to the orchestra play the pieces to see how they sounded. Later she discovered that this was a common practice for him. It was his way of giving new composers a chance to be heard. He would choose several new works and have his orchestra sight-read them at rehearsals to determine which were worthy of performance. It was admirable of him to give aspiring composers a chance, Phillips thought, but what about his orchestra? What about giving the poor players a chance to get their teeth into the program they would have to perform that week? Or didn't these speed kings need that? Were they so skilled they could master what the maestro wanted that quickly? What in God's name was she doing there? she asked herself. How could she continue under such demanding circumstances? Now she had to sight-read works in front of the maestro and the orchestra. It was just too much.

Sight-reading is an especially difficult task for a harpist. Like music for the piano, music for the harp is written on two staves, which adds a complexity, but the harp presents an additional problem. It has no black keys to serve as sharps or flats like the piano. Instead, a harpist must raise or depress one of seven pedals at the base of the harp to change the pitch of a particular string to create its sharp or flat. That means that the harpist must continually read ahead in the music to set the sharps and flats correctly before playing the notes and then keep changing the pedal settings as the music dictates. Obviously, this can be challenging, especially in a dense, complicated piece that one is reading for the first time.

According to Phillips, Salzedo had "mollycoddled" his students when it came to sight-reading. He always gave them plenty of time to figure out a piece before they played it for him. That approach was fine for a soloist who would be able to plan out the correct pedal settings before playing a piece in public, but it made it difficult for someone to play new works on the spot. As time went on, Phillips taught herself to read music for the harp almost as fast as if she were reading a newspaper, but she couldn't do it at her first rehearsal.

Smallens, an energetic and capable conductor in his own right, plunged into the task of conducting the unfamiliar music without wasting time, leading the orchestra through several short works. Phillips managed to negotiate her way through them, although some were doubly hard to figure out because they were written by hand. Just deciphering what the composer meant by the squiggles on the page was a trial in itself. Somehow Phillips limped along, keeping up as best she could. Then, for a reason Phillips never understood, Smallens directed the orchestra to play a portion of *Swan Lake*, which she had never played. At first, she was able to carry on, but then came a long cadenza for the harp. Hundreds of notes covered the page. It was just too overwhelming. Her mind went blank. She knew Smallens was standing there on the podium, waving his baton at her, and everyone was watching, waiting for her to play, but she couldn't move. She just sat there, too confused and overwrought to play a note.

Eventually, the rest of the orchestra finished the work, and the rehearsal was over. None of the men said anything to Phillips as they left the stage. Sure that those who didn't want her there were gloating over her failure to play, she began to gather herself together in preparation to leave. Just then the maestro brushed past her as he headed back to the podium to collect his scores. Stopping beside her and speaking very low, he pointed to the still-open manuscript on her stand.

"You didn't play a note."

Then he held up both hands, flexing his fingers at her. "You do have all the technique, don't you?"

Now he asks, Phillips thought. Tempted to cave in and tell him that she was in way over her head, she struggled to find the right words. Then she stopped. As long as she had come this far, she decided, she might as well play the game to the end.

"Yes, Maestro, I do."

Stokowski gave her a long look. Then, seeming to conclude that she must have been suffering from a case of nerves, he asked, "On which finger do you get the best tone?"

"Well, I think it must be my second finger," Phillips answered, wondering what on earth he meant.

"Then play everything with your second finger," he said and walked on.

That, apparently, was his way of breaking the tension.

A few minutes later, thoroughly drained, Phillips gathered up her coat from where she had hung it in her dressing room and prepared to go home. After much consideration about what she should wear that day, she had borrowed an outfit from her sister Peggy that consisted of a gray tweed skirt, gray silk blouse, and matching gray coat. She had chosen the somber outfit with Salzedo's warning in mind that she must enter the orchestra like a "little queen." It looked very proper, she thought, but after that high-pressure rehearsal she felt so drained she recalled that "It probably made me look like an oyster."

It was a wonder her hair didn't turn as gray as her outfit, she said. The intense momentum and the high level of concentration that Stokowski and the orchestra had maintained left her feeling thoroughly exhausted as she made her way back to Panama Street, still stinging with shame at not having been able to sight-read the *Swan Lake* cadenza and resenting Salzedo's failure to introduce her to important works like that.

Her first rehearsal, a terrific jump from anything she had ever experienced, had gone by "like an express train." She hadn't had a second to take an extra breath. The road ahead looked bleak indeed. She had been fearful before, but now she came close to despair.

"I realized as I hadn't totally before that this was no happy family I was entering," she said. "Not at all. Everyone was there in the severest professional capacity. It was sink or swim, and I was on the brink of sinking."

## CHAPTER 5

# One Step Ahead
# of the Sheriff

On the Friday afternoon of her first concert, Phillips had no choice but to "head down the track without looking left or right, like a racehorse with blinders on." There was nothing to do but steel herself and go forward. Much to her surprise, she made it through the concert without any gaffes. She didn't come in at a wrong place or get lost or lose count or commit any of the terrible errors she feared she might. Instead, she found herself totally absorbed in the music, following the maestro's lead almost as if she belonged there.

But even though she got through the concert fairly well, she did get the scare of her life afterward. She decided to take a shortcut to her dressing room, a "dingy, moth-eaten" room among the dressing rooms reserved for soloists and guest conductors next to the stage. Since the orchestra had never had a woman in its ranks before, there were no other accommodations to offer her but a small, unused room in the soloist section, which was situated stage-right while her placement in concerts was stage-left.

Phillips's shortcut led her through the deep, dark backstage area, where strange shapes loomed in the darkness, and teasers and tormentors—huge horizontal and vertical mechanisms used to facilitate the changing of stage sets—hung menacingly in the vast expanse overhead. Knowing that the Academy of Music was used as an opera house as well as a concert hall, she wasn't concerned about the dark shapes she saw in the gloom. She assumed they were parts of opera sets that were always lying about. Then she heard voices and laughter coming from among those shapes.

Suddenly out of the gloom, one, then two, then four of her colleagues emerged in front of her in various stages of undress. Phillips's heart began to pound so hard she could hardly breathe. Memories of the Roxy flooded back. Oh no! Was this the same breed of pups after all?

Then the half-clothed figures caught sight of her and started yelping. They hurried to take cover, ducking behind the bass fiddle cases that were standing around and anything else they could find. Phillips soon discovered that she had stumbled upon the spot that the men of the orchestra used for changing into their street clothes. It was their dressing room of convenience. They had an official dressing room downstairs but found it more convenient to change after concerts in the deep backstage area, next to their instrument cases. And why not? Before her arrival, the whole place had been theirs. They didn't have to worry that a woman might catch them in their BVDs. But now she had invaded their territory, and their yelps told her they didn't like it one bit. In fact, she said, they seemed more embarrassed by the episode than she was!

At the beginning of the concert that afternoon, the audience had greeted Stokowski with a standing ovation as he strode onto the stage. Clearly delighted to have their glamorous conductor back after the summer break, they rose to their feet spontaneously as Stokowski leapt onto the podium "like a lion tamer entering the ring."[1] Phillips had to smile, though. In the midst of his glamorous entrance, the lion tamer took a moment to dart a look at her as he mounted the podium, "as if he were worried that I might be wearing green sequins or some other outlandish thing," but he needn't have worried. There she was in the decorous black afternoon gown that Salzedo had chosen for her, blending into the orchestra like one of the men.

Assured that everything was in order, Stokowski stood for the briefest moment, his posture perfectly erect and his arms spread wide as he swept his eyes over the orchestra, riveting the concentration of every player on him. Then he brought his arms downward, and, Phillips said, "We were off to the races."

Reviews of the performance were enthusiastic, which delighted Phillips, who made it her business to read every one she could find the next day. Samuel L. Laciar, the *Philadelphia Public Ledger*'s critic, undoubtedly pleased her when he commented, "The four new firsts acquitted themselves well." As one of those new firsts, she had to have been happy to receive his approval, however muted. It must also have amused her to find that Laciar seemed as confused as she was about the mystifying *Prometheus*. "The difficulties of performance and interpretation are equal to those of comprehension," he said. Reserving his highest praise for the orchestra's "dramatic and highly impassioned reading" of the Tchaikovsky Fifth, he did note "the somewhat questionable experiment . . . of adding a harp to reinforce the pizzicato of the strings," but Phillips didn't worry about that.[2] It was the maestro's decision to have her play, not hers.

Many of the critics commented on what one called Stokowski's "eloquent hands and agile digits." Those hands were news because the maestro had put aside his baton the year before. He was now conducting the orchestra using only his graceful and expressive hands, which caused quite a stir among orchestra watchers. Phillips heard rumors that he had developed neuritis in his right hand and found himself unable to grip the baton, but there was no official explanation of why he had given it up. Perhaps his innate sense of drama prompted the change. It didn't really matter. What mattered was that his hands were as eloquent as his baton had been, and he was able to communicate his intentions to the players with astounding clarity.

Relieved that her first series of concerts was behind her, Phillips still had huge challenges ahead. She faced a strenuous schedule in the upcoming months that included a number of works with prominent parts for the harp that she had never played. *Scheherazade*, *Ein Heldenleben*, works by Ravel, Debussy, and copious amounts of Wagner were on the schedule, as well as new compositions the maestro planned to premiere that season. It was a daunting lineup that required her to devote almost every moment of every day to intense practicing. She barely had time for sleeping and eating. All she did was practice and perform. Diversions of any kind were out of the question.

As a harpist, Phillips was in one sense fortunate to be playing under Stokowski, whose largely Romantic repertoire and interest in French music led him to program numerous works that called for the harp, an instrument that he appreciated and understood more than many conductors, she said. He liked its sound and considered it to be an emotional instrument that should be given its due in the orchestra.

In another sense, however, she also felt somewhat cursed by his interest in the harp, for the maestro's choice of repertoire required much from his principal harpist. He wanted a lush, full sound with subtle gradations of tone and gradual diminuendos from her and often offered quick suggestions in rehearsals to help her produce what he was looking for. "Some conductors treat the harp as if it has rubber strings," Phillips said, "but Stokowski allowed it to bloom."

On top of her orchestral challenges, Phillips learned to her dismay early in the season that certain peripheral obligations came with the position she occupied as the principal harpist of the Philadelphia Orchestra. Already racing to "stay one step ahead of the sheriff" and hold her own in the orchestra, she found on many occasions that she had to divert her energies to perform in outside concerts, making her life even more challenging.

Foremost among her outside duties was the requirement that she assume the principal harp position in the orchestra of the Philadelphia Grand Opera Company, which flourished for several years in the early 1930s. Members of the Philadelphia Orchestra were expected to play in the opera orchestra, and that was no small commitment for Phillips, for the harp is often featured in opera scores. On the docket for the 1930–31 season were several major works, including *Aida*, *Tosca*, *Lucia di Lammermoor*, and *Lohengrin*. She was able to get the second harpist to take over some of them, but her load was still heavy. The main conductor of the Philadelphia Grand Opera was Fritz Reiner, a maestro whose reputation for being exacting was so terrifying that years later when the Chicago Symphony's players learned he was to be their new conductor, Phillips said, "They all got diarrhea."

In addition to her opera commitments, Phillips was also expected to play at various social gatherings for prominent orchestra supporters anxious to hear and see the young lady who was such a novelty in the musical world. That meant she had to prepare for Sunday afternoon soirees and such when she had much else to do. Those command performances always seemed to crop up just when she wanted to concentrate on preparing a particularly difficult piece for the orchestra or when her schedule was already crammed to the breaking point.

Overwhelmed with work, exhausted, and often furious at Salzedo for getting her into such a difficult spot, she soldiered on, straggling back to Panama Street after rehearsals and concerts, loaded down with piles of music she had to learn and polish. Often, to her later regret and shame, she took out her frustrations on her mother and sister by "throwing tantrums over nothing of any importance." It wasn't fair to them, she said, but they put up with her bad behavior with great forbearance, calming and supporting her as best they could and propping her up with her mother's ubiquitous eggnogs to get her ready for the next battle.

———•———

It's never easy for a newcomer in an organization to learn the routine under which it operates, but for Phillips it was especially difficult. Without having the luxury of serving under a first-chair player who might tell her how this or that was done or having any natural allies to mentor her, she had to learn most of the ins and outs of being a Philadelphia Orchestra member on her own. At the Curtis Institute she had attended sessions on proper concert behavior led by Samuel Arthur King from Bryn Mawr College. He regaled the students with passages from Shakespeare and showed them how to bow properly and flip up their coattails before sitting down. Obviously, little of that was helpful to Phillips. Salzedo offered more practical advice, but even he didn't prepare her for a challenging aspect of orchestral life that she encountered early on—patrols from the women's committees.

One might have thought that the members of the Philadelphia's Women's Committees would be proud and delighted that a woman had joined their beloved orchestra, but they appeared to be more than a little dubious about this innovation. The original Women's Committee of the Philadelphia Orchestra, the first permanent organization of its kind in the United States, was founded in 1904. In its first year, the committee raised desperately needed funds to keep the orchestra going and brought numerous subscribers and benefactors into the fold. Its activities soon became so important to the success of the orchestra that additional committees from different areas of the city and its environs were developed under the aegis of the original committee to expand its reach. Together those committees became vitally important to the orchestra.[3]

The committees' members worked so hard and so successfully at supporting and promoting the orchestra that they had developed a somewhat proprietary attitude toward it. Everything about the orchestra and its members seemed to be their business, especially the young woman who had entered the ranks of the players as one woman among one hundred men. The possibilities for scandal inherent in that experiment galvanized the women into action, especially their president, Frances Anne Wister, who had long watched over the orchestra like a godmother.

Miss Wister began her surveillance campaign at eight o'clock each morning by telephoning Phillips and offering a greeting that was usually supportive but that sometimes contained a not-so-veiled hint about the proper behavior befitting a young lady in her position. Then at the other end of the day, Miss Wister's chief accomplice, the committee's corresponding secretary, Mrs. William W. Arnett, a daunting woman, would call with her thoughts. These were often more critical than Miss Wister's. In one conversation, Mrs. Arnett wondered ever so coyly (not at all her normal approach) if Phillips wasn't worried that she would catch a cold in the drafty Academy of Music. After all, her sleeveless evening gown with its V neckline didn't give her much protection, now did it? Perhaps she should consider wearing something with a higher neckline and longer sleeves to keep warm.

Half annoyed and half amused by her remark, Phillips thanked Mrs. Arnett for her concern and told her she would be just fine. Later, she and Salzedo had a good laugh about the dowager's comment. "Really," Phillips said. "That was the tiniest V neckline you ever saw."

Soon other ladies from the women's committees began making unannounced forays backstage. What they were really doing, of course, was patrolling to make sure that no monkey business was going on. Unfortunately for the men of the orchestra, the ladies sometimes ran across them changing into their street clothes backstage after concerts just as Phillips had done after the first concert of the season. Having learned her lesson from that unexpected meeting, Phillips never again took that shortcut to her dressing room, taking the long way around instead, happy to allow the men their privacy. But the women from the committees were on a mission. Nothing could stop them. The men would be backstage changing into their street clothes, and along would come a delegation from one of the committees. The men would yelp and run for cover just as they had with Phillips, but that didn't faze the ladies. They were not to be deterred from doing their duty.

Slowly, the reality of the situation dawned on the men. Just as the orchestra was no longer their private club, the backstage area was no longer their private clubhouse. Eventually, the men retreated to their dressing room to change their clothes. It was the only thing they could do. The gender barrier had been breached, and patrols from the women's committees were among the consequences.

---

Meanwhile, the season was unfolding at a heady pace with Stokowski making news, as usual, by introducing new works to his often-reluctant audiences. He was also ramping up his technological experiments with the making of recordings and radio broadcasts. Devoted to the goal of carrying great music beyond the confines of the concert hall to the wider public, he was deeply involved in trying to perfect the technologies that promised to make that possible.

Two weeks after her first season began, half the orchestra, including Phillips, journeyed to New York on a Sunday to make a coast-to-coast live radio broadcast of a symphony orchestra performance. Although

Stokowski had always had an interest in promoting technological advances in music transmission, he had originally been reluctant to involve the orchestra in live radio broadcasts, believing that the technology of broadcasting did not do justice to orchestral music. He hated the thin, metallic tone that came over the wires and thought the receivers were too crude to take in the sound of the whole orchestra.

He also didn't like the idea of turning over the controls that regulated the volume and quality of sound that went over the airwaves to radio engineers who might not understand the carefully modulated tones his orchestra was producing. To get around those problems and overcome some of broadcasting's technical limitations, the maestro studied radio engineering and worked with officials at NBC to create a "top-secret" soundproof glass booth outfitted with a battery of knobs that allowed him to act both as conductor and radio engineer.

As a result, fifty-four orchestra members found themselves in the NBC studio on the roof of New York's Amsterdam Theater one Sunday afternoon in mid-October with Stoki directing them from inside a glass booth with his right hand while adjusting the knobs on his "top-secret" machine with his left to regulate the sound that was going over the airwaves.

Phillips heard a rumor that the engineers had fooled the maestro and were regulating the broadcast from a hidden booth, but whether that was true or not, critics were most impressed with the improvements the maestro had wrought in the sound that came over the radio, with the *New York Times* reporting that "the Stokowski device marked a great advance in the broadcasting of a symphony orchestra. It brings out and maintains the voice and tonal color of each component choir of the orchestra."[4]

The broadcast marked a definite step forward in radio transmission and grew out of Stokowski's intense interest in improving the technological means of reproducing sound, for which he deserves recognition from music lovers the world over. Commenting on the maestro's achievements fifty years later, Hans Fantel, founding editor of *Stereo Review* and a *New York Times* columnist, wrote, "Far ahead of almost anyone—and surely long before most musicians—[Stokowski] realized that music in the 20th century would be heard mostly through electronic means rather than in the presence of the performer, and this prescience spurred an intense concern for the techniques of broadcasting and recording which at times occupied him nearly as much as his musical activities."[5]

Sergei Rachmaninoff was another great musician who early on appreciated the significance of recording and preserving the music he and his contemporaries were making, although he did not involve himself in the technology that allowed it to happen as Stokowski did. Like Stokowski, Rachmaninoff originally disliked the sound of music that came over the radio. To his ears, the piano he heard over the airwaves had the thin, tinkling tone of a balalaika, and he didn't want to have anything to do with it, but he loved and was grateful for the gramophone. "A gramophone record can preserve forever the playing and singing of the world's most distinguished artists. Think what it would have meant to us today could we possess records made by Liszt, the greatest pianist who has ever lived," Rachmaninoff said with touching gratitude in an interview in *Gramophone* magazine in 1931.[6]

"Of all our own music-making, silence must someday be the end," he said. "Formerly, the artist was haunted by the knowledge that with him the music also must vanish into the unknown. Yet today, he can leave behind him a faithful reproduction of his art, an eloquent and imperishable testimony to his life's achievement." Rachmaninoff also extended his past praise of the Philadelphia Orchestra into the realm of recording. "To make records with the Philadelphia Symphony Orchestra is as thrilling an experience as any artist could desire," he said. "Unquestionably, they are the finest orchestral combination in the world; even the famous New York Philharmonic, which you heard in London under Toscanini last summer, must, I think, take second place."

The electronic age had begun and was on the way to revolutionizing the world of music, a phenomenon that Stokowski recognized and enhanced with serious research, study, and promotion. But whatever the technical and historical ramifications of radio broadcasts and phonograph records, Phillips, as a member of the orchestra, often saw the less lofty, more quotidian side of the equation. After the New York broadcast, Marshall, the lone stagehand on duty that day, stood in front of the orchestra members who were heading toward the door. Holding two folding music stands in his beefy hands, he demanded, "Whaddsa madder wid youse guys? Got sore hands?" He needed help putting away the chairs and music stands, and once the players realized his problem, they helped clear the area quickly. They all had great affection for Marshall and relished the contrast that his rolled-up shirtsleeves and big, hairy arms provided to the maestro's elegant, aloof presence. They loved it when he referred to Stokowski as "boss."

"Boss," he would ask, "ya want duh Wagner now?"

It was never *Vahgner*, as Stokowski would pronounce it. To Marshall, it was *Wagner*, as in a dog's tail. Titles of particular works often became hilariously tangled in Marshall's mouth, Phillips said, but Stoki never blinked an eye, and everyone understood what he meant. Marshall was Stoki's special project. He had formed the burly stagehand into just the kind of right-hand-man he needed. Famous for his uncanny ability to spot talent in a musician and develop it, the maestro apparently had the same ability with those who weren't musicians, and Marshall was a prize example.

The day after the broadcast, the orchestra was back in the Academy of Music rehearsing that week's program. Stokowski, a master arranger and transcriber, had transcribed a piano prelude by Debussy, *La cathédrale engloutie (The Sunken Cathedral)*, for full orchestra. To Phillips, who loved most of the maestro's transcriptions, it sounded "like a giant with too-big boots on." Maybe that was because it caused her to put her foot in her mouth.

In the middle of rehearsing the piece, Stoki told her to play a harmonic on a very high note. Phillips didn't think it would work. Playing a harmonic produces a sound an octave higher than the string that is touched, but this note was already up so high she was positive a harmonic could never be achieved.

"That's impossible," she blurted out without thinking.

"Try it," he said, glaring at her.

So Phillips tried it, and the impossible happened. It worked!

Which was lucky for Phillips, she later realized, for if it hadn't, everyone would have been embarrassed. This way the maestro was satisfied in front of the orchestra, and she was put down where she belonged for having the nerve to question his authority. But she never played a harmonic in that spot again because it really wouldn't work in normal playing, she said, and he never asked her to do it again because he probably knew that.

Her "impossible" remark was bad enough, but when Stoki called for the next work they were rehearsing that day, Phillips did something she had been trying not to do since the season began. The work was the César Franck Symphony, and when it was announced, Phillips caught the eyes of two of her friends from Curtis who had come into the orchestra with her, Bob Bloom, second oboe, and Robert McGinnis, second clarinet. They grinned at each other and pantomimed their relief. Here was a piece they knew! They had worked on it for months. Finally, they didn't have to struggle to master strange, new rhythms or startling dissonances. They smiled at each other and pretended to wipe their brows.

Just then Phillips noticed the maestro, who was always alert to what was going on in the orchestra and could catch the slightest thing, looking from one to the other of the trio. He was taking in the interplay, she realized, and he could be interpreting it the wrong way. She had never forgotten Salzedo's warning not to allow herself to become involved with any of the men, particularly Stokowski, the "ah-hem," lest she be thrown away like an old shoe. Did he think she was making a date with these fellows? What ideas might that put in his head or the heads of her colleagues?

She immediately turned her eyes back to her music stand and brought a stop to the exchange. It had been her practice from her first day in the orchestra to keep strictly to herself. She had done it partly because she had too much on her mind just keeping up with her huge workload to take much notice of her colleagues. She also knew that some of them regarded her as an intruder, and she didn't want to subject herself to the sting of their disapproval. But most of all, she wanted to prevent any passes from coming her way in case a few "Roxy Romeo" types had slipped in among Philadelphia's players.

To do all this, she had created her "own little island," where she kept to herself and interacted with the others as little as possible. Not that she was rude to the men, but she stayed slightly apart from them and went about her business. Now the Franck Symphony had made her forget her plan for a moment.

After rehearsal, Bob Bloom headed straight for her. A good friend, he was dating one of her friends in the harp department at Curtis.

"What on earth is the matter with you, Edna?" he said, putting his arm around her shoulder. "You won't have anything to do with us anymore. Back at Curtis, you were as much fun as anyone, but now you act as if we have leprosy. What's going on?"

Just then, Phillips noted, one of the older men walked by and gave the two a quizzical look.

"Now look what you've done," she answered, drawing away. "He saw you with your arm around my shoulder. He might misunderstand, and I don't want that since I'm the only female around here. I don't want to be mean or aloof, but I just have to be a little bit alone until I get my bearings."

It was lonely staying on that island, Phillips said, but she was so overwhelmed with all she had to do that she didn't mind. In fact, she barely looked at the other members of the orchestra, she recalled. "I just knew some wore mustaches and some didn't." If only the ladies from the women's committees had known that, they might have saved themselves some patrol time!

Soon a situation cropped up that Phillips hadn't thought about before joining the orchestra—touring. At that time, each season the orchestra played ten concerts in Carnegie Hall, five in Washington, D.C., and Baltimore, and one in Hartford, Connecticut, which meant train rides, late-night returns, and sometimes, overnight hotel stays. It was more new territory to navigate as the lone woman among one hundred men.

Once again, Phillips relied on the island she had created around herself. She always sat alone on the train and tried to look as occupied as possible, rarely entering into conversations and never inviting anyone to sit with her. Fortunately, the kindly Marshall took it upon himself to look out for her on the orchestra's tours. There were many late, dark nights when she had to make her way to hotels, trains, and taxis, and he took on the role of bodyguard, acting as a bulwark against problems that might occur, making sure she got taxis and smoothing the way for her wherever he could.

———•———

After her first Carnegie Hall concert, Phillips took a small break from her intense work routine when Salzedo and Lucile invited her to stay overnight at their Riverside Drive apartment so they could take her to a glamorous postconcert party at their friend Jules Bouy's apartment. It was a party that made her understand why Salzedo insisted on commuting from New York to Philadelphia to teach at the Curtis Institute rather than living full-time in Philadelphia. Obviously, his life in New York was much too exciting to forego for the quiet propriety of the Quaker City. For the young woman from Reading, the supper party was an eye-opening affair. She had lived in New York when she played at the Roxy, of course, but then she had barely seen anything except the inside of the theater and her hotel down the block. This time she was not only among glamorous people; she was also among people of real artistic accomplishment. To Phillips, this was the epitome of sophistication, and she drank it in with gusto.

Salzedo was an active and important figure in New York's avant-garde musical circles. In 1921, he cofounded the International Composers' Guild to promote new music with Edgard Varèse and others. He also established a magazine, *Eolus*, which was devoted to contemporary music, and was heavily involved in organizing, preparing, and publicizing performances for other new music organizations, including the International Society for Contemporary Music and the League of Composers. It was partly through his myriad associations in forward-thinking music circles that he had come to know Stokowski, who often conducted premieres of works championed by Salzedo and his associates at New York's Town Hall.

The party at Bouy's apartment gave Phillips a peek at this avant-garde world and allowed her to step away from her demanding schedule for at least one evening. After the dazzling job of decorating Bouy had done on Salzedo's apartment, she was eager to see what he had done to his own and found that he had made it into an equally stunning example of the *moderne* style of design. There were few residences like it in Philadelphia—certainly none that Phillips had ever visited. Two stories high with "a kind of floating balcony where supper was served," it provided a sophisticated and elegant setting for Bouy's guests.

Phillips watched in awe as one famous person after another entered the room. When Martha Graham, as exotically beautiful and dramatic offstage as she was on, arrived, she made a beeline for her old friend Salzedo, which thrilled Phillips, who got to meet her. Then, Stokowski swept into the party in all his glory, the hero of the evening. Passing Phillips, he paused briefly with a startled look on his face at seeing her there. Then he nodded and walked on. She was just a member of his orchestra, after all, too new and too young to honor with much attention at such a party.

Not long after their Carnegie Hall appearance, Phillips faced another challenge when the orchestra presented Rimsky-Korsakov's *Scheherazade*. Sensing that his new principal harpist might need bolstering, Stokowski had decided to have two harps play where one usually does in order to generate more sound. Due to tight scheduling, he didn't have enough time to work with Phillips to get her playing up to where he wanted it, so he had the second harp play with her. In fact, the orchestra had only two rehearsals on the work before the first performance. Phillips had to take a score into the concert to make sure she was ready when it was time for her to come in, something she had to do often, given Stokowski's tendency to assume his players could handle the details themselves.

At the Saturday night performance, a group of Phillips's friends from Curtis were in the audience. Afterward they hurried backstage to tell her that they finally understood why Salzedo's students kept raising their arms. They had always made fun of the practice when the harp students did it in recitals at Curtis, but now, they told her, they understood the reasoning behind Salzedo's method when they saw Phillips and the second harpist playing at the same time.

After a loud chord, they watched Phillips raise her arms high. Then as the chords got softer, they noticed that her arms would rise a little less high, and a little less, then up again after a louder chord, and so on. At the same time they saw the second harpist, who played in the traditional way, dropping his hands straight down to the sounding board after each chord. Phillips would go up. He would go down. Up. Down. Up. Down.

"Now we know what Salzedo meant," they told her. Not only were her gestures pleasing to look at, they expressed the music and made it more meaningful. By that point, Phillips was unconscious of the nuances of her arm movements. Salzedo had so thoroughly indoctrinated her with his technique that it had become automatic, but she was happy that her skeptical schoolmates had finally been won over.

By the time the orchestra took the work to Washington, the next venue in their touring schedule, Phillips had a better grasp of *Scheherazade*, but she still had some lessons to learn. They played in the district's Constitution Hall, a terrible place to hold a concert, Phillips said, where a player could barely hear the player next to him. It made Phillips so nervous she was doubly on edge, afraid that, not being able to hear well, she could get out of step with the instruments around her.

In the work, the harp often accompanies the violin, which plays the role of Scheherazade. At one point, the harp was to play right after the violin's first note. Phillips was so anxious she didn't give Stokowski a chance to give her the signal before she plunged ahead. She got ahead of him, so "he almost had to put his hands in his pockets"—twice. That, she knew, would not please the maestro.

Then in the second movement, disaster struck. "In the very dreamy part about the prince and the princess, in the quietest of places," she explained, "a string on my harp broke. Bang! It was a very taut string, and it let out a terrific noise that sounded out with a boom just when Stoki had lowered the orchestra to the softest pianissimo."

Shocked, Phillips felt a surge of panic, but Salzedo's training came to the rescue. "Never look behind you, even if a bomb goes off!" he had said.

Remembering that, she sat perfectly still as if nothing had happened. In fact, she sat so still that the second harpist began to think it was a string on *his* harp that had broken. He started looking all around, trying to see which string it was. All the while, Phillips continued to sit there outwardly calm, although she knew "damn well" it was her string. The second harpist kept frantically fidgeting until Stokowski looked over and glared at him. Then Phillips knew she was safe.

Afterward, as the men filed out for intermission, the second harpist made haste to tell as many as possible that it wasn't his fault. It wasn't *his* harp string. It was Miss Phillips's, he explained to anyone who would listen. But it didn't matter. The damage had been done. Later, one of the older players came over to Phillips with a twinkle in his eye. "You're learning how to do it quickly," he said with an approving chuckle.

When they got back to Philadelphia for their next rehearsal, Stoki made a rare comment to the two harpists. Phillips's new *moderne* harp designed by Salzedo, which she had ordered from Lyon and Healy, had arrived while they were on tour. Until then she had been using the orchestra's harp, which wasn't much to her liking. Now she was delighted to have a sleek new instrument to play and proud when Stokowski noticed it from the podium. "Is that a new harp?" he asked. Phillips nodded yes. Then, turning to the second harpist, he said, "Now you must get a harp like that."

"I have a far more beautiful harp at home, and I'm going to bring it in," Nicoletta announced proudly. "It's got lots of gold on it and a snake woman wound round the column."

Phillips wondered if he noticed Stoki's suppressed smile.

In time, Phillips began to relax enough to notice the differences among the regular audiences in the Academy of Music. She said she could shut her eyes onstage and tell which audience—the Friday afternoon, the Saturday night, or the Monday evening—they were playing for, just by the atmosphere in the hall. On Friday afternoons, the atmosphere was restrained and proper. That audience, made up mostly of women, had been taught their concert manners by the maestro through his podium speeches. By the time Phillips joined the orchestra, they were fairly well-behaved (except for those who still sneaked out early to catch their train home), and their responses to the music were restrained and polite in comparison to those of the other audiences. As Marshall used to say, they "clapped with their kid gloves on."

The Saturday night audiences, on the other hand, had much more zip. They came to the concerts "dressed to the nines," the women in long dresses, the men in black tie. Everything about Saturday night was sparkling and elegant. It was always an occasion, and the audience reacted to the orchestra's playing with great and voluble enthusiasm. Its members were even enthusiastic about showing how much they *dis*liked some of the new music Stoki offered them, hissing loudly and walking out when the orchestra played a piece they found especially unpalatable.

The Monday crowd was the most intellectual and academic, Phillips said. It was made up of serious music lovers, who scorned "Friday as being too much garden club."[7] She could feel them listening intently and thoroughly as the concert progressed. They responded in a more contemplative way than the Saturday audience, and they didn't object as much to Stoki's presentations of new music.

After the Monday concerts, groups from the audience would congregate onstage with their friends from the orchestra, chatting in distinct circles, Germans with Germans, Russians with Russians, French with French, and so on. As the great amalgamated orchestra it was, the Philadelphia contained musicians of many nationalities, and each of the groups seemed to have their special friends to talk to.

After one Monday night concert, Salzedo, as usual, joined his French compatriots from the woodwind section onstage, especially his good friend Marcel Tabuteau. They were standing in a little group when Phillips sailed by with her "nose in the air," looking neither left nor right and not realizing that Salzedo was in the group.

Suddenly a loud "Ed-naa!" sounded out behind her.

Embarrassed, Phillips tried to apologize for not seeing him, but Salzedo was having none of it. Finally, he offered to walk her home, and on the way, she explained her situation. "Don't you remember how you told me to behave in the orchestra? 'Come in like a little queen and *stay* that way,' you said. Well, I'm just doing what you told me to do." There wasn't much he could say to that, but he had still more advice for her.

"You've gotten too thin," he told her. "You look terrible. You need to eat more and get some rest."

As if she could help losing weight and looking tired with all the strain she was under! It took an almost reckless expenditure of energy to hang on in the nerve-racking, over-her-head position he had gotten her into. No wonder she was losing weight. How could Salzedo be so blasé about it? Didn't he know what a spot he had gotten her into? The other Curtis recruits who joined the orchestra when she did were looking pretty frazzled, too. They were all under pressure. It wasn't easy for any of them to fit into that high-powered institution.

"Eat more and get some rest"—now when would she find time for that?

## CHAPTER 6

# A Season of Firsts

Six weeks after Phillips joined the orchestra, she faced a thundering giant who struck fear into her heart—and also into the hearts of her colleagues. Arturo Toscanini came to town as part of a highly publicized maestro exchange between the Philadelphia Orchestra and the New York Philharmonic that had been set up by Arthur Judson, manager of both orchestras. A canny businessman who understood the value of a good public relations ploy—as did both Stokowski and Toscanini—Judson arranged to have his star conductors each lead the other's orchestra for two weeks. Music aficionados of the day loved to argue about who was the better conductor. What better way to capitalize on the attention such an exchange would bring, than to send Stokowski to New York and Toscanini to Philadelphia?

As planned, Judson's idea ignited enormous curiosity and excitement among a press and public anxious to find out who would emerge the victor in this battle of the maestros. Would it be the classicist Toscanini, who cultivated a reputation as an artistic purist, centering his repertoire on the established masterworks, and proclaiming that the only way to make music was to play every note "as written"? Or the romanticist Stokowski, who advocated freedom of expression and made a habit of introducing new music and new ways of making music to his audiences?

Outside the Academy of Music, anticipation about Toscanini's turn on Philadelphia's podium mounted as the day for his first concert approached, but inside during rehearsals, fear and dismay reigned among the players. A great ball of fire had descended on them, and they were suffering the consequences.

Accustomed to Stokowski's quietly intense demeanor in rehearsals, they now found themselves the brunt of one explosive outburst after another from Toscanini. Stoki's comments to his players could be sardonic, which often discomfited them, as Phillips had discovered with his Foolish Virgins ploy, but he rarely subjected them to public dressings-down, and he never raised his voice. He drove his players hard to produce what he wanted, but he did it in an even, unemotional manner.

Toscanini, on the other hand, screamed at the players and subjected them to vituperation for their mistakes, breaking batons in perfect fury so often that Marshall groused, "If he breaks anudder one a dem sticks, I'm gonna get him an iron stage brace. We'll see what he can do wid dat."

Immediately upon his arrival, Toscanini rearranged Stokowski's seating plan for the orchestra. Stoki, in his restless search for the best way of projecting and blending the orchestra's sound, had rearranged the orchestra's seating. He had devised a plan that departed from the European model then in use by putting the first and second violins next to each other on the left side of the podium and the violas, cellos, and double basses on the right side.[1] Toscanini wanted none of Stoki's experiments. He ordered everybody back into the more traditional arrangement, with the first violins on the left of the conductor and the second violins on the right. In so doing, he placed the harpists back within the orchestra, not out in front as they were under Stoki. Phillips was grateful for that. At least it gave her some cover.

The first time the orchestra played for Toscanini in rehearsal, he seemed genuinely impressed. "This is the Stradivarius of orchestras," he told the players. But not long afterward the eruptions began.

"What was I thinking?" he exclaimed. "This is anarchy!"[2]

What was bothering him was the practice of free bowing, which was one of Stokowski's hallmarks. Against standardization in any form and wanting to maintain a continuously flowing musical line, Stoki had his string players move their bows across the strings according to their individual inclinations rather than in unison, which was the usual practice. Stoki thought that string players who used uniform bowing or wind players who used uniform breathing produced a combined sound that was interrupted by slight diminuendos when they all raised their bows or took a breath together. Free bowing and free breathing, he decided, would produce a more continuous sound because the individual cessations would be more diffused and less noticeable. Toscanini, on the other hand, thought bows going every which way and individual breathing represented anarchy. There would be no more of that while he was in charge!

Having settled that point, Toscanini proceeded to create his own form of anarchy by screaming and aiming invectives at different members of the orchestra, even Philadelphia's most seasoned and celebrated players. Phillips could see uneasiness in the face of the orchestra's revered solo flutist, William Kincaid, widely acknowledged as "one of the greatest virtuosos the flute had ever known."[3] Anton Horner, the first horn, also looked disconcerted, as did many of the other distinguished veterans. It didn't seem to matter how eminent a player was. Toscanini went after everyone. Stokowski had sought to develop the virtuoso qualities of his great players, encouraging them to play freely, almost like soloists, within the framework he laid out for them, but Toscanini wanted them to "put their corsets on," Phillips recalled, and he screamed until he got them to pull themselves in.

Actually, that wasn't all bad in Phillips's view. Sometimes in his effort to enrich the tone of an instrument, Stoki could push a player a little too far, she said. The sound would get too big and exaggerated. He was encouraging Marcel Tabuteau to play with such a big, fat sound that his oboe sometimes sounded like an English horn. But when Toscanini came to town and put Mozart on the program, Tabuteau scaled his playing way back. It went right down to where it belonged, Phillips said. He didn't have to be told. He knew that was what Toscanini would want because he had played under him before.

When Toscanini first came to the United States as conductor of the Metropolitan Opera from 1908 to 1914, he chose Tabuteau, who had been brought to the States by Walter Damrosch in 1905 to play in the New York Symphony, as principal oboe in the Met's orchestra. The next year Toscanini and Gatti-Casazza, the Metropolitan Opera manager, imported Carlos Salzedo from France (like "a piece of cheese," Salzedo told Phillips). The two young Frenchmen, both great natural talents, shared rooms in New York and were equally devoted to perfecting their art. But they could never please Toscanini, who often berated them in rehearsals and made them quite miserable. Finally, they gathered their courage to speak to him during an intermission.

"Maestro, we try our best, and we know we're not playing badly, but we cannot please you. Yet you never say a word to the first clarinet, and he doesn't play well at all."

Toscanini's answer was short: "There's hope for you. There's none for him."[4]

Knowing how demanding Toscanini was, Salzedo must have been concerned when he realized that his wobbly former pupil had to play

Richard Strauss's great tone poem *Ein Heldenleben*, a work that presents serious challenges for the harp. He told her he was going to speak to the maestro and tell him to be nice to her because she was just starting out. Of course, she knew he was just talking. He would never do it. Besides, after she saw Toscanini at work, she knew it wouldn't help. In the fire of rehearsing, "the maestro would forget if a player were male, female, or fish" and wouldn't care how long she had been with the orchestra. The player was just an instrument under the conductor's command, and that instrument had better play well, or else.

To help prepare Phillips, Salzedo coached her on *Heldenleben*, offering some helpful and some not-so-helpful advice to familiarize her with the daunting work and with Toscanini's way of handling it. A proud moment came for Phillips with the first sound she had to make when they started rehearsing. During the tremendously beautiful violin solo, there's a place where the harp suddenly has to play a chord, she said. She was following very carefully and played the chord just as it should be. But somebody else came in at the same time, and Toscanini yelled for him to stop.

"It's hers," he hissed.

When they came to a part where Salzedo had told her to play with great strength, she came in loud and sure like a trombone, and the whole orchestra turned and looked at her as if they were surprised the little girl could do that. She was in her glory until it was time for the second harpist to come in. He fumbled his entrance, she said, but she could tell Toscanini knew it wasn't her fault.

She discovered that Salzedo had given her a bad steer in one place. Near the end of the piece, when everyone in the huge orchestra is playing at full tilt, there's a "whole lot of business for the harp," she said, a lot of notes scrambled together. It was really a handful, and Salzedo had told her to slide it across the strings as a glissando. At the rehearsal, she did just that, but Toscanini, in the midst of all the orchestra's thunder, looked over at her with a suspicious look as though he were a detective ferreting out a clue. Suddenly, she realized that he wanted the notes fingered separately as an arpeggio, not a glissando as Salzedo had told her. She quickly switched to fingering the rest of the passage, and Il Maestro nodded his head.

Happy to have escaped Toscanini's thunder so far, Phillips was still confused about several places in the score where she had to play between his beats. The maestro's dressing room happened to be not far from hers, since she had been put with the conductors and soloists in her lone-woman status, so after rehearsal she decided to ask him about one or two places to make sure she was on the right track. She caught him coming out of his door and thrust the miniature score she had toward him to show him where she was confused, but she had forgotten how myopic he was. During rehearsals, he would put the score right up to his nose when he looked at it, and he always conducted concerts without a score. (Stokowski also conducted without a score, a practice both conductors prided themselves on.) Obviously, Toscanini couldn't see the print on the little score Phillips had in her hand. He took one look at it, patted Phillips on the shoulder, and went on his way. It turned out that she managed to get through the *Heldenleben* unscathed, even though she felt overwhelmed by it. She "just put on those blinders again and made it through."

However, she wasn't so lucky the next week. For the second half of his time in Philadelphia, Toscanini programmed works that were very much associated with Stokowski, which, he seemed to imply, would now be played the correct way. An autocrat who brooked no competition, Toscanini didn't think much of most other conductors, especially Stokowski. Whether he was jealous because Stoki had garnered so much attention for his musical achievements or aghast at his interpretations, Toscanini seemed more than ready to challenge him in any way he could. Wagner's music was one of Stoki's specialties, so Wagner took center stage in Toscanini's program for the second week.

Apparently, in Il Maestro's opinion, the orchestra had learned nothing the week before. During his second week with them, he shouted even more insults in Italian, stamped his feet, and broke more batons to show his fury than he had the week before, but now, Phillips said, the players had enough experience with him to be able to discern the signs that indicated he was about to erupt. They would watch his face as he yelled at someone or something. If his face was just flushed, they were OK, but if it got redder and the color started to rise toward the top of his head, they prepared themselves for the worst. When it reached his bald pate, they knew pandemonium would soon break loose.

A young English horn player, who Phillips said was as new as she was, found himself in a terrible spot in the *Liebestod* from *Tristan and Isolde*. His instrument just didn't speak at one point, perhaps because he was nervous. Toscanini rapped on his stand and had the orchestra repeat the part, but the English horn still didn't speak.

By the third time, with the red flush nearing the bald pate stage, Toscanini looked down at the poor fellow and asked in a fierce voice, "First time you play in orchestra?"

"Yes, maestro."

"Well, I, too, play first time in orchestra, but I use this," Toscanini answered, jabbing his chest.

Phillips's own heart went out to the hapless player. It wasn't easy to be new and vulnerable in a great orchestra.

Toscanini had a special way he wanted to have the last chord of *Liebestod* played that was different from the way Phillips had heard Stokowski do it. Luckily for her, Salzedo knew what Toscanini wanted. He told her to "count just like arithmetic" to make the chord work, and to come in before the measure. Toscanini looked over at her when the time came, and she was ready for him. He was probably puzzled because it was his unique way of doing it, but he never said a word.

So far Phillips had avoided attracting Toscanini's wrath, but that was not to last. It soon descended on the harp section in a complicated spot in Siegfried's Death from *Götterdämmerung*. According to the music, Phillips, as first harpist, was to play the part straight, and the second harpist was to fit in around her. God help him, she said, it wasn't easy, but if he really followed the beat he could do it. However, that didn't happen. The first and second harps were supposed to get to the crossroads together, but they never met. Three, four, five times they tried and failed until Toscanini's face turned bright red. He was screaming and fuming, and they knew they were going to get it for sure. In desperation, Phillips shushed the second harpist and took a stab at playing the whole thing herself. The minute she did that, Toscanini stopped yelling. What a relief! The harp section had escaped the line of fire for the time being.

And so it went. Toscanini got so angry at the violins at one rehearsal that he stalked offstage and refused to come back. To make amends, he sent them a message of apology before the first concert. But that night when the orchestra was assembled on stage ready to perform, he looked down at the violins and hissed, "I was right!"

Another time the maestro kept yelling in Italian at a horn player who was also Italian. The more he raged, the more obviously nervous the player got. This went on over several rehearsals. Whenever the orchestra got to a certain spot, Toscanini would shout at him. The poor fellow was calling on every patron saint in heaven and a few others, Phillips said. He was a wreck. Finally, in the last rehearsal he got it right. But Toscanini tempered his yelling only a little.

Afterward, Phillips asked the Italian-speaking second harpist to translate what the maestro had been shouting at the poor man. "'I'll get you yet! I'll kill you!'" he explained.

In spite of all the terrors they had endured under Toscanini, there was little doubt among the orchestra members that they had witnessed a remarkable musical mind at work. They recognized what a supreme artist he was. But after two weeks of having a madman exploding in their ears, they looked forward to the quieter rehearsals of Stokowski, who they had heard did not have an easy time with the New York Philharmonic.

Although Toscanini's stormy demeanor rattled them, the Philadelphia players had tried their best to please him even when he terrorized them. The Philharmonic players, on the other hand, were not so cooperative with Stokowski. In fact, they were obstinately uncooperative. First of all, a number of the players had been hired by the Philharmonic after being fired by Stokowski, and they were not inclined to cooperate with him now. On the contrary, they did their best to embarrass him. "They actually sassed him like school children," Phillips said, and he had to banish two of them for the duration.

Beyond the fact that Stoki had enemies within the ranks of the Philharmonic, that orchestra had a reputation for giving all guest conductors, not just Stokowski, a hard time. Forced to expend so much energy performing for Toscanini on a regular basis (after two weeks, the Philadelphia players could well imagine how hard that would be!), they tended to slack off, giving less than their full effort when guest conductors took over. They were also proud to belong to the great Toscanini's orchestra and determined to prove the superiority of their leader over his archrival Stokowski.

Thus, Toscanini appeared to emerge the winner in the great conductor exchange, but Phillips always thought it was because the Philadelphia Orchestra behaved so well for him and the Philharmonic behaved so badly for Stokowski.

———•———

Back on the podium in Philadelphia, Stokowski presented another of his experimental concerts, just the kind that Toscanini scorned. This one featured a young French inventor, Maurice Martenot, and his new electronic instrument called the *ondes Martenot*. Addressing the possibilities of what he called "electric" music and expressing his belief in its future, Stoki spoke to the audience before the performance to explain this extraordinary departure from the orchestral music they were used to.

"Music," he said, "consists of four dimensions—high and low, loud and soft, short and long, and what for lack of a better name we call color or timbre. The new electric instrument has developed the first three to a high stage, but the last lies in the future. It may take a hundred years to develop it, but in time it will imitate all instruments of the orchestra and all voices and add new as yet unimagined effects."[5] At the time, the idea of music made by an electrical machine seemed crazy to most people, including Phillips. Few had Stokowski's vision of the future.

Switching from the future to the past, an all-Bach program, featuring two of the Brandenburg Concertos, the Prelude in E-flat minor and the Toccata and Fugue in D minor, was next on the agenda for the orchestra, but that programming carried with it its own controversies. Trained as an organist at the Royal College of Music in London, Stokowski loved Bach and believed the master's works could be played to great effect by a modern orchestra, but his transcriptions shocked the purists. In high dudgeon, they pointed out that Bach didn't write for a modern orchestra but for the organ, other solo instruments, or a smaller baroque orchestra using ancient instruments. Of course the great master didn't, Stoki countered. He couldn't. He didn't have all those wonderful modern instruments and those big, splendid orchestras available to him. But if he had had them, Stoki asserted boldly, he would have used them.

Whatever the critics thought of the Bach-Stokowski transcriptions, audiences loved them. Before Stoki, Bach's works had remained largely unknown to general audiences, but those controversial transcriptions, so frowned upon by purists, introduced the wider world to Bach, bringing some of the greatest works in musical history to the attention of many who might never have heard them otherwise.

Halfway through Phillips's first season with the orchestra, Stokowski took a leave for six weeks of travel, as had become his pattern. On his leaves, he often visited exotic places, where he would research native music and seek out indigenous instruments. Ossip Gabrilowitch, a gifted pianist but not a terribly inspiring conductor according to Phillips, took over the orchestra in the interim.

Always the operator in matters of musical politics, Salzedo advised Phillips to find an opportunity to speak to Gabrilowitch about something or other so that he would get to know her. "That's the way to do it," he told her.

So one day after rehearsal, Phillips went up to the podium and made "a terribly obvious remark to the poor man." In return he gave her a funny look over his spectacles, as if to say, why are you doing this? Phillips got the hint and took her leave as quickly as possible. Why, she asked herself, did she let Salzedo talk her into these things, anyway?

During Gabrilowitch's time on the podium, the Philadelphia Award, which was given each year to a distinguished citizen, was presented to Paul Philippe Cret. A French-born architect, who incidentally had redesigned and upgraded Rittenhouse Square in 1913, Cret was an influential force in Philadelphia architecture during the early twentieth century. At the presentation ceremony, the orchestra sat on the stage of the Academy of Music, which was draped with red, white, and blue bunting, and played suitably heroic music to enhance the program. What Phillips remembered most from the event was not Cret's moment of glory, but the special mention, made with much fanfare, of Cornelius McGillicuddy, who had received the award the year before, but had not been given it because the ceremony had been canceled after the benefactor who made the award possible, Edward Bok, died. Now in January 1931, the ceremony resumed and kudos went to the Philadelphia Athletics, who had won the World Series for the second year in a row that fall, and to the mysterious Mr. McGillicuddy. But why, Phillips wondered, didn't they salute the man responsible for the championships—Connie Mack? Buried as she was in music, even she knew he was the team owner and manager.

After the ceremony, as the dignitaries on stage milled about, a nice-looking gentleman with smiling blue eyes struck up a conversation with her. Upon learning of her concern about the slighting of Connie Mack, he tactfully explained that outside the rarefied atmosphere of the Academy of Music, Cornelius McGillicuddy was known as "Connie Mack." The gentleman's name was Samuel Rosenbaum. He was a member of the orchestra board of directors, and his explanation was so diplomatic that Phillips barely felt the sting of embarrassment her naïveté might otherwise have caused her.

———•———

Stokowski arrived back in Philadelphia in March 1931 ready to proceed with a huge project that would rival the great *Symphony of a Thousand* spectacle that he had staged in 1916. This time, he combined the forces of the Philadelphia Orchestra, the Philadelphia Grand Opera, and the Curtis Institute of Music to produce the U.S. premiere of Alban Berg's tragic opera *Wozzeck*, an atonal work that represented a radical departure in the world of music. As he had with his premiere of the *Symphony of a Thousand*, the maestro engineered this groundbreaking project with such skill that he drew the attention of musicians, critics, and the musical public from near and far to his *Wozzeck* premiere and made it necessary, according to Phillips, for "everyone who was anyone in music to come to Philadelphia to see it."

On the night of the first performance, Phillips was amazed to see a huge aggregation of musical personages: "Every well-known conductor, every musician of any consequence seemed to be there." A special train carried notables from New York to Philadelphia, and others came in on their own from as far away as Chicago, Cleveland, and Boston. Critics from the major newspapers as well as from European papers were dispatched to Philadelphia to cover the momentous occasion.[6]

Such an undertaking was too large to be staged at the Academy of Music, so the production was presented farther north on Broad Street in the Metropolitan Opera House, which was built in 1908 by the first Oscar Hammerstein, grandfather of the famous lyricist. Possessing a beautiful, 4,200-seat auditorium, it was in use as a movie palace at the time. The massive production Stokowski staged at the Metropolitan was underwritten by a gift of forty thousand dollars from Mary Louise Curtis Bok, founder of the Curtis Institute of Music, and required eighty-eight preparatory and sixty on-stage rehearsals. Work had begun the previous fall, with Stokowski leading all eighty-eight of the preliminary rehearsals before he left for his midwinter travels. While he was gone, his assistant Sylvan Levin carried on with the vocal and orchestral preparation, and the faculty and students of the Curtis Institute immersed themselves in all aspects of the production.[7] When Stoki returned two weeks before opening night, he brought all the disparate parts together with breathtaking efficiency and authority.

*Wozzeck's* libretto is brutal, uncompromising, and very sad, and its musical language is expressionistic. The story of a poor soldier who is exploited and humiliated by his superiors until he is driven to kill his mistress, it was and is a revolutionary work. Stokowski made the most of its dark drama in a powerful presentation of its compellingly modern music. With the help of expert consultants—including stage designer Robert Edmond Jones, who, Stokowski said, "understood the power of darkness and where to put one little spot of light"—the maestro was able to create a production of immense atmosphere by amplifying the bleakness of the opera on a stage enveloped in shade.[8]

From her seat in the crowded pit below the Metropolitan stage, Phillips couldn't see the scenes of betrayal and murder being portrayed on stage, but she could see the flickering shadows of Stokowski's hands on the ceiling of the auditorium as he directed the orchestra. They were magnified by a small light on the lectern that cast them onto the theater's domed ceiling and added to the eerie feeling of the production.

The audience was quickly drawn into the opera's compelling web, a web so strong that the orchestra had to call on all its powers to keep from getting trapped in it. The players struggled with Berg's difficult modern music, which they had to perform having had far fewer rehearsals than their counterparts at the Berlin State Opera had for the world premier of the work in 1925. It was a wonder they managed to carry it off, Phillips said, but somehow they did under Stokowski's intense direction—or at least most of them did.

Unfortunately, "the second harpist couldn't catch on to *Wozzeck* for anything," she recalled. And this time Phillips had no suspicions that "he was trying to make me look bad," as she thought he might have done at other times. He just couldn't get the hang of Berg's atonal score. At one point in the first performance, she could see that he was about to play in the wrong place. To stop him, she had to lean over and take his hands off the strings.

Throughout the performance, the illustrious audience sat rapt, totally absorbed in the tragic story of exploitation and cruelty unfolding before them. After the final note sounded, they let out a loud, agonized gasp in unison and continued sitting in silence for several moments. Then they broke into tumultuous cheering. Stokowski had scored another triumph. He had not only conducted a magnificent performance, he had introduced an important modern masterpiece to a new and receptive audience.[9]

After the performance as the audience milled out of the auditorium, Phillips was putting the cover on her harp before leaving the pit when a man leaned over the railing above her. He introduced himself as Nikolai Sokoloff, conductor of the Cleveland Orchestra, which at that time was gaining much attention although it was not yet considered a major orchestra, having been in existence for only a decade.

With people jostling him as they passed by, Sokoloff asked, "Where do you come from? Are there any more like you? I need a harpist."

Then the surging crowd intervened. Not wanting to let the opportunity pass, Phillips slipped out of the pit and pushed her way through the crowd until she found Salzedo, who was bursting to tell her that he had seen her take the second harpist's hands off his harp and how proud he was that his student understood more about this challenging music than a supposedly seasoned professional.

"But I have to tell *you* something," Phillips yelled above the din, "Get hold of Maestro Sokoloff. He's looking for a harpist for Cleveland."

It didn't take Salzedo long to do that. He recommended his student Alice Chalifoux for the position, and she became Cleveland's principal harpist, a position she held for forty years. Chalifoux became one of the leading orchestral harpists in the country as well as a legendary teacher. Coincidentally, it was Florence Wightman who had left the Cleveland position vacant. She had recognized that the Roxy Theatre Orchestra was a dead end not too long after Phillips departed and had left the Roxy to take the principal harp position in Cleveland. Now she was moving on to the job of principal harpist in the New York Metropolitan Opera Orchestra, which left the spot open for Chalifoux. Salzedo was on his way to filling the top U.S. orchestras with his students, and Phillips had become one of his coconspirators in the process.

———•———

After *Wozzeck*, Stokowski launched into another premiere of a modern work. This time he teamed the League of Composers with the Philadelphia Orchestra to present Igor Stravinsky's opera-oratorio, *Oedipus Rex*. For this production, he had Robert Edmond Jones create another stark stage setting. This one called for the four oratorio singers featured in the work to wear dark blue robes on an unadorned stage while a puppeteer operated huge fifteen-foot figures that represented the tormented psyches depicted in the music.

It was an altogether exalted and serious undertaking, but Phillips observed some pretty ordinary orchestra business in the midst of it. First was the celebrated Hungarian mezzo-soprano Margarete Matzenauer, who played Jocasta, saying as she was shown the chair she was to sit in, "Now, Leopold, you know I can't sing sitting down." It gave Phillips a chuckle and made her wonder just how close their relationship was.

During that production a mix-up occurred in the harp section, which led Phillips to make an embarrassing blunder in rehearsal. She had decided to divide what the harps were to play in one part of *Oedipus Rex* into two sections to make it simpler and more effective. She told the second harpist to play the first section, and she would play the second. It was her prerogative as principal to do that, but whether he was being diabolical or just didn't understand her, the second harpist did nothing when it was time for him to play in the first rehearsal. When the maestro signaled for the harps to play, nothing happened. Dead silence.

"Where are the harps?" he asked, a question she later realized was meant to spur action, not an answer.

"Well," Phillips said, "I was waiting for the second harpist, who is to play first, and then I will play second."

"I don't want to know how you're doing it. I just want to hear it," Stokowski snapped at her, obviously annoyed.

At the break, Salzedo's friend Tabuteau came over to Phillips's music stand. "*Nevaire* speak," he said, holding his finger to his lips and shaking his head. "*Nevaire* speak."

Phillips appreciated his trying to give her advice, but she didn't understand what she had done that was so wrong.

Then Marshall stopped her backstage. "Ya did somethin' bad," he said. "You're not supposed ta talk back. Ya gotta apologize."

Well, I'd better do it, she thought, even though she didn't think it was all that bad. She waited by the stairs Stoki used to get to his dressing room high above the stage, to talk to him. The players called Stoki's lofty perch his aerie nest, thinking it an appropriate place for an eagle like him. When the maestro came down the stairs and saw her, he immediately said, "You were a naughty girl today."

"I'm terribly sorry. I didn't mean to speak out," Phillips began her apology. "I see that it was not the thing to do. I should not . . ."

"You know," he answered, stopping her in midsentence, "that's such a pleasant speech. I think you ought to give it to the ladies on Friday afternoon."

Now it was Phillips who was annoyed. She turned on her heel and walked off. Curiously, she recalled, Stoki caught up with her and began talking about something to do with the harp. Why he did it she didn't know, but in the end she was glad he didn't seem to be taking her misstep too seriously.

Later, after she thought about the incident, she understood why it had been wrong to speak in rehearsal and certainly wrong to air harp department business in front of the whole orchestra. No one ever spoke except the maestro, unless he asked a direct question that required an answer from one of the players. The maestro gave short directives, using succinct musical terms that got his intention across clearly and efficiently. That was all. No time was wasted on chatter, not even on a word of praise for achieving an effect that he wanted. He told the players what he wanted, and when they did it correctly, whether after the first or fourth try, he would jump immediately to another section without comment.

Phillips had learned her lesson: "*Nevaire* speak." Talking wasted time, and rehearsal time was precious. Finally, she understood why Stokowski banned any talk and insisted on jumping through a score. He wanted to concentrate on areas that needed work. That's where he wanted the attention of the players to be focused. Listening to long-winded explanations or playing through an entire piece would have been an indulgent waste of time. Efficiency and effectiveness were what Stoki was after, and his players, if they wanted to remain with the orchestra, had to learn his rules and stick to them.

A colleague, John Minsker, an English horn player and oboist, who played with the Philadelphia Orchestra for twenty-three years, also spoke of Stokowski's drive and intensity in rehearsals. "He was very, very strict and imposed severe discipline. Everybody had their parts memorized. When he stopped the orchestra, he'd . . . [throw his elbows down]. With most orchestras, you hear somebody play an extra note or two. When *he* did it, you could hear a pin drop. Every man stopped immediately. Then he'd say, 'Three bars after C.' You knew where C was. You anticipated what he might ask. You were ready to play. That orchestra was disciplined like no other ever was."[10]

Jumping through a score like that in rehearsal was challenging for harpists because they had to reset their pedals before playing if there happened to be a change of key in the bar the maestro wanted them to jump to. But that was Stoki's way. He concentrated on the problem areas and gave the players the responsibility for mastering the less complicated parts of a work on their own. Then he would pull everything together in the actual performance, a practice that kept the players on the edges of their chairs to follow his cues. It was nerve-racking, but Phillips came to believe that one of Stokowski's great strengths as a conductor was his ability to command the rapt attention of his players. They had to focus every ounce of their attention on him in concerts precisely because they weren't over-rehearsed, and that led to remarkably flexible and intense performances.

In rehearsal, the maestro sat on what looked to Phillips like an old wooden bar stool, directing with the same impassive look on his face he had when she auditioned for him. The rehearsals usually moved forward in a businesslike manner, quiet but very intense. Stokowski was polite, but he wasn't easy on the players. In fact, he was incredibly demanding. He would make them go over and over particular phrases to get them right, sometimes forcing each player in a section to play alone and not letting up until perfection was reached, which made them feel, Phillips said, "like they were being put through the wringer."

In ways, she pointed out, Stoki was even more demanding than Toscanini. He had a fellow in the second violin section taking down notes for him, and during rehearsals Stoki would make sotto voce comments to the note taker about the players. Once she heard him whisper "Harp, flat." He didn't need to do that, she said. She knew it and was about to fix it. Those darn drafts from the wings kept her in a constant battle to keep her harp in tune.

The notes Stokowski had the second violinist take sometimes had much harsher consequences for players than Toscanini's tantrums ever had, Phillips said. Toscanini might unloose a terrible barrage of invective on a player in a rehearsal, but he seemed to forget about it later, leaving the player with little more than a bruised ego. But Stoki had a more lethal way of registering his disapproval. He had those notes, and if the notes piled up too high on a player, Stoki fired him. That was how he had built the Philadelphia Orchestra. He began by weeding out the stiff, unmusical players he had inherited in 1912, and he didn't hesitate to fire others who failed to live up to his standards in the years that followed, at least until the musicians union began to assert itself more firmly later in the 1930s.

Phillips said he even had the note-taking fellow keep records on players when a guest conductor was on the podium so that he would always know what was happening. "We knew Stoki knew if we weren't prepared or if we committed some other musical sin," she said. "And he would remember it." Toscanini retained players that Stoki wouldn't have, she said. The fierce Italian insulted, berated, and terrorized players, but that was usually it. Stoki, on the other hand, stayed cool during rehearsals, but he might take action afterward.

At the same time, Phillips recalled, Stoki worked harder with his players to train them and help them improve their tone than any other conductor she knew. He was "a magnificent molder and builder of talent," she said. If a player was receptive, Stoki took great pains to help him or her grow. He was a masterful teacher, she said, and he produced some of the finest virtuosos in the orchestral world, but if he decided that a player was inflexible, unwilling, or unable to learn from his suggestions, then God help that player. "In those days you could be fired at the end of the season on the whim of the conductor. There was no safety or security, no redress, no help from the union. It wasn't strong then, and even the best players sometimes felt uneasy about their positions."

As the season drew to a close, the young harpist was looking pretty haggard.

"Ed-naa, you're too thin," Salzedo told her every time she saw him. But what could she do? Obstacles kept arising that required a big expenditure of her energy. That year she had already lost twenty-five pounds. Stokowski's spontaneity and intensity put a great deal of pressure on all his players, but especially on those new to the game. One day almost at the end of the season, the maestro surprised Phillips with a telephone call. A recording session had been scheduled for Monday morning, he said, and he wanted her to play Debussy's *Danses sacrée et profane*. This was Saturday morning. They had a concert that night. Phillips had not looked at the piece in year. It was a major work for the harp, and she had less than two days to refresh it and get it up to performance level.

"The time is short, I know," Stokowski told her. "Perhaps the second harp can help you out in the second movement."

"Oh no, I'd rather do it myself, " Phillips blurted out. She didn't need to carry that fellow along. It would only add to her worries. And so she shed more pounds that weekend, practicing almost nonstop for two days, taking time out only for the orchestra performance on Saturday night.

Rather than making the recording in the Academy of Music on that Monday morning, April 4, 1931, the members of the orchestra crossed the Delaware River to Camden, New Jersey, to a Sunday school room on the second floor of a Baptist church, where Stoki chose to record when the Academy wasn't available. Having never participated in a recording session, Phillips knew nothing about the process. She followed the maestro as best she could, but when he cut her off abruptly because they had almost reached the maximum length of the first side of the record, she asked, "Shall I let it vibrate," oblivious of the fact that her voice was being recorded.

"I think we ought to keep that one," Stoki said, smiling.

A good psychologist, he realized Phillips didn't understand that her remark would necessitate the rerecording of that side, and he didn't reprimand her. Partly because of Phillips's inexperience, it took a long time to make the recording that morning, and it was a warm spring day. All the windows had to be closed to keep out street sounds, making the room in which they were working almost unbearably hot and stuffy.

During a break, Phillips heard someone say in a vexed voice, "Blow the other way!" She looked over and saw that it was Bill Kincaid. His second flutist was Italian and enjoyed his garlic, Phillips said. Apparently, the stuffy room and the garlic were too much for the great Kincaid!

For all the heat and pressure involved in its making, the recording turned out to be a success. It got good reviews and sold well, which Phillips thought was a lucky break.

At about that time, Stoki announced that he had plans to build what he called a Temple of Music on Logan Circle in Philadelphia. It was to be an imposing edifice devoted solely to the orchestra, one that would no longer be shared with other organizations for such annoyingly pedestrian purposes as political speeches and high school graduations, as was the Academy of Music. His new temple would have better acoustics and better sight lines than the Academy, and, best of all, the orchestra wouldn't have to travel to Camden to make recordings. The new building would contain all the proper recording facilities and be the perfect site for pursuing experiments in electrical music and methods for recording and broadcasting.[11]

It was another of Stoki's big dreams, but it didn't meet with much enthusiasm from the people who had the power to make it happen. In fact, it was vociferously opposed by one of his biggest supporters—Frances Wister. She made it clear to all who would listen—and many did, since she had long played such an important role in the affairs of the orchestra—that she was astonished and shocked at Stoki's words and found them completely "out of order." No hall could be more beautiful than the Academy of Music, she asserted. The women's committees agreed in full voice. It would be a sacrilege for the orchestra to leave the Academy. But Miss Wister and her allies needn't have worried. The Depression soon brought an end to Stoki's plan for his Temple of Music.

A few days after the Debussy recording was finished, Stoki stopped Phillips as she walked to her dressing room after a rehearsal. She thought he might make a comment about her playing on the recording, but he didn't.

"I want to commend you on your fine deportment this year," he said.

Deportment? What about her playing? Wasn't that the important thing? She had worked so hard to master her instrument and learn the routine of the orchestra. Wasn't he going to say something about her playing? Had it improved? she wanted desperately to know. Was she becoming a worthy player in his orchestra? No comment on any of that, she said. Just her deportment, whatever that meant.

Then she realized with surprise and some amusement that the introduction of a woman into his orchestra had concerned even the iconoclastic Stokowski. He must have had at least a twinge of worry about whether his experiment would actually work. Perhaps he thought Phillips might cause a scandal in his orchestra after all. It was good, she concluded, that she had decided to remain aloof from the men. She had been so determined not to socialize with them that the personnel manager had asked her whether they had done something to offend her. No, she assured him, secretly glad that her signals had been read correctly and no one had made a pass at her. Distancing herself also insulated her from being rebuffed by those in the orchestra who objected to having a woman as a colleague. At least it kept her from ruffling too many feathers.

However, she couldn't help ruffling one set of feathers. The second harpist resented her presence, and he had made those feelings clear from the beginning. The best news Phillips got at the end of the season was that she wouldn't have to worry about him anymore. He was fired.

Stokowski the taskmaster had struck again. Phillips was relieved that she might have a more amenable second harpist to deal with in the future, but she knew she couldn't rest easy in her own position. She was still very much on trial. The maestro reinforced that idea by sending her a message that "it would be advisable" for her to play in the outdoor concerts planned for that summer in Philadelphia's Fairmount Park, just west of the center of the city. She had hoped to restore her energy and have an extended time to work on the harp with Salzedo in Maine over the summer, but Stoki obviously thought she needed more orchestral experience. If the maestro thought that, she had no other choice but to do it.

And now Phillips's year of firsts was over. Only the end-of-season luncheon for orchestra members given by the orchestra's great patron Alexander Van Rensselaer was left. As she sat in the grand ballroom of the old Ritz-Carlton Hotel surrounded by her colleagues from the orchestra and the distinguished members of its board of directors—including that nice Mr. Rosenbaum with the smiling blue eyes who was sitting at her table—Phillips silently thanked Salzedo for urging her forward. She knew that if he hadn't chosen her to audition, she would never have had the opportunity to be there.

She had grown to love the sound of the harp in the orchestra and felt honored to be part of the magnificent music the Philadelphia Orchestra produced. Surviving her first season had been the hardest thing she had ever done, but it was also the most rewarding. She had cursed Salzedo many times as she struggled to hang on, angry to the point of despair at her lack of preparation. But she had survived. Whether she could continue to do so or end up falling by the wayside, she didn't know, but whatever happened, it wouldn't be for want of trying.

## CHAPTER 7

# "Answer Yes or No"

For eight steamy weeks, night after night, with conductors coming and going and mosquitoes crawling up her arms, Phillips played that summer under the stars in Fairmount Park. Taking part in the summer concerts provided good on-the-job experience, she knew, but coming at the end of an exhausting first year, it was taxing. The entire enterprise was an experiment started that summer by the players and a group of friends of the orchestra called the Philadelphia Summer Concerts Association. Its purpose was to increase the number of weeks the orchestra members played—and got paid for—each year.

Although the orchestra board of directors didn't officially sanction the project, a few of the members saw the need for it and did what they could to help. One of them, Sam Rosenbaum, seemed to understand the financial difficulties the players experienced more than the others. He helped the summer series get off the ground:

> While the [regular season] pay-scale offered the players was good by symphony standards (the weekly minimum . . . was ninety dollars), the contract with the men provided only thirty to thirty-two weeks' employment, from October to May in each year. This made them vulnerable to siren voices from other jobs [since] they and their families insisted on eating fifty-two weeks in the year. To help bridge this gap, and also to provide Philadelphia good musical provender during the lean summer months, the [Philadelphia Summer Concerts] association chose a natural amphitheatre called Robin Hood Dell in Fairmount Park and erected a stage with a sound-projecting shell . . . designed for the site by that master of acoustic, Leopold Stokowski himself.[1]

According to the *New York Times*, the musicians union allowed the orchestra members who participated in the project to be paid from gate receipts rather than preset wages. The gate receipts were then divvied up among the players from the total amount received at the end of the summer.[2] The players didn't end up making much that first season, but it was a start.

The urbane and attractive Mr. Rosenbaum was often at Robin Hood Dell in his efforts to help the project succeed, and his path and Phillips's crossed often. She frequently found herself chatting with him when she was waiting offstage while the orchestra played a piece that didn't call for the harp. As witty as anyone she had ever met, Rosenbaum kept her happily entertained with his often-irreverent commentary on the state of the world, and he impressed her with his expansive knowledge of music. Although he was almost twenty years older than she was, he had such nice blue eyes and made such wise and funny observations that she found herself looking forward to his company, finding him far more interesting than the younger men she knew, who now seemed rather dull when seen from the heady arena she had been thrust into when she joined the Philadelphia Orchestra.

One Sunday, Rosenbaum invited her to lunch at his home. Picking her up at her house on Panama Street, he drove them along the picturesque east bank of the Schuylkill River out to School House Lane in the Philadelphia neighborhood of Germantown, about five miles from Center City. Phillips felt that they had left the city far behind them when they arrived at the Rosenbaum home, Roxboro House, which dated back to 1779 and was surrounded by big, old trees and lovely flowers.

A charming little girl with braids accompanied Rosenbaum on the journey—his eight-year-old daughter, Heather. Another daughter waited at home. Edna knew that Sam was a widower whose English wife had died seven years before, but she had never met his daughters. The older girl, Rosamond, whom the family called Peggy, was fourteen, just ten years Edna's junior. She had recently returned from boarding school in England, and was so sophisticated and worldly-wise that Phillips felt like a country bumpkin next to her.

Edna hadn't attended an official high school, let alone an English boarding school. Anna Phillips had been so anxious to encourage her musical development that she had arranged for her daughter to study with the Misses Bessie and Anna Stewart, who ran a little day school in Reading, rather than having her attend the public high school. That left Edna free to concentrate more of her time on studying the piano, but it also left her with a lifelong feeling of inadequacy. The Stewart sisters drilled grammar, Latin, and Shakespeare into their students, but not much else. At the time, that was fine with Edna. It gave her plenty of time to practice, practice, practice, and then have a happy time with her friends, unhampered by the responsibilities of mathematics, history, biology, and the rest, but later in life she felt the lack of a broader education.

She had certainly never been exposed to the cultured world that was so evident in the Rosenbaum household. Luckily, Sam's irreverent sense of humor took the edge off the situation and put her at ease, and Heather's curiosity and little-girl outspokenness were hard to resist. Her older sister greeted Edna with more reserve, but all in all, "it was a sweet day," and a happy respite for the young harpist from the hectic work schedule of the past year.

---

Then the Robin Hood Dell season ended. Now it was time for Phillips to do what she had been waiting for all summer—get herself to Camden, Maine, where Salzedo's Harp Colony was in full cry. That year Cher Maître had moved his summer coaching sessions from Seal Harbor, where he had been for several years and where Phillips had gone the year before, to a home in Camden, which he had christened, the Summer Harp Colony of America, a grand name indeed. Anxious to work with Salzedo without the pressures of her orchestral duties, Phillips also wanted to see what was happening with his new venture. Several of her friends from Curtis were there. They had written glowing letters about all the fun they were having on the cool coast of Maine while she "was steaming away in Philadelphia."

With her harp stowed in the baggage car, she traveled by train to Rockland, Maine, where a man with a distinct down-east accent and a truck met her at the railroad station. "You here to see the Count?" he asked, obviously on the lookout for a young woman with a harp.

The "Count," Phillips soon learned, was the locals' name for Salzedo. The debonair Frenchman with his distinctive accent and "continental" manners fascinated them, as did the fact that he had a pretty wife half his age and was surrounded by young and mostly female students who had been coming and going from his Harp Colony all summer. At the post office or bakery or passing each other on the street, the townspeople loved to swap tales about the Count's exotic ways and speculate about the intriguing things that must be going on at that "colony" of his. They were especially interested in the changes taking place in the house itself after Salzedo's friend Jules Bouy gave the traditional Maine cottage one of his "Art Deco do-overs."

As Phillips's driver ferried her from the train stop at Rockland to nearby Camden and the comfortable white clapboard house on Mountain Street where she was to stay while studying at the Harp Colony, he alluded to mysterious goings-on at the Count's. Apparently, he and his friends thought things were "mighty strange" there.

Anxious to see the strange doings for herself, Phillips quickly unpacked and walked the several blocks to the handsome shingled home on Marine Avenue overlooking Penobscot Bay that Salzedo had chosen. Surrounded by tall pine trees and ferns, the house stood on a hill that sloped gently down to the craggy rocks at the water's edge. It had a full view of the sailboat-dotted bay sparkling before it in the sunshine as well as the gray-green islands that hovered offshore. And there, digging away to create a garden, was the normally impeccable Salzedo—with his jacket off, his suspenders exposed, his shirtsleeves rolled up, and what looked like a Spanish mantilla comb holding back his usually slicked-back hair.

It was a shock to Phillips to see him looking so humbly normal (except for the comb, of course), and even the house he had chosen seemed at first rather unimpressive. It was a big traditional New England home with weathered shingles and dark green trim, handsome but nothing out of the ordinary. Not chic and *moderne*, as she had come to expect from the Salzedo-Bouy team. Then Salzedo took her inside, and with the opening of the door, she left traditional New England behind to enter the world of Art Deco.

Salzedo proudly gave her a tour. The front rooms on the first floor, one of which he used as his studio, shone in vivid yellow, while the dining room was swathed in dark burgundy with heavy draperies to match (all the better to encourage intimate conversation, Phillips learned). Other rooms followed suit with dramatic colors and built-in furniture, the latest in *moderne* lighting fixtures, made-to-order woven rugs, and on and on. It was dazzling, but after a while Phillips began to notice that there were no sofas anywhere. "I looked," she said, "but I couldn't find any." The only things to sit on were austere bamboo chairs with linen cushions, very attractive, but all straight up and down, not particularly comfortable-looking.

"Where are your sofas?" she asked. "Haven't you a single sofa here?"

"Oh, Ed-naa, don't be so Oriental," Salzedo answered.

The harp students, who were the raison d'être of the whole enterprise, were farmed out to houses in the village, mostly on Mountain Street, as was Phillips. There were about ten or twelve that first summer. Later, as word spread, many more would take part. The students would take their lessons at his house, for which Salzedo required that they dress as they did at Curtis, which meant that the young ladies had to wear nice dresses, gloves, and high heels. After their lessons, they would return to their various residences to practice for five hours every day. Phillips said she could start at the top of Mountain Street and hear harpists practicing all the way down the street.

Salzedo kept the students busy putting on recitals and festivals in the churches and parks in Camden, and people came from all around to hear them. It created quite a happy musical life for the area, adding to the already active musical life in that part of Maine in the summer. Just south of Camden along the coast is the seaside village of Rockport, where Mrs. Mary Louise Curtis Bok had a summer home, and a number of cottages that she leased "for a song" to some of the prestigious musicians associated with the Curtis Institute. One of them was Fritz Reiner. Apparently the cottages that surrounded Maestro Reiner were filled with many practicing people, Phillips said, just as the homes on Mountain Street in Camden were. When someone later asked him where he had spent the summer, she heard that Reiner answered, "In C minor."

It was a wonderful time to be musical and in Maine, and Salzedo worked hard with his students to develop their technique and interpretive abilities. In spite of his many eccentricities, Phillips considered him a brilliant teacher. "He had great integrity in the studio," she said, but that didn't prevent him from playing every angle he could think of to promote his Harp Colony, including joining the Lions Club of Camden.

"Ed-naa," he said one day, "I go to their luncheons, and I *r-r-roar!*"

---

When the orchestra's season got under way that fall back in Philadelphia, Phillips was pleased to have the assistance of Flora Bruce Greenwood, a Salzedo student who had been chosen for the second harp position. It gave Phillips comfort to have a female ally, and Greenwood was definitely more cooperative than her predecessor had been. Her being there seemed to be a good omen to Phillips that her second season would proceed more smoothly than the first.

But that wasn't to be.

The season started off on a controversial note when Stokowski treated Philadelphia audiences to a mini-festival of music by living composers. The program included Mossolov's *Soviet Iron Foundry*, a Toccata by Alexander Tansman, two Etudes by a Russian named Vladimir Vogel, Robert Russell Bennett's *Abraham Lincoln: A Likeness in Symphonic Form*, and Anton Webern's *Symphony for a Small Orchestra*.[3] To say that his audiences did not appreciate the new music Stoki offered them would be an understatement. They hated it. At the opening concert of the festival, the Friday afternoon women didn't much like taking the medicine Stoki administered, but at least they kept their disapproval within bounds. However, the Saturday night audience was not so restrained. As usual, the men had on tuxedos and the women long gowns, but they had left their formal concert manners at home. They grew restive with the first piece on the program and got more vociferous during the second, the Webern symphony.

While it was being played, a segment of the elegantly outfitted audience, obviously displeased, started hissing and booing and even laughing out loud. Then the most brazen of the lot got up and walked out—loudly and in large numbers. Phillips had seen some of that behavior before when Stoki presented modern music, but it had never been so obstreperous. Things were getting out of hand. She was just finishing a part that ended with a "way-down bottom note and a way-up top note" when Stoki, bristling with anger, signaled an abrupt halt to the playing and stalked offstage.

Dumbfounded, the players stayed in their places, not knowing what to do. The remaining audience also sat waiting. But nothing happened. Stokowski did not return. Both audience and players waited in puzzled silence. After awhile the wait became unbearable, and the audience started clapping to try to woo him back. Finally, after the maestro had let them plead long enough, he brushed back through the curtains and resumed his place on the podium. But if the audience thought the Webern was well over, they were wrong.

Stoki signaled the orchestra to play it again. Da capo. They had almost finished the short work the first time round. Now the audience had to sit through the whole of it again from the beginning! Only this time, Phillips was so rattled that "instead of going boom-ba, from bottom to top, [she] went ba-boom, from top to bottom," when the orchestra reached the crucial point again. Afraid that her mistake would be noticed, she looked sheepishly around, but everyone was in such a state, she said, it didn't seem to register.

Stokowski's commitment to new music had been ruffling the feathers of those with conventional tastes for years, but it had been tolerated because he had built the orchestra into such a revered institution. However, the deepening Depression had started to change that equation. By the fall of 1931, money was scarce and nerves were taut. People, whether they were audience members, board members, or members of the press, were now emboldened to express their disagreements with the maestro more muscularly. The all-embracing exuberance of the 1920s had faded, and grimmer times brought changes to the atmosphere of the Academy of Music.

A few weeks after the furor over Stoki's new music festival had died down, Toscanini was scheduled to come back to Philadelphia for two weeks of guest conducting. "We were all quaking in our boots at the prospect," Phillips said. "But then, one week before what was to be our first rehearsal with him, he developed neuritis and had to regret."

Il Maestro's cancellation was to have momentous impact on the future of the Philadelphia Orchestra.

"A young conductor named Eugene Ormandy, who had previously led a few summer concerts at Robin Hood Dell but who did most of his current work on the CBS radio network in New York, was presented as a last-minute substitute, not without trepidation on everybody's part, except his own," Herbert Kupferberg writes in *Those Fabulous Philadelphians*. Manager Arthur Judson had not been able to find anyone from among his stable of leading conductors to take Toscanini's place on such short notice. As a last resort, he offered the job to Ormandy but warned him that he would be taking a great chance if he agreed to substitute for the renowned maestro. "'Here's the opportunity to start your career or break your neck,' he said. Ormandy, always a quick study, accepted on the spot."[4]

To stand in for the great Toscanini was both brave and bold, especially for Ormandy, who at the age of thirty-two had little experience in conducting a full orchestra. His youth and lack of experience plus the brief amount of time—a matter of days—he had to learn and master the program for that week's concerts made his task even more daunting.

On the day of Ormandy's first performance, Phillips was invited to join a few people having lunch with the young conductor and his wife at Child's Restaurant on Broad Street. Ormandy's Viennese-born wife, Stephanie Goldner Ormandy, a professional harpist, was the woman who held the second-harp position in the New York Philharmonic. Apparently, someone in Judson's office thought that Phillips and Goldner would have much in common, but the two harpists didn't have much of a chance to talk that day. Child's—"a big, china-clattering kind of place," according to Phillips—was not exactly a relaxing interlude for the young conductor in the hours before he had to lead an immensely difficult program. Stokowski always repaired to his isolated aerie above the Academy of Music stage to meditate in majestic silence before a concert, but Ormandy, with an enormous job ahead of him, behaved fairly normally under the circumstances, she observed. He appeared a little distracted perhaps, but not overly so. Steffi (as his wife was known) seemed more nervous than her husband.

Less than two hours after that lunch, Ormandy led the orchestra in a triumphant concert. Philadelphia audiences, still smarting from Stokowski's new-music festival, were instantly impressed with the young conductor. The program Ormandy led included Brahms's Symphony No. 4, Richard Strauss's *Till Eulenspiegel* and *Rosenkavalier* waltzes, and the polka and fugue from Jaromir Weinberger's *Schwanda the Bagpiper*. The *Philadelphia Record* reported ecstatically: "An audience that was genuinely pleased to hear a program of beautiful music, instead of foundry imitations and noises from the nethermost depths, accorded Eugene Ormandy, guest conductor of the Philadelphia Orchestra, an enthusiastic welcome yesterday afternoon at the Academy of Music."[5]

The fledgling conductor had not committed career suicide, as Judson had warned he might. Instead, he had accepted a challenge that would propel him toward a dazzling future. Within two weeks he was appointed conductor of the well-respected Minneapolis Symphony (now the Minnesota Orchestra), whose conductor, Henri Verbrugghen, had recently been incapacitated by a stroke. He was to remain there for the next five years.

On a lesser scale than Ormandy, Phillips had to deal with her own last-minute call to perform early that season. Salzedo had been scheduled to perform the Mozart *Concerto for Flute and Harp (Concerto in C major, K 299)* as soloist with the orchestra's principal flutist, William Kincaid, but three weeks beforehand, Salzedo and Stokowski had a tiff about something Phillips wasn't privy to. With no warning, Stokowski removed Salzedo from the schedule and informed Phillips that she was to take his place. She had never played the extremely complex work, one of the harp's few masterpieces from the classical period. Now she had less than a month to learn it and bring it up to a soloist's level.

Adding to the pressure, Phillips had recently been appointed chair of the harp department at the Philadelphia Conservatory of Music, which was accredited by the Juilliard Foundation of New York. Salzedo's younger compatriot, the prestigious harpist Marcel Grandjany, had unexpectedly decided not to come to Philadelphia that summer after he had been scheduled to take the harp position at the conservatory. Later he became head of the Juilliard School's harp department in New York and eventually developed a following of students as loyal to him as Salzedo's were to their Cher Maître. Grandjany's decision not to come had left the conservatory without a prominent harpist on its staff, and nothing would solve that problem, it seemed, but to have the Philadelphia Orchestra's principal harpist fill the position. It was the last thing Phillips wanted to take on, but the musical politics of the situation dictated that she accept the appointment, even though it threatened to be the straw that broke the camel's back. She needed all her free time to work on the Mozart, but her new duties plus her normal rehearsal schedule for the orchestra's concerts kept hampering her progress.

She had struggled with Debussy's *Danses* when Stoki gave her two days' notice for the recording session at the end of last season, but she had played that work before. It was in her head and heart and fingers. She could revive and refresh it even though she didn't have the luxury of doing the job as thoroughly as she would have liked. But the difficulty of that experience paled before that of learning the Mozart from the ground up. Mastering such a complex work in three weeks would be considered by any standards an almost impossible task. "It was god-awful to try to unravel that concerto and cook it into my fingers in the time Stoki gave me," she said. "To be honest, I don't think I did a very good job of it. I didn't make any huge mistakes, but my performance wasn't what I would have wanted it to be."

Fortunately for Phillips, Kincaid, although he was considered the preeminent orchestral flutist of his era, was also very kind. He gave up much of his time to hold extra rehearsals with her, going over and over difficult sections without complaint, but he could do only so much. She had to master the concerto on her own.

During a rehearsal before the concert, the wise Tabuteau, another of the orchestra's great virtuosos, noticed Phillips's obvious anxiety and proffered another of his "nevaires" to her, but this time he wasn't chastising her, as he did when she spoke out during a rehearsal. This time he meant to encourage her. "*Nevaire* worry, mademoiselle. *Nevaire* worry," he told her. "Just listen."

Stokowski seemed oblivious to the extraordinary pressure he had put on Phillips, but that wasn't unusual. He was always springing things on his players and expecting them to do the impossible. Phillips wasn't the only first-chair player he had surprised with a last-minute assignment. That was life with Stokowski. For the most part, the players accepted the demands placed on them by their spontaneous leader as part of their job, even though they had to struggle mightily at times to meet them. Their lives under Stokowski weren't easy, but they were never dull.

———•———

As the season progressed, Phillips began to notice a change in the maestro's demeanor toward her. In her first year with the orchestra, he had maintained a professional, detached attitude toward her—at least after the foolish virgins incident—but in her second year she couldn't help feeling a certain heat radiating her way from the podium. "Even a ten-month-old baby would have sensed something was up," she said.

She tried to ignore it and wish it away, until one morning her fears came to a head. The orchestra was rehearsing Stokowski's synthesis of the Love Music from act 2 of *Tristan und Isolde*, a particularly sensuous piece, when Phillips felt strong sparks coming her way from the podium. At the end of the rehearsal, she heard the words she feared might be forthcoming.

"Harp, please come here."

That was it. Now she would have to talk to him face to face. Knowing what she did about Stoki's reputation as a ladies' man, the last thing she wanted to do was find herself alone with him after the rest of the orchestra had left the stage. Not with those sparks flying. So she grabbed her music and moved to the podium as fast as she could. The men were still filing out, gathering up their instruments and chatting with each other, and the associate conductor was standing on the other side of the podium. With that many people around, Phillips felt somewhat protected as Stoki smiled at her and took her proffered music.

"I want you to play an arpeggio here," he said, turning to the correct page and proceeding to write on it, which appeared to be perfectly legitimate.

Handing back her music, he asked, "Do you think that will work there? Do you understand it?"

Looking down at her music, Phillips was dismayed to discover more than the expected notation at the bottom of the page. The maestro had also written, "Will you take lunch with me today? Answer Yes or No."

What could she do? If she said no, she might lose her job. If she said yes, she might lose it in the end anyway. The possibilities swirled before her. What to do? She needed time to think, but she had to answer right away.

Grasping for time, she answered, "Yes."

"Are you sure you understand?" he asked again, eyeing her carefully.

"Yes, maestro."

Looking very pleased, Stoki turned to confer with the associate conductor.

Phillips had gotten what she wanted—time to think. But now what? She had to think of a way out fast. With Salzedo's warning about the possibility of being thrown away like an old shoe playing in her mind, she cast about for a solution.

From gossip about town, she knew that Stokowski had recently taken an apartment on Lincoln Drive in Germantown after his second wife, the pharmaceutical heiress Evangeline Brewster Johnson, had chosen to live in Manhattan rather than in their home in Chestnut Hill, so that their children could attend the Dalton School. That gave Phillips a sliver of an idea. Assuming that Stoki was planning to take her to his apartment, she devised a plan, which she quickly put into motion.

Before the maestro could descend from his dressing room to take her to lunch, she hurried over to Marshall, who was in charge of everything to do with Stokowski, and told him she needed to see the maestro right away. Looking skeptical and maybe disappointed in her, Marshall gave her permission to go upstairs. Without wasting a second, she ascended to Stoki's secluded aerie, which was strictly off limits to orchestra members except by special appointment. When she arrived at his door, Stokowski looked surprised, but pleasantly so.

"Maestro, I just remembered I have to teach at two o'clock today," Phillips began immediately. "You've taught me how important punctuality is, so I don't want to arrive late for the lesson. I might be setting a bad example for my student. Do you think I can be back in time from lunch?"

"Well," he answered slowly, "it's a little far where I live. I'm afraid there wouldn't be enough time to go out there and come back by two o'clock."

"Wouldn't it be possible to have lunch in town?"

"Oh, I don't think so," he answered. "I don't think people would understand."

"Well, I don't see why not," Phillips said, putting on her most innocent face. "What is there to understand?"

She had him there, and they both knew it. After pausing a moment, he gave her a bemused look and muttered, "Some other time."

What a relief! Her plan had worked even better than she had hoped it would. She quickly took her leave, praying she had dampened that fire for good and not endangered her future.

To Phillips, Stokowski was an extraordinary leader and teacher and a magnificent, exciting conductor. He was almost a god. The music he brought forth from his orchestra was so enthralling all else could be forgiven. Well, almost all else, she said. But this was really too much. Just six months before he had complimented her on her deportment. What kind of deportment did he have in mind for her now?

At least, she said, after the aborted luncheon, he appeared to accept that she was not someone to be toyed with. His behavior toward her reverted to the purely professional, and no repercussions fell on her for having resisted his overture. The sparks stopped flying toward her, and she was able to continue her work in his orchestra as a professional. Stokowski kept on working with her in rehearsals, giving her suggestions to help her enrich her tone and improve the flexibility and responsiveness of her playing, just as he worked with his other first-chair players. She was grateful for that, she said, because aside from Salzedo, Stoki was her most valuable teacher.

As for her own teaching, which she had used as an alibi to escape the tryst Stoki had planned, Phillips wasn't actually scheduled for a two o'clock lesson that day, but she did have to teach too often for her comfort. Up until the moment she used it as an excuse, she had regarded the time and effort she had to spend on teaching as a burden, especially when she was such a newly minted harpist herself. But now that teaching had offered her a way out of the awkward situation with Stokowski, she vowed to give it more of her attention and slowly began to revise her attitude. Over the years she grew to love working with promising young musicians.

———•———

Stokowski had by then led the orchestra for nineteen years and was insisting on ever-longer breaks in his schedule of conducting so that he could travel and pursue what he called his "researches" into native music and instruments around the world. A series of guest conductors took over the podium while he was away, and Phillips enjoyed observing and comparing them.

During one of Stoki's absences, Fritz Reiner conducted both the Philadelphia Orchestra and the Philadelphia Grand Opera, which gave Phillips many opportunities to observe him. As demanding as he was, she said she considered Reiner, like Stokowski, an excellent teacher. She learned a great deal by trying to live up to his exacting standards. "If you could do what Reiner wanted, you knew you had really gotten it right," she said.

However, she recalled a lighter moment with him one morning when the orchestra was rehearsing *Liebestod*. Reiner, as was his wont, led with a small, precise beat, moving just the tip of his long baton in miniscule patterns, in great contrast to Stoki's expressive conducting style. That morning the players were following Reiner's tiny little beat almost to the point of becoming hypnotized, and they failed to provide the surging feel the music called for. Suddenly, the maestro erupted.

"Don't you know vaht dis iss?" he asked. "It is a paroxysissum uf luf!"

"Believe me," Phillips laughed, the players understood very well the "paroxysm of love" the music called for after following the emotive Stokowski through so many concerts, but they were so mesmerized by Reiner's precise baton movements they forgot themselves until he brought them back to their senses.

Another guest conductor the orchestra faced that year was Bernardino Molinari. Although he was generally regarded as a good conductor, Tabuteau couldn't stand him. The great oboist glowered during Molinari's rehearsals, looking so sour that the other players kidded him about it, but Tabuteau insisted that he never showed his feelings. "I have a *pokeaire* face," he bragged, which made them laugh because it was absolutely not true. His scowl was plain for everyone to see, much to the enjoyment of all. Except Molinari, of course.

The orchestra played three concerts in Philadelphia under Molinari, and Tabuteau tormented the poor conductor by leaving a different little something out at each performance. Phillips said the hapless conductor kept trying to figure out what was wrong. He knew something was missing, but what? Where?

"Tabuteau was so subtle, so deadly," she said with a twinkle in her eye. "He had Molinari looking as if he were batting at a fly buzzing around his head. But when we got to Carnegie Hall, Tabuteau stopped his mischief. Molinari was a protégé of Toscanini, and the great maestro was in the audience that night. Tabuteau knew he couldn't fool the master, so he gave up his prank."

Tabuteau must have been going through a blue period at that time, Phillips said, because she heard him complaining to Salzedo as they left the Academy of Music one Monday night.

"I am so weary," he moaned, donning the beret he always wore and fitting a cigarette into his long cigarette holder for the walk to his apartment. "I think I will quit *la musique*."

"Then what would you do, Marcel," Salzedo asked, completely unsympathetic, "sell neckties at Wanamaker's?"

Finally, Stoki returned to Philadelphia for his spring concerts. In the midst of a rehearsal, Phillips thought she smelled smoke coming from somewhere near the stage. She immediately scanned the area and soon spotted a bearded man she didn't recognize lounging comfortably with his feet up on the railing of the proscenium box behind her, puffing on a cigar. It turned out to be the maestro's good friend, the noted painter Arthur B. Carles.[6] As dignified as Stokowski appeared to be to the general public, Phillips explained, he was an artist and bohemian at heart, and his true friends were also artists, who shared with him a passion for the art of their day. Carles, a brilliant colorist and an early American modernist helped organize three exhibitions at the Pennsylvania Academy of the Fine Arts in the 1920s to introduce modern art to Philadelphia, getting his friend Stokowski, whom he called Sto, to write the introduction to the catalog for the first. In it, "Sto" likened the painters in the show, Cézanne, Gauguin, Picasso, and Matisse, to composers Debussy and Stravinsky and urged viewers to accept their work just as he hoped his audiences would accept the music of modern composers.

The second exhibition gave nearly one hundred modernist U.S. artists a chance to be seen, and the third displayed seventy-five works that art collector Albert Barnes had recently acquired in Europe. All the exhibitions drew huge crowds as well as much consternation and squawking from the public and the press, but the final exhibition was pilloried so rudely that Barnes recoiled in anger and vowed to close his collection to everyone but his chosen guests.

---

In the spring of 1932, Stokowski staged two important premieres, hoping they would reach the successful heights that *Wozzeck* had the year before. However, the response was more muted this time. The orchestra performed Arnold Schoenberg's massive *Gurrelieder* in Philadelphia's Metropolitan Opera House, as it had *Wozzeck* the year before, and Carlos Chávez's *H.P.* (Horse Power) in the Academy of Music with a stunning backdrop painted by Diego Rivera, but neither met with the popular and critical success *Wozzeck* had.

Worried about the loss of revenue due to the effects of the Depression and the high cost of Stokowski's ambitious premieres, the orchestra's board of directors urged the maestro to reel in his musical experiments. Thinking that audiences would appreciate soothing, familiar music in hard times, many on the board pushed him to scale down the number of contemporary works the orchestra played, but Stokowski would have none of it. Good music was good music, he insisted, and it didn't have to be old to be good. He firmly believed that audiences should be introduced to the music being written by their contemporaries. It was the duty of a great orchestra to lead the public's taste rather than follow it, he asserted, whether times were hard or not.

It wasn't that Stokowski was indifferent to the hardships brought on by the Depression. He involved himself in the Robin Hood Dell summer concerts that supplemented the incomes of the Philadelphia Orchestra players and led many free concerts around the city, including one featuring two hundred unemployed musicians, called the Jobless Band, which entertained thousands in Reyburn Plaza at city hall, and another in Convention Hall, an all-Sousa concert, to benefit unemployed musicians.[7] He accepted no payment for those concerts and others like them, which was certainly commendable. However, there happened to be an awkward fact about his own income that couldn't be ignored: it was quite high.

The *Philadelphia Record* ran a story about it that aroused much interest. Claiming that Stokowski earned Philadelphia's highest salary, which the paper estimated to total $200,000 with his radio and recording contracts and other extras, columnist Norman Abbott wrote:

> There's a phase of the economic situation that doesn't annoy the blond maestro, and that's the wage cut. Almost everywhere salaries are being shaved down these days. Mr. Hoover has offered to do his chores for $1 a year. Mr. Babe Ruth is socking home runs with all the old verve and éclat for a measly $75,000 a year. But those who pay Mr. Stokowski a stipend which might be called princely—except that princes aren't doing so well either this year—have little thought of asking him to accept a reduction. How come? They're afraid he might quit! And they insist that he's worth every nickel he gets and probably more.[8]

Abbott must not have known what was going on behind the scenes between the maestro and his board of directors at that time. The natural divide that had long existed between the artistically adventurous Stokowski and the conservative board grew during the Depression, and the board began to increase its level of resistance to his ideas, feeling its responsibility for keeping the orchestra's financial ship afloat and seeing that ship start to list under the weight of its first deficit. Many members laid the blame for the financial problems on Stoki's insistence on presenting new music, which, they believed, discouraged ticket sales. They were determined to bring him under control.

Without consulting Stokowski, the board gave the newspapers a bombshell story (at least in musical circles) about the upcoming season. It read in part: "The programs will be almost entirely devoted to acknowledged masterpieces. The directors feel that in times such as the present, audiences prefer music which they know and love, and that performances of debatable music should be postponed until a more suitable time."[9]

When Stokowski learned about the announcement, he exploded—also in the newspapers—saying that he had not been told about such a dictum and vowing that it would not deter him from pursuing the plans he had for premiering a new Shostakovich symphony. Then he threw down the gauntlet by announcing that he would open the 1932–33 season with another new piece, Werner Josten's *Jungle*, which, he gleefully pointed out, was filled with primitive sounds representing the jungle, and promising to play it twice so that listeners could better understand it.

In one of his famous podium speeches, Stoki challenged the board still further. "It all boils down to this, whether Philadelphia wishes to keep an open mind—whether Philadelphia wishes to hear the best in music—whether Philadelphia wishes to keep an open attitude toward what the world is doing today—or whether Philadelphia, artistically, wishes to stagnate."[10]

"Debatable music," harrumph. He wasn't going to let the board dictate to him on that subject.

Although Phillips was immersed in the world of music, she couldn't avoid the harsh realities of the Depression bearing down around her. As a young woman with a salary and a family of somewhat comfortable means, she escaped the true desperation that many felt, but she took a 10 percent cut in her salary, as did all of the orchestra members, to share the burden of lost revenue the orchestra was facing. She also couldn't avoid seeing the empty seats that began to show up in the Academy of Music, like stitches pulled out of a sweater, as more and more people found themselves unable to afford tickets. For years the orchestra had played to sold-out houses. Tickets had been so hard to come by that people joked about their scarcity. When Stokowski had married heiress Evangeline Brewster Johnson in 1926, humorists said she had to marry him to secure a seat to the orchestra. But by 1932, times were very hard. The giddy days of the twenties were well over.

As for the feelings of the players toward Stokowski in the board-versus-maestro controversies, Phillips allowed that there were some gripes here and there about the demands Stoki put on them, but for the most part, she said, the players were grateful to have such an inspiring leader to follow. Not involved in the battles between the maestro and the board, they kept their heads low, hoping to avoid the crossfire. While Stoki and the board sparred, the players went about their business, hoping that peace would prevail. One day Phillips overheard a comment that summed up the players' attitude toward Stoki, especially because it came from the hardest of the group to please—Marcel Tabuteau.

On a homeward-bound train after a performance in Hartford, the players were talking from seat to seat about one of their favorite topics: who was the greater conductor—Stokowski or Toscanini? Tabuteau had played extensively under both maestros, and he offered an opinion that brought nods of understanding from all who heard it.

"I could play seven concerts with Toscanini," Phillips recalled Tabuteau saying, "and those seven concerts would be perfect. They would be impeccable. When I would leave my house to play, I would say to myself, this is going to be a perfect concert. I anticipated perfect concerts, and they were perfect concerts.

"But with Stokowski, I play seven concerts, and six are colorful and glamorous and fascinating and beautifully interpreted, but in the seventh concert, something strange happens. A kind of brush fire goes through the orchestra. It becomes incandescent, and the music goes to the stars."

English horn and oboe player John Minsker echoed that same feeling over seventy years later. Wanting to preserve his memories of "the alchemistic relationship between conductor and orchestra," he spoke about Stokowski to the *Philadelphia Inquirer* in 2007. "When you played a concert with him, you were so proud of yourself, because you realized you had done something great . . . there was always that feeling when we played for him."[11]

Sometimes, however, Stokowski pushed his players too far. Laila Storch, in her fascinating biography of Tabuteau, mentions a time when the great oboist "felt that Stokowski had been riding the orchestra too hard, and so he headed to the Academy of Music early enough before a morning rehearsal to locate some props stored underneath the stage from the previous night's performance of *Aida*. Finding the yoke from the scene where the Ethiopian prisoners are paraded by to become the slaves of the Egyptians, he hauled it up to the stage and linked it around the whole oboe section. 'You know,' [he told Storch,] 'when Stokowski came in to begin the rehearsal and saw us, he got the idea!'"[12]

Tabuteau's colleagues must have savored that moment.

## CHAPTER 8

# "Mortally Wounded"

Now it was Edna's younger sister's turn to be the center of the Phillips family's attention. Peggy had waited patiently, somewhat on the sidelines, as Edna struggled to maintain her position in the orchestra. Not that she didn't have her own fun, zipping back and forth to college in her roadster and just being the happy, sunny person she was with lots of friends and a growing romance to occupy her time. Her infectious good humor had cheered her sister many times when she felt overwhelmed by the pressures that confronted her. Edna was happy to stand aside while Peggy stepped into the family spotlight.

Peggy's budding romance with Christy Mathewson Jr., son of legendary pitcher, Christy Mathewson Sr., and, according to Edna, "as handsome and nice a young man as could be," had blossomed into an engagement. But a problem emerged. Young Christy had become enamored of flying after he graduated from Bucknell University, and that led to protracted separations. After joining the Army Air Corps, he had gone to flying school in Texas and then on to Mitchel Field on Long Island to complete his required period of service. Peggy thought that would be it. She had waited for him for four years, through all the steps he had taken. Now she was graduating from college; he had finished his service, and they would get married and settle down. That was the plan. But, in the spring of 1932, young Christy was asked to teach flying in the Chinese Central Aviation School at Hangchow, as "part of a quiet American effort to build up China's fledgling air force."[1]

After Japan invaded Manchuria in 1931, it had become apparent that the Chinese air defenses needed to be strengthened, and fourteen U.S.

Air Corps pilots were assigned to train Chinese pilots in the new school. Christy was one of them. His tour of duty was set for three years. Captivated by the adventure that lay ahead of him, Christy told Peggy the news. She was heartbroken. Three years—it was just too much. How could she wait for him that long?

Then Christy suggested that she come to China. They could marry and live there while he taught flying. That immediately appealed to Peggy, who was brave and young and full of adventure herself. Edna was proud of her sister for being so determined and daring, and surprisingly, Mrs. Phillips was, too. She gave her consent with only a few protestations about her youngest daughter traveling so far from home. When Christy's mother, Jane Mathewson, decided to accompany Peggy on the long and arduous trip from Philadelphia to Hangchow, Mrs. Phillips's fears were quieted, and she entered into the plans for the wedding with enthusiasm.

Edna and her mother both admired Christy, who had been a friend of her brother ever since they were at Bucknell together. Good-looking in an all-American, clear-eyed way, he was unassuming and genuinely kind. He didn't put on airs about being the son of a great sports hero, Edna said, and he won their hearts with his wholesome friendliness. Christy Mathewson Sr. had been more than just a terrific baseball player when he pitched for the New York Giants from 1900 to 1916. His sportsmanship and fine character had earned him the respect and devotion of countless fans and made him such an idol of the press that he helped elevate the game of baseball in the eyes of fans across the country.

"In a time when baseball was known for its hard-living, hard-drinking players," journalist Philip Seib wrote, "there was Christy Mathewson to prove that there was another way for athletes to live. He was the role model after whom every parent wanted their children to shape their lives."[2] When Mathewson died in 1925 after suffering for years from the effects of being gassed in the First World War, he was mourned across the United States as a national hero, "the first great hero of the modern age of American sports."[3] The *New York Times* announced his death on its first page: "Christy Mathewson, idol of the nation's baseball fandom over a span of more than two decades, and one of the greatest pitchers the game has ever known, was a symbol of the highest type of American sportsmanship."[4]

In spite of his father's fame, the young Christy chose not to follow his footsteps into baseball. "They would always point to me as my great dad's son," he said, "and besides you don't know how awful a baseball player I am."[5] He set out on a different path that would take him all the way to China.

Once Peggy had made up her mind to travel to China to marry Christy, the Phillips household began to buzz with preparations, the most important of which was to assemble her trousseau, which, Edna said, was great fun. Peggy was a pretty young woman who took great joy in choosing the outfits she would wear. She and her mother would bring selections home, and Peggy would model them while Mrs. Phillips stood by beaming.

There were times, however, when Mrs. Phillips wasn't beaming, and that was when Sam Rosenbaum would stop in to see Edna, whom he had first spoken to two years before on the stage of the Academy of Music when he gently explained to her that Cornelius McGillicuddy's nickname was Connie Mack. An older man, a widower with children, Jewish—he was not what Anna Phillips had in mind in the way of suitors for Edna, and her disapproval showed in her icy demeanor toward him.

Jane Mathewson and Peggy set off for China on November 24, 1932, Thanksgiving Day. At the train station in New York—they traveled across the country by train before boarding a ship from San Francisco for the rest of the journey—a *Times* reporter asked Peggy what her thoughts were on her departure, and Peggy told him, "I think it's all very exciting to travel halfway around the world for your wedding."[6] Edna agreed with her. It was to be a wonderful adventure.

On Christmas Eve 1932, Peggy and Christy were married in Hangchow in a double ceremony with Christy's flying mate Ellis Shannon and his bride. Christy and Ellis's aviation school friends helped them celebrate, and good cheer and happiness prevailed. After the ceremony, the couples traveled to Shanghai for their honeymoons. Two weeks later, when it was time to return to Hangchow on January 8, the Shannons elected to go by train, but Christy had arranged a special surprise for his new bride. As a wedding present, he had been given the use of the Sikorsky amphibian airplane belonging to T. V. Soong, then China's finance minister, for the short flight. When it came time for the young couple to leave, a group of friends, including the Shannons, gathered in the plane's hangar to see them off. Delighted at the prospect of flying with Christy for the first time, Peggy told their friends how excited she was and laughed about how funny Christy looked in his flying helmet, which she called his derby hat. All cheered as they took off.

Thirty seconds later, the gathered company were horrified to see the plane lose control. Christy struggled to keep its nose in the air but couldn't hold it steady. It dove into the Whangpoo River, skimming along on top of the water for several moments before it hit a mudflat at a bend in the river, where it overturned. Peggy was crushed in the wreckage.

Christy suffered two broken arms and a broken leg. His first words when the rescuers got to him were: "Look after my wife."[7] But nothing could be done. Peggy's injuries were too extensive.

The Phillips family received the cable informing them of Peggy's death on Sunday morning, twelve hours after the accident. Edna's older sister Caroline was visiting the Panama Street house for the weekend. She took the cable in and carried it upstairs to a place on the landing where there was a big window. Not fully comprehending what she read, she stood there, holding the cable up to the light to try to see it better.

Then she gave it to Edna, who saw the terrible words "mortally wounded."

Because the Mathewson name was so famous, word of the tragedy spread quickly in radio reports. It was also front-page news in the New York and Philadelphia papers. Not long after the Phillips family received the cable, the orchestra's personnel manager, Paul Lotz, who had already spoken with Stokowski, called Phillips. That Monday evening, the very next day, the orchestra was scheduled to play a concert that had the César Franck Symphony on the program, which the second harpist had not rehearsed with the orchestra.

Stokowski asked Lotz to convey a message to Phillips for him. "As a man," the maestro said, "I'd tell her not to play, but as an artist, she must if she possibly can."

And so Phillips played the concert on Monday night. "They didn't think to move me back into the orchestra, but left me out in front as usual," she said. "So I took my harp, turned it into the orchestra with my back toward the audience and played the Franck. Ever since, that piece has brought tears to my eyes when I hear it."

She also had to leave Philadelphia on Tuesday to travel with the orchestra to Ohio for a long-scheduled performance in the Toledo (pronounced *Tolaydo* in Stokowski's "orchestreze") Museum of Art. Phillips was in shock. She could play, but everything else was blank. She heard later that some of the men in the orchestra criticized her because she didn't cry on the train, but they didn't understand, she said. "I was too numb to cry."

In the days and weeks following the crash, many news reports contained speculations about what had happened to Peggy and Christy, adding to the Phillips family's grief. They eventually learned that the plane had been sabotaged in an attempt to assassinate T. V. Soong, a member of one of China's most powerful families. China was experiencing intense internal strife as well as escalating threats from Japan at the time, so it was difficult to know who had been responsible. There was never an official inquest or verification of what caused the crash, but the Phillips family came to believe that it was the Japanese who had sabotaged the plane and that Peggy and Christy were among the earliest victims of the Second World War.

Mrs. Phillips was devastated by the tragedy. She had now lost five of her eight children. Overnight she turned into an old woman who wanted only to be left alone, Phillips said. The little house on Panama Street, which just over a month before had brimmed with laughter and high hopes, was now enveloped in sorrow. It felt too bleak for Mrs. Phillips to stay there, and the family decided she might find more solace living with Caroline in her home in Wernersville, near Reading.

Although Edna's grief over Peggy was deep, her work in the orchestra couldn't be ignored. She had to go forward, and she did. Her orchestral duties were as demanding as ever, and that was good because "Stoki kept everyone so involved and so on our toes all the time, I didn't have time to dwell on my sorrow."

Having known much sorrow himself, Sam was a great help to her at that time. Not only had his wife died nine years before, he had also lost a young son the year before that. In spite of those tragedies, he had gone on with his life, raising two daughters, the younger one only nine months old when her mother died, and building a strong career and a fine reputation for himself. He emanated a sense of strength, wisdom, and security that Edna came to rely on. It was good to have his frequent company. His playful sense of humor also refreshed her spirit. "Stick with me, baby," he once told her, "and I'll keep you in rhinestones."

Edna respected greatly Sam's encyclopedic knowledge of music. For her, music was instinctive. She didn't bother much about its history or other specifics. She felt it, loved it, and played it. Sam, on the other hand, had amassed a raft of information about the history and theory of music. As an undergraduate at the University of Pennsylvania, he had run a popular lecture series on opera and since then had continued to be a music patron, supporting numerous musical endeavors, "really supporting them," Edna said, "by rolling up his sleeves to solve problems and raise money and get things going."

That he was a member of the orchestra's board of directors presented a barrier to the possibility of a romance developing, however. It put him on the other side of the equation from Phillips. As he wryly pointed out, he was capital and she was labor. It was awkward for both of them: he with his fellow board members and she with her orchestral colleagues.

Beyond that, there was another person they were sure to be on the wrong side of—Stokowski. His relationship with the board was growing rockier by the day. Having a member of his orchestra involved with a member of his troublesome board of directors would surely not please the maestro.

But Sam had those wonderful blue eyes, and he was so witty and so fascinating that Edna found herself disregarding the obstacles and agreeing to marry him in spite of the possible consequences.

Deep in mourning, Mrs. Phillips could not rouse herself to support the marriage, which left Edna with no one to help her make arrangements for the wedding. Caroline tried to help out, but she lived too far away to do much. Then Mary Louise Curtis Bok, the founder of the Curtis Institute, stepped forward.

Two years before, after Edna's first year in the orchestra when she had to stay in the city to play at Robin Hood Dell, Edna was alone in the house while her mother and Peggy spent the summer at their usual cottage in Mt. Gretna. Without so much to do for once, Edna began thinking about all the wonderful things that had happened to her because she had attended the Curtis Institute. One day, she sat down and wrote Mrs. Bok "a bread and butter letter," thanking her for her generosity in founding and funding the school. Ten days after Mrs. Bok received the letter, she wrote back, remarking that Phillips's letter was the only one she had ever received.

After that, Mrs. Bok took a special interest in Phillips. Along with her good friend Mrs. Charles Griffith, she proposed Phillips for membership in the Cosmopolitan Club of Philadelphia, a newly established club for women on Latimer Street, a block away from the Academy of Music. Its membership was made up of women who were involved in "creative or professional work . . . cosmopolitan and civic affairs and the world of arts and ideas."[8] Unafraid to be avant-garde in conservative Philadelphia, the club's founders had hired Jules Bouy, that master of *moderne* again, to turn the interior of their clubhouse into an Art Deco showplace, and Phillips enjoyed interacting with the lively women she met there. Although her orchestral commitments demanded much of her time, whenever she could she enjoyed attending their soirées, which were really salons that brought together stimulating people to exchange ideas. Among those who took part in the soirées were Edna St. Vincent Millay, Thornton Wilder, Stokowski, and Salzedo, as well as other artists and scholars.

By chance at one of the club's functions, Phillips told Mrs. Bok that Sam and she were planning to marry. One thing led to another, and Mrs.

Bok and Mrs. Griffith stepped forward to help her with her wedding arrangements. It made things much easier, Edna said, "especially since my mother was absenting herself."

She and Sam postponed the announcement of their engagement until the very last minute in order to keep the ceremony private. The last thing they wanted was "a wedding with a lot of folderol so soon after Peggy's death." They also wanted to keep any announcement of their marriage plans quiet until the orchestra's season was over. Fearing that Stokowski might object in some way, they wanted to make sure he was well out of town on his summer travels before he found out about it.

The two were married on May 17, 1933, in Sam's azalea-and-dogwood-filled garden at Roxboro House. Phillips was twenty-six. Sam was forty-five. Only a few family members and close friends attended the ceremony. The *Philadelphia Inquirer* carried the announcement of the engagement just ten days before, on May 7, noting at the end of its announcement that: "The orchestra office said it had no indication that Miss Phillips intends to resign. At the time of her engagement by the orchestra, she said that if she chose the right kind of husband, she did not see why marriage should interfere with her career."[9]

That was true. Phillips did make that comment in answer to a reporter's question in 1930 after her appointment to the orchestra had been made public. "I really haven't thought about marriage," she said in that interview. "So far, my one love has been my harp. I suppose I will marry though, and I don't see why, if I have chosen the right kind of husband, it should interfere with my career."[10]

Whether or not she had chosen well would soon be tested.

## CHAPTER 9

# War on Broad Street

"Don't leave. Don't go home." Marshall rushed to stop Phillips as she left the stage after the first rehearsal of the 1933–34 orchestra season. "Ya gotta go back."

Puzzled, she turned around and stepped back onto the stage, whereupon Maestro Stokowski gave the downbeat for the Wedding March from Mendelssohn's *Midsummer Night's Dream*, and the orchestra serenaded her with it. Phillips was grateful and relieved, for it meant that at least outwardly, and certainly graciously, Stokowski had accepted her marriage to Sam without recriminations.

Sam was a highly involved, active member of the board. Younger than most of his colleagues, whose resistance to Stoki's avant-garde ideas seemed to increase with their advancing years, he respected the maestro's many innovations and his huge musical gifts, but he also felt his fiduciary responsibilities as a board member. Although he recognized the maestro's genius, he understood the difficult financial situation the board was facing in the Depression years and knew that a certain amount of belt-tightening was called for. The orchestra's deficit didn't frighten him as much as it did others on the board. "What do you think you're running—Woolworth's?" he once asked. "It's not a 'deficit,' it's a 'got-to-get.'" But he still represented the other side as far as Stokowski was concerned.

The maestro had long advocated that the orchestra reach out to audiences beyond those who frequented the Academy of Music. He wanted to take the orchestra on national and international tours to show the world how magnificent it was, but the board refused to back his plans, content to keep its shining jewel within the confines of the Academy and the limited touring schedule then in place. The board was also reluctant to support Stokowski's desire to make more extensive use of phonograph records and radio broadcasts to fulfill his ultimate mission: spreading the gospel of classical music to listeners far and wide.

Always fascinated by sound, Stokowski strove from his first days with the orchestra to increase its sonority by choosing players who could produce a beautiful tone and working with them to perfect it. He also experimented with different seating plans for the orchestra, searching for an arrangement that would best project the rich, full, deep sound he was seeking. No detail seemed too small for him to act on, as with his insistence on free bowing to create a more sustained sound, or too technical, as with his creation of sound reflector panels to be placed around the stage.

"As a result of . . . [his] innovations, the Philadelphia Orchestra under Stokowski achieved the unique sound—dark yet luminous—that became its hallmark," Hans Fantel, an authority on high fidelity, said.[1] Having created the Stokowski Sound, Fantel noted, the maestro then strove to "impart some of this sonic splendor to recordings," pursuing many experiments with scientists from Bell Laboratories of Camden, New Jersey, the research and development branch of American Telephone and Telegraph Company (AT&T). Those experiments helped lead to the development of stereophonic sound.

Convinced that technology would help him spread his gospel, Stoki agreed to write an introduction to an advertising brochure for the Victor Talking Machine Company in 1927. "I am often asked," he wrote, "Will the Victrola altogether replace concerts and opera? Exactly the opposite is happening. Each stimulates interest in the other. . . . We must make machinery even finer . . . an intelligent use of machinery can make our lives longer and deeper and richer and give us more leisure for the most ideal of occupations—to cultivate the mind and the soul."[2] Still, however spirited his campaign was, he could not convince the board of directors to expand the orchestra's recording schedule beyond its limited scope.

Stokowski also participated in experiments on broadcasting technologies and was anxious to put what he had helped develop to greater use by lining up big broadcasting contracts. However, the board and the orchestra's manager Arthur Judson also resisted entering into those big contracts, and they eluded the Philadelphia orchestra. Much to Stoki's dismay, the New York Philharmonic often ended up with them, which was a bitter pill for him to swallow.[3] He argued that the Philadelphia Orchestra had achieved first-class status and deserved to be heard throughout the country and the world, but in the midst of the Depression, the bankers on the board held to their commitment to conserve funds. They weren't interested in expanding the horizons of the orchestra at such a difficult time.

With those disagreements simmering, Stokowski couldn't have been happy to have Phillips marry someone from the enemy's camp, but he never outwardly showed his displeasure. He even managed an enigmatic smile when Phillips told him that she and Sam had made a pact: Sam wouldn't tell her what went on in board meetings and she wouldn't tell him what went on within the orchestra. In Sam's words, they would "keep capital and labor separate."

Some of the men of the orchestra also seemed disturbed by the marriage, and that surprised Phillips. She hadn't thought they would have a reaction to it, but she said, "Some of them began to treat me as if I was in a glass box that needed special handling." In the course of the three years she had been with the orchestra, her relationship with the men had become more relaxed, although it would never be completely collegial, possibly due to the distance she placed between herself and the men when she first joined or to the lingering resentment some still felt toward having a woman in their ranks. Now, after her marriage, some of the men became even more reserved toward her. Her first-chair colleagues, like Tabuteau and Kincaid, who had become good friends, didn't change their attitudes after her marriage. "But some of the others" she said, "seemed to think I might spill the beans by telling Sam about squabbles within the orchestra or that I would find out things from him I shouldn't know."

They need not have worried, for Phillips quickly found herself so absorbed in trying to adjust to the complicated life she had taken on as a bride that she had no time to pry into board business or tell Sam tales about bickering within the orchestra. Besides, the newspapers delighted in exposing every detail of the tiffs between Stoki and the board, so there wouldn't have been much for her to tell in that regard.

In truth, Phillips was finding her marriage quite complicated. At times, she felt almost as challenged on the home front as she had been on the professional front when she first joined the orchestra. Once again, she was a novice expected to perform in an arena she wasn't prepared for. As disarmingly witty as Sam was, he was also a highly accomplished man with many responsibilities and aspirations. At the time of his marriage to Phillips, he was serving as vice president of the Banker Securities Corporation as well as president of WFIL Broadcasting Company. A graduate of the University of Pennsylvania with both law and master of laws degrees, he had been a Gowen Fellow in the Middle Temple of the Inns of Court in London and was widely recognized for his erudition. Phillips always spoke of his achievements with great pride, regarding them as especially praiseworthy in light of the difficulties he had to overcome.

When Sam returned to Philadelphia from England with his prestigious law degrees and his first wife, Rosamond Rawlins Rosenbaum, he encountered great difficulties in establishing himself in a career, Phillips explained. The major Christian law firms wouldn't hire him because he was a Jew, and the prominent Jewish law firms wouldn't hire him because he had married a Christian. Yet, in spite of the prejudices that confronted him, Sam managed to work around those obstacles and become an important figure in the commercial and cultural life of Philadelphia, making use of his law background in business enterprises and practicing law on his own. By the time he married Phillips, he was an active participant in the city's intellectual life, and he expected his new wife to step into that role with him, especially as hostess for the dinner parties he often gave in historic Roxboro House, his beautiful frame and clapboard home, for the accomplished and urbane people he knew. Their neighbor Francis Biddle, who later became attorney general of the United States, was only one of the distinguished friends Sam socialized with and brought into his home. Others included important artists, influential jurists, and, of course, famous musicians. But Phillips was not yet ready for the role he wanted her to play in those heady circles.

"I blush to think of the gaffes I made," she said. "I had to make conversation with people years older than I was and much more sophisticated, and I'm afraid I didn't make much of a splash at it."

She also hadn't acquired the managerial skills needed to run the kind of dinner parties Sam was used to attending. After several near-disasters, "he realized he couldn't stretch me that far yet, and he gave it up for awhile," Phillips said, "but I think he missed the social life he had led as an eligible bachelor."

Before they married, Sam had told Phillips that he was marrying her before she was "half cooked." Now he was seeing just how true his words were, she said, but luckily for her, he was an extremely capable, organized man. "He took a great deal off my hands, letting me concentrate on practicing, which I continued to do for many hours every day. I was also able to continue with all my other musical responsibilities." To keep the house running in the midst of all this, Sam relied on the English housekeeper his first wife had brought to the States, who "was marvelous at saving the day when things fell apart." He also employed a nanny for Heather, a cook, and a gardener, all of whom made it possible for his complicated household to function and for Phillips to continue her career. Even with all that help, the adjustment wasn't easy for the young harpist.

It took her awhile to adapt to the role of stepmother. "I'm sure Heather, who was only nine at the time, wished she had a more motherly step-mother than I was," she said. "She had a little friend whose father had also remarried, and the two of them would go upstairs to Heather's room and whisper about their wicked stepmothers. They were pretty obvious about it, so I knew what they were doing, but I didn't know what to do about it."

As the years went by, a deep bond of love developed between Heather and Edna. Still, Edna always regretted her inability to offer more mater-nal comfort in the beginning to the little girl who had lost her mother when she was just a baby. She had a different kind of relationship with Sam's older daughter, Peggy, who was already a beautiful, brilliant, and independent young woman when Edna married her father. Peggy, who later chose to be called by her given name, Rosamond, was used to be-ing on her own by the time her father remarried, having spent years in boarding school in England and traveling in Europe. Well on her way toward becoming a woman of great accomplishment, she didn't need or want much attention from her new stepmother, who, after all, wasn't that much older than she was.[4]

Realizing that it was hard for Edna to find the peace and quiet she needed for practicing in his busy household, Sam converted an old stone barn at the back of the garden into a studio, equipping it with a furnace, rugs, two pianos, a couple of benches and chairs, and her harp. "It was a grand place," she said. "One hour in that studio was worth a hundred in the house, where there were so many distractions." Salzedo was most impressed when he came out from Center City to see it. "Ed-naa, it's just like Maine," he exclaimed, standing at the door and gazing at the beautiful old trees in the garden that surrounded the barn.

In another generous move, Sam gave Edna's mother a dachshund puppy. That seemed to soften Mrs. Phillips's attitude toward him and lifted a burden from Edna's heart. Sam's father did not agree to accept Edna, however. An Orthodox Jew, he had not forgiven Sam for his first marriage to a Gentile and had read him out of the family. It took many years for that breach to be bridged.

However complicated their life was, Edna said, Sam was always there to support her. "At a time when a husband could squelch a wife's career with the snap of his fingers. Sam supported my art in every way. He had a great love of accomplishment, and he sincerely wanted to see me succeed, just as he wanted to see everyone he was close to succeed. He was willing to sacrifice his own time and comfort to make sure that we all achieved what we were capable of doing."

---

Back on the orchestral front, Stokowski's disagreements with the board of directors were having surprisingly little effect on the players. They read stories in the papers about the spats he and the board were having, but Stoki didn't speak of them, and the players went along pretty much as usual, except, Phillips said, they noticed that the maestro did in fact program a little less "debatable music" that season than usual.

Of course, Stokowski always had his Bach-Stokowski transcriptions to feed his restless soul. They were enough to stir up controversy among the critics, which one has to suspect he enjoyed doing, but they didn't irritate audiences so much as his forays into modern music did. In fact, the opposite was the case. Audiences loved the transcriptions. While musical purists railed against Stoki for sullying the works of Bach by transcribing them for modern orchestra, audiences adored them. Critics may have derided the Bach-Stokowski *Toccata and Fugue in D minor* as being excessive, but audiences relished its drama and grandeur. They also loved his impassioned interpretations of other great works that purists criticized as departures from what the composers had intended. One day in rehearsal, Phillips heard Stoki almost agree with the critics. "When I get to Hell, what Bach, Beethoven, and Brahms will do to me!" he said. But that didn't stop him from continuing on a path that drove his critics crazy.

He also drove his players crazy at times, not with his interpretations but with his impetuosity. After his transcription of Bach's chorale "Come Sweet Death" was finished, the maestro proudly brought it to rehearsal one morning for the orchestra to run through. Then it was supposed to be put into the file to be scheduled for a future program. At least that's what the players thought. But that very evening, after Phillips had finished playing the first half of the concert, she was preparing to go home because she wasn't scheduled to play in the next half—"a Brahms symphony or something"—when Marshall came rushing out to get her.

"Get back to your harp," he panted. "He's gonna play the new Bach piece. Get out there!"

Phillips already had her galoshes on, the old-fashioned rubber kind that had a line of buckles up the center, which she had not finished fastening. She had no time to take them off.

"I had to waddle to my place with my partially buckled galoshes poking out from under my long velvet dress and tune my harp right away to be ready to play," she said. "I worried that I might ruin everything by inadvertently altering a chord while I was changing pedals with those damn galoshes on. Thank heavens that didn't happen."

Good old Stoki, she said. He was always full of surprises.

In the fall of 1933, Stokowski set up a new series of concerts for young people, this time between the ages of thirteen to twenty-five. A gifted teacher, he loved to work with young people, whether they were musicians or audience members. Their flexibility and openness to new ideas intrigued him, and his faith in youth was well-placed, for those who attended his youth concerts eventually became his most devoted and ardent fans.

The youth concerts were immediate sellouts. They featured talks and demonstrations in addition to the orchestra's performance, and the maestro wisely turned over the operation of the concerts to the youths themselves, which only increased their enthusiasm. They jumped at the chance to run things and happily wrote publicity, made posters, sold tickets, composed their own program notes, and took on the ushering duties. So successful were the concerts that rules soon had to be made to keep adults disguised as teens from sneaking into the Academy of Music, just as they had been needed to prevent adults from infiltrating the children's concerts back in the twenties. In response to complaints that some youths had to be turned away because "of older people attending in no official capacity at all," a notice in the *Philadelphia Evening Bulletin* warned adults to stay away unless they had ten children in tow and an official OK from the Concerts for Youth Committee. "Any elderly person trying to 'crash' the next Philadelphia Orchestra Concert for Youth will risk an encounter with a bouncer," the article began.[5]

Some adults, however, weren't so sure about the youth concerts, suspecting that Stoki might be creating a hotbed of supporters for modern music and other dangerous ideas. When he announced a program for an upcoming concert that included the "Internationale," the anthem of international socialism and the Soviet Union's unofficial national anthem, irate citizens and the local American Legion chapter rose up to denounce Stokowski as a "Red" and demanded a change of program.[6] After much huffing and puffing, a compromise of sorts was finally reached with the anthem being sung in French, its original language, and the youth concerts continued unabashed and unabated.

In the regular concert series that year, another lineup of guest conductors appeared before the orchestra. Back at Curtis, Phillips and her friends used to question how important a conductor was to an orchestra. Did the players actually need that person up there waving his arms? Stokowski and Toscanini with their awesome abilities quickly answered that question for Phillips, but some of the conductors who occupied the podium in the 1933–34 season brought it back. Some, like Fritz Reiner and Eugene Ormandy, did a beautiful job at the helm. But not all the captains were up to keeping the ship on course, Phillips said.

One conductor, Werner Janssen, was definitely not equipped to conduct the virtuosos of the Philadelphia Orchestra, in her opinion. "Tall and good-looking, he decked himself out in expensive clothes and looked the perfect picture of a conductor, but the picture was better than the product," she said. "At the final rehearsal of Sibelius's *First Symphony*, he got so frantic his shirttails came out of his pants, his hair fell onto his forehead, and he looked a total wreck." He was so confused that Phillips thought Tabuteau was going to throw his oboe at him. But the worst was yet to come. At the concert, the bottom fell completely out. Phillips had never felt so insecure during a performance, a feeling she knew the rest of the orchestra shared. It was as if the players had nothing underneath them. No one was in charge.

"Instead of leading us, Janssen would give us tentative looks, seeming to ask us whether we should come in or not, and he lost all sense of time," Phillips said. "If Kincaid hadn't pounded on the floor with his foot, we'd still be there finishing that symphony!"

"What a splendid conductor," Sam commented as he and Edna drove home after the performance.

A splendid conductor! The man was lost all the time! But he made a fine appearance with those fancy tails of his, she said, and the orchestra did the rest of the job. She was amazed that Sam hadn't caught on to him.

Then there was Vladimir Golschmann, who was a delightful man, very musical, and generally recognized as a fine conductor, Phillips said. In rehearsal for Ravel's *La valse*, which the orchestra had not played before, he made the work sound fascinating. He talked about it so intelligently that Phillips was looking forward to the performance. But when the players arrived at the concert, they saw the score on the podium, which indicated to them that he was not quite up to the situation. Stokowski and Toscanini insisted on conducting without a score, a practice that other prestigious conductors of the day also followed. The Philadelphia players had come to expect it of the top conductors. By relying on the score, poor Golschmann suffered in their eyes. On top of that, Phillips said, "he led us through a lukewarm performance."

"Same old story," she heard Anton Torello, the principal double bass player who had played under many a guest conductor, say afterward. "One hundred percent in rehearsal. Fifty percent in concert."

Another time, Clemens Krauss, who claimed to be the illegitimate son of Richard Strauss and "wore a romantic, wide-brimmed hat and had the most fascinating sideburns," tried his hand at conducting Strauss's "Dance of the Seven Veils" from *Salome*. At the beginning of the work, a long oboe solo establishes the atmosphere. In the orchestra's first rehearsal, Tabuteau was playing it "so evocatively," Phillips said, "with a languorous sensuality that developed the theme perfectly." Then Krauss broke in.

"Monsieur Tabuteau, we must remember that Salome was a lady," he said in a reproving tone.

"A very *rough* lady," Tabuteau shot back, looking at Krauss with daggers in his eyes. That was it for Krauss, Phillips said. He got off on the wrong foot by challenging a master, and he never regained his standing with the orchestra.

The relationship between an orchestra and a conductor is like that of a teacher and a class, Phillips said. If students sense a weakness in their teacher early on, they quickly lose respect, and who knows what they'll do? It's the same with an orchestra. If something goes wrong at the beginning, things probably won't go well for the poor conductor later on.

"I don't know why someone would want to be a conductor," Edna said. "They have to impose their will on the orchestra, and if they don't know the score, know what they want to do with it, know every nuance, every little note of it, they won't get respect from the orchestra, just like a weak teacher won't get respect from the students."

A very great conductor, Eduard van Beinum, leader of Amsterdam's Concertgebouw Orchestra, proved Phillips's theory in reverse, she explained. When he arrived to conduct the Philadelphia Orchestra, the players hadn't heard much about him. He was an unknown quantity, and he had the misfortune of having to conduct his first rehearsal with them in Baltimore while they were there on tour. They were tired and not particularly enthusiastic about rehearsing an upcoming concert on the road, but in order to fit the rehearsal in, they had to do it there. When the rehearsal began, the players looked generally disgruntled and unwilling to play. "But within four measures, they sensed the magic of the man," Phillips said. "Suddenly, they were all right there with him. They just woke up and played as if they had had fifteen hours of sleep because he was so wonderful, and they knew it in four measures. That's the best example of the schoolroom psychology theory I can give."

As the 1930s wore on, the skirmishes with Stokowski on one side and the board of directors and Arthur Judson on the other escalated to full-fledged battles. Before long their differences exploded into the open, and a virtual war broke out.

The relationship between Stokowski and Arthur Judson had begun on a high note, but it deteriorated over the almost twenty years they worked together. With Judson's multiple roles as manager of the Philadelphia and New York orchestras, president of Columbia Concerts Corporation, and major stakeholder in Columbia Broadcasting System (CBS), he exercised immense power in the world of music, and Stokowski began to feel that power was working against him in the later years of their association. In 1930, the New York Philharmonic made the first U.S. orchestral tour to Europe and soon thereafter obtained an extensive contract with CBS to present ninety-minute concerts on Sunday afternoons, just the outlets Stokowski had long pleaded for, while the Philadelphia Orchestra was left to wait on the sidelines.

Stokowski's appetite for innovation increased over the years that the two worked together, while Judson's conservative tastes solidified. Their different attitudes and ambitions eventually drove them apart. Judson, who according to Abram Chasins, "regarded all experimental art as anarchy and was convinced of its poisonous effect on the box office," invariably came down on the side of the conservatives on the board of directors in their resistance to Stoki's innovations, and Stokowski grew to think of him as "a natural enemy of new music."[7]

Early in the 1934–35 season, Judson decided to give up his position in Philadelphia. "Manager Resigns in Stokowski Rift," read the headline in the *New York Times*. "Dissension in the Philadelphia Orchestra Association over management policies, involving among other things, the extent of the power to be accorded Leopold Stokowski, the conductor, has led Arthur Judson to submit his resignation as manager, according to reports which have been in circulation . . . since last week."[8] Upon learning the news, Stokowski immediately asked the board of directors to choose a manager more amenable to his way of thinking than Judson had been, but the board wasn't inclined to do so. "What Stokowski was really seeking was the power to hand-pick a successor to Judson, and the board was resisting," Herbert Kupferberg explains.[9] It balked at Stoki's first suggestion for a replacement.

He was already seething over another of the board's refusals, this time to grant him the yearlong sabbatical he had been asking for. Always a restless soul, Stokowski argued that he deserved a sabbatical after so many years with the orchestra to free him to pursue his musical "researches," but the board refused to grant him one, saying that it could not afford to have him away from the orchestra for such a long time. Ticket sales would suffer too much.

Well then, Stoki countered, if the board wanted to increase ticket sales, they should hire truly distinguished guest conductors like Bruno Walter and Wilhelm Furtwängler during his absences rather than hiring "men of less experience and less established fame." After much back and forth, Stoki grudgingly acceded to their wishes and agreed to forgo his sabbatical, adding one more thing to his list of grievances with the board.

Finally, on December 8, 1934, Stokowski's resentment boiled over. He fired off an open letter of resignation and made sure that it appeared in all the newspapers. In it, he listed his grievances with the board of directors in detail. First, he said, the board had not yet hired a manager he could work with to plan for the next season. Plus, it had refused to enter into the broadcasting and recording contracts he felt were so important. Plus, it had rejected his plans for taking the orchestra on tours of Europe and Russia. Plus, it had chosen to back a disastrous opera season that had taken $250,000 from the orchestra's coffers. Plus, it wouldn't allow him to take the sabbatical he had requested. Plus, it had refused to lower ticket prices in the face of the Depression so that more people could attend concerts. Instead, he charged, it ran the concerts "as social functions for the wealthy."[10]

In sum, Stokowski said, the board was "too elderly and too conservative." He could not work with it as it was constituted and could not accept the new contract it had offered him for the next season.

Shock swept through the city. Stokowski was leaving! It couldn't be. The next afternoon, when he strode onto the stage of the Academy of Music to conduct Dvorak's *New World Symphony*, the orchestra stood en masse to pay him tribute. The Friday afternoon women also stood and burst into applause, clapping as hard as they could and settling down only after the maestro had tried to quiet them many times. After the concert, in another of his podium speeches, Stokowski thanked the orchestra and the audience and craftily enlisted them on his side of the argument.

"You of the audience and we of the orchestra have often been united by the magic of music," he said. "Somehow—at present I do not know how—I hope we can all be again united through music."[11]

Once more the usually decorous ladies broke into vigorous applause.

The furor quickly spread. Music lovers marched down Broad Street, demanding that Stokowski's wishes be granted. Mass meetings of subscribers and youth concert disciples took place in various hotels and gathering places and produced demands from the youth for "the immediate resignation of the present board of directors"[12] and threats from the subscribers to "force a showdown on the entire situation by recourse to the bylaws of the association."[13]

Mary Louise Curtis Bok, one of a minority of board members on Stokowski's side, issued a statement that merited a headline in the *Evening Bulletin*: "For Philadelphia to Lose Stokowski Is Unthinkable." Her son Curtis Bok, who was the president of the board of directors and also a supporter of Stokowski, convened the board and presented a plan that called for "the resignation of the present board and the creation of a new board, which will be sympathetic to Mr. Stokowski, his philosophy, and his musical policy."[14]

Unsurprisingly, the rest of the board would not agree to that, so Curtis Bok and his mother resigned, as did two other board members. On December 14 and for days thereafter, the city's newspapers covered the story as front-page news, calling the situation, "a collision of an irresistible force and an immovable object" and wondering, "whether or not Leopold Stokowski shall continue as musical director of the Philadelphia Orchestra."

In response to calls for its resignation, the board expressed "its full appreciation of Stokowski's 'musical genius,' but refused to depart from its stand, saying, 'the board is convinced that matters of business policy must be directed by it.'"[15]

Someone had to find a middle ground. Finally, the board sent a committee made up of Orville Bullitt, Frances Wister, and Sam Rosenbaum to meet with Stokowski privately in an attempt to reach a compromise. Sam's special expertise as a lawyer was in finding common ground between the different sides of a dispute. He played an important role in the negotiations, but he never revealed much about the proceedings to his wife.

"Musicians," he exclaimed one night upon returning from a meeting. "It's a mistake to get to know them."

"Well, thank you!" Phillips said, reminding him that she was guilty of that crime herself. He smiled briefly, she said, but then the telephone rang, and he closeted himself in the library to talk.

Throughout all the unpleasantness, Stokowski maintained his usual professional attitude at rehearsals. He worked with the orchestra as if nothing else was happening and didn't reveal his displeasure. However, one day as he was leaving a rehearsal, Phillips could tell he was very much out of countenance. Perspiring from conducting, he flung his jacket around his shoulders and left the podium, giving her a nasty look on his way out.

"Mr. Rosenbaum is coming over to talk to me," he snapped as he passed her. It was the only time the maestro ever communicated his feelings about board matters to her, she said.

In spite of the public fireworks, progress was being made behind the scenes, and finally, on December 26 at the close of the last concert of his fall stint with the orchestra, Stokowski announced that he had been invited back for the next season and had agreed to come as "guest conductor."

"I shall be with you in October," he said with his usual dramatic flair.

In the resolution that ended the impasse, the board agreed to reduce its size from twenty-four to fifteen and to add a representative from the orchestra and one from the youth concerts committee to its roster. Reginald Allen, a member of the board who was agreeable to Stokowski, got the job of manager, and Dr. Thomas Gates, president of the University of Pennsylvania, was elected president of the board. Sam Rosenbaum became one of the board's two vice presidents.

A peace treaty of sorts had been struck. Stokowski was coming back, but only for the first half of the season, with an abbreviated visit in the spring. His usual six weeks off in the winter had been extended, and he would return for only a few weeks in the spring. Still, at least he was coming back. On January 6, 1935, the *Philadelphia Record* wrote, "For the first time in 22 years Leopold Stokowski leaves Philadelphia with his future permanent relationship with the orchestra in some doubt."[16] And that was where everyone was left: in doubt.

In the midst of the war between Stokowski and the board of directors that fall, Phillips had to confront Stokowski with a personal situation that she feared could end her own career. She was pregnant, and her doctors, extra cautious in line with the practices of the day, insisted that she take a leave from the orchestra for much of the second half of the season, long before her due date at the end of April. But how was she to do that? Nothing in her contract said she could take time off in such a situation and expect to come back to her position. She had already seen the second harpist during the 1931–32 season give up her position in such a circumstance. When Flora Greenwood McCurdy discovered she was pregnant at the end of that season, she decided to resign from the orchestra, and Stokowski answered her resignation with a kind letter.

"I am so sorry that you cannot be with us again this winter," he wrote, "but I am sure you will find a first baby more interesting than a second harp."[17]

But Phillips didn't want to resign from the orchestra. She saw no reason for it. She knew she would have enough help at home to watch over the baby, and she wanted to continue her career. There had to be a way to get this done, but how? No maternity-leave policies were in place at the time, and Phillips doubted the union would be interested in advocating for her on that issue. There seemed to be no other way to resolve the situation other than by petitioning the maestro directly.

She did it in November. It was a very awkward time, what with the war between Stokowski and the board heating up, but it had to be done, so Phillips made an appointment to see the maestro after a rehearsal and climbed to his aerie nest above the stage of the Academy of Music at the appointed time. She found him sitting at a long table in front of the Navajo rugs he had hanging on the walls and rather shakily began her plea. Not mentioning that she was pregnant, she told him that she had gone straight on after marrying, never looking right or left and keeping on with all her harp and orchestra duties, but it had been terribly hard, and now she found that she needed some time to orient herself in her home and her marriage. Would it be possible for her to take a leave of absence?

As soon as she finished, she realized that she had made a weak argument and felt embarrassed. Stoki was an old-timer in the marriage and family department. Undoubtedly, he would realize what the situation was and tell her to resign as Flora had.

But to Phillips's surprise, he pounded the table and jumped up from his chair.

"A sabbatical! You need a sabbatical! Of course, you do. Everyone should have a sabbatical!"

And there it was, Phillips laughed in telling the story. Stoki's desire for a sabbatical led him to grant her one! Of course, she knew she probably wouldn't have gotten that kind of treatment if Sam hadn't been on the board of directors and Stoki hadn't wanted to send a message to him about the board's rejection of *his* request for a sabbatical, but it was still a victory. No one had heard of a maternity leave back then, but that's just what Phillips got. For the second half of the season, Marjorie Tyre, the second harpist, another of Salzedo's students from Curtis, would fill in for her, and Phillips could look forward to retaking her old position in the fall.

Daughter Joan was born at the end of April. After a happy summer at home, Phillips was ready in September for the orchestra's 1935–36 season to begin, curious and slightly apprehensive about what it would bring.

In the meantime, just as the hullabaloo between Stokowski and the board was quieting down, Otto Klemperer came to town to conduct a series of concerts to be held the first week of 1935. Sam, with his many friends in the musical world, knew Klemperer well, and invited the maestro and his wife, Johanna, to his home while they were in Philadelphia. Edna had grown more comfortable with Sam's illustrious friends and was beginning to enjoy, rather than fear, having them as guests in her home and at the dinner table. However, Klemperer wasn't easy to talk to, and the holidays weren't a propitious time for additional visitors. But the orchestra schedule was what it was, and he had to be in Philadelphia to prepare for his upcoming concerts. So the Klemperers were guests at Roxboro House over the New Year's holiday.

Maestro Klemperer had a strange temperament, Phillips said. He was blunt and unnerving. When he arrived in Philadelphia, she explained, one of the reporters who interviewed him asked him how he liked the city. He answered, "Vy should I?" At times his caustic temperament seemed out of control, and the battles between husband and wife, accompanied by butter balls thrown across the dinner table, were disconcerting to the Rosenbaums, but nothing the maestro did diminished Phillips's respect for him as a fine conductor.

An esteemed Beethoven specialist, Klemperer stood six feet, seven inches tall, so tall he didn't use a podium, and everything about him seemed oversized. He was to conduct an all-Beethoven program and, through some scheduling complexity, had the misfortune of having to conduct the first rehearsal of Beethoven's Fifth Symphony the morning of New Year's Day. Sam drove him to the Academy that morning, and Edna went along to observe.

Settling into a seat in the auditorium, Phillips chuckled as she watched the members of the orchestra "straggle onto the stage like condemned prisoners, dragging their instruments behind them." One by one, they dropped onto their chairs, grumbling to themselves and to each other and making it obvious that they felt dreadfully wronged to have to rehearse on New Year's Day.

Klemperer made little attempt to commiserate with the sullen players, aside from offering a few sardonic remarks that didn't seem to improve the situation. Then he straightened up to his full height and gave the downbeat for the beginning of Beethoven's Fifth Symphony—the famous *da da da DUM.*

"It's a very difficult beginning, always hard to pull off," Phillips said. Unsurprisingly, Klemperer didn't get what he wanted from the orchestra the first time, so he tried again. No, that wasn't right either. Again. No. Still not what he wanted. Again. No.

The players could not or would not give the towering conductor what he wanted. Unfazed, Klemperer gave the downbeat for the opening phrase again, and again, and again, and each time, what the orchestra gave him wasn't what he wanted.

This was becoming a war of wills, Phillips realized: the recalcitrant orchestra versus the imperious maestro. She edged forward in her seat, wondering how it would end. Who would cave in first? Unrelenting, Klemperer kept at it. Equally unrelenting, the orchestra failed to produce the sought-after phrasing. She was beginning to think they would be there all day. Then on the thirty-eighth try, she said, the orchestra finally gave the maestro what he wanted.

From there the rehearsal went forward without incident, except during a break when Klemperer walked over to Tabuteau's chair and bent over to speak to the illustrious oboist. Phillips couldn't hear what he said, but Tabuteau's face turned bright red. Afterward Kincaid told her that throughout the first half of rehearsal Tabuteau had been making derogatory comments in French, and since Klemperer didn't use a podium, he was close enough to hear him. Worse still, Klemperer had spoken to Tabuteau in French, letting him know that everything he said had been overheard and understood.

"Dear Tabuteau," Phillips said. Like Stokowski, he kept things interesting.

## CHAPTER 10

# Honor among Women

After the previous year's unpleasantness, the reconstituted board of directors set out to establish a happier tone in their relations with Stokowski
in the 1935–36 season. Sprucing up the Academy of Music's shabby stage
furniture was one step, and it became Sam Rosenbaum's job to procure
new chairs and music stands as well as a new podium. Although stage
design wasn't one of his specialties, Phillips said, Sam took his redeco-
rating role seriously, marshaling the best advice he could from designers
and others who understood such things. The result was a sleek new stage
set chosen to please Stokowski. Out went the scratched wooden chairs
the players were used to. In came new chrome-plated models with bright
Caribbean-blue seats. Out went the old black music stands. In came
shiny chrome-plated models. And out went the bulky wooden podium,
to be replaced by a cylindrical, chrome-plated model that looked as if it
had come straight out of a Hollywood set.

In the process of selecting the podium, Rosenbaum had studied Stokowski's movements carefully. To his surprise, he found that the maestro
stood almost stock-still when he conducted. He appeared so balletic and
graceful on the podium that he seemed to be moving his entire body,
Phillips said, but it turned out that "all that terpsichorean stuff was only
from the waist up." That discovery led to the selection of the stylish cylindrical podium. Stylish it might have been, but its contours reminded
Phillips of something a little less glamorous—"a round of cheese with
bites taken out for steps."

Though Sam's choice of stage furniture seemed somewhat incongru-
ous, sitting as it did between the stately Corinthian columns and red

velvet curtains of the Academy of Music, its sleek modernity was perfect for the forward-looking Stokowski. However, it did present one problem. The chrome plating on the music stands magnified the sound when anything brushed against it, which meant that the players had to be extra careful, especially when something was being recorded. If a bow should brush against a music stand, the sound would be caught and magnified, possibly ruining the recording.

During the 1935–36 season, Stokowski took another important step in eliminating the gender barrier that still stood firm in the orchestral world: he hired Elsa Hilger, a young woman from Austria, on the fourth desk of the cello section. The Philadelphia Orchestra now had two women on its roster in addition to Marjorie Tyre, the second harpist who played often with the orchestra but was not listed as a full-time player.

One might have thought that Hilger and Phillips would bond as happy companions in the struggle for female acceptance in the orchestral world, but they did not, especially after Hilger began describing herself as the first woman, "other than an occasional harpist," to join a major orchestra. That made Phillips furious. What had she been doing playing solo harp for five years before Hilger joined the orchestra? Hilger's claim was an insult to herself and to her instrument, Phillips said, and she resented it mightily.

"What do you think the harp is—a goddamned ukulele?" Phillips demanded years later when she encountered Hilger after hearing her call herself "the first woman other than an occasional harpist" on a radio program yet again.

A sturdy woman who wore her blond braids wound around her head peasant style, Hilger never ceased making her claim. In an interview on her ninety-eighth birthday in Shelburne, Vermont, she repeated her story to the *Shelburne News*. She even expanded on it by explaining how she came to be a member of the Philadelphia Orchestra. "I played solos on the Academy of Music stage for two hours for Leopold Stokowski and he hired me. . . . I had no idea what I was in for! Because then the Orchestra gave a lot of tours—Carnegie Hall, all over the United States, Europe, South America and Mexico. And always they had a big article, usually in the front of the paper, about the first female in any major orchestra—me."[1]

Aside from laughing at Hilger's claim that Stokowski sat in the Academy of Music and listened to her play solos for two hours, which Phillips could not imagine him doing, she also said that Stoki would never have approved of Hilger's dismissal of the harp's value if he had heard her claim. He viewed the harp as an emotional catalyst in the orchestra, believing that its cascades and spirals of sound created warmth and color that joined the different orchestral elements together, making it vitally important in the overall texture of a composition. "To disparage the harp as Elsa did was unmusical," she said. "Obviously the harp doesn't play as often as many other instruments do, but when it does, it is an integral part of the music and it matters."

Violinist David Madison, associate concertmaster and a member of the orchestra for fifty-one years, agreed. The harp frequently plays alone at crucial points, he pointed out. "When that happens," he said, "it's for publication."[2]

Although harpists were the first women to break the gender barrier in virtually all orchestras, they get little credit for their trailblazing efforts. Writers who specialize in the history of women in music seem to reserve their kudos for women who played more "manly" instruments, like the cello or the flute or the horn. But that does the pioneer harpists a disservice. They stepped into the places of men who held the harp positions before they arrived and became the lone women in all-male orchestras, which left them in difficult, sometimes hostile circumstances. Their perseverance in their positions paved the way for others to follow by proving that women could withstand the pressures of orchestral life and that orchestras could function with female players in their ranks without losing vigor or prestige.

The woman who most often is credited as the first principal player in a major orchestra is Doriot Anthony Dwyer, who became first-chair flutist with the Boston Symphony Orchestra in 1952.[3] That was twenty-two years after Phillips became a principal player in the Philadelphia Orchestra.

As for other principal harp pioneers, after Florence Wightman left the Cleveland Orchestra for the Metropolitan Opera Orchestra, Alice Chalifoux took over in Cleveland as principal harpist in 1931 (as noted in chapter 6). Chalifoux took a different tact from Phillips in dealing with the problems she faced as the lone woman in an all-male orchestra. While Phillips chose to remain aloof to shield herself from unwanted advances as well as the scorn of male players who resented having a female on board, Chalifoux, whom Phillips described as "tiny in stature but big in spirit," plowed right into the fray. Once, when some of her male colleagues were harassing her, she gave them a piece of her mind in a way that amused Phillips greatly when she heard about it.

"You sons of bitches keep your mouths shut, your hands to yourselves, and leave me alone!" Chalifoux told them.

Another member of what Phillips called "the sisterhood of pioneer firsts" was Sylvia Meyer, who joined the National Symphony Orchestra in 1933. Perhaps because the NSO at that point was only two years old and therefore not so firmly established as an all-male bastion, Meyer reported enduring only "minor ribbing by male colleagues" when she and Phillips led a discussion on "Women's Role in the Orchestra" at the American Harp Society national conference in 1982.

One of the most revered members of the Philadelphia Orchestra from 1921 to 1960 was principal flutist William Kincaid. Since harp and flute complement each other so well, Phillips often had the good fortune of working with Kincaid, as she did in the *Mozart Concerto for flute and harp*. She described his playing as being so magical that it appeared to be almost effortless and as full of colors and nuances as the finest singing voice. A student of the eminent French-born flutist, Georges Barrère, Kincaid is credited by Nancy Toff, author of *Monarch of the Flute*, a biography of Barrère, with being "the most influential flute teacher of his generation, perhaps of his century, surpassing his own teacher in the rigor of his methodology and the sheer number of his students placed as orchestra principals."[4]

Once when Phillips was struggling to master something she and Kincaid were working on together, she joked that compared with the complexities of the harp, the flute would be "a walk in the park." Kincaid countered by pointing out the subtle difficulties of his instrument. When she asked him which of all the instruments he thought was hardest to master, he wouldn't choose, but his answer impressed her. A serious student of any instrument who really worked hard could usually learn to play that instrument at the 85 percent level, no matter what the difficulties, he told her, but the last 15 percent on any instrument requires "something out of the ordinary" from a player.

As a fortunate member of the Philadelphia Orchestra, Phillips felt she was surrounded by "out-of-the-ordinary" people much of the time, whether they were her colleagues or visiting soloists. One of the extraordinary musicians she worked with was Sergei Rachmaninoff. He had had such happy associations with the Philadelphia Orchestra over the years that he often premiered new works with it. Not only would he bring with him a new composition, he would perform it with the orchestra. "That was a special treat because he was a great piano virtuoso with a terrifically scintillating style of playing," she said.

It amused her to watch the often-haughty Stokowski treat Rachmaninoff with the utmost respect, even obeisance. With his flair for the dramatic, the maestro was normally the most compelling person on stage, and he liked to keep it that way, no matter how stupendous a particular soloist might be. But when Rachmaninoff came to town, Stoki toned down his star power, deferring to the composer's greatness.

Never was that deference more apparent than when Rachmaninoff premiered his *Rhapsody on a Theme of Paganini* with the Philadelphians. On the afternoon of the first performance, Stoki, minus his usual lion-tamer bravado, stepped quietly onto the podium behind the piano, allowing all attention to focus on Rachmaninoff. Then he waited patiently, even meekly, while the great composer-pianist turned the knobs on the side of the piano bench with his long-fingered hands, moving the bench up, then down, and back again several times while the audience sat in pin-drop silence. Finally satisfied with the bench's height, Rachmaninoff's deep Russian voice sounded out magisterially: "I am ready." His words must have reached "all the way up to the peanut gallery," Phillips said. The silence was so absolute.

Like Stokowski, Phillips also worshipped Rachmaninoff and was surprised to discover how cooperative and unassuming he was to work with. With his deeply hooded eyes and tall, almost gaunt presence, he appeared to be somewhat unapproachable, but one day, in a simple, direct manner, he asked to speak to her about the specifics of writing for the harp. He wanted her opinion on the best notation to use for indicating harmonics and other details that would help him utilize the harp more effectively in his compositions. It amazed Phillips that such a great artist, with all his accomplishments, would still care to learn more about the instruments he used in the works he composed. The bane of a harpist's existence, she said, is that many composers don't understand how to write for the harp. They write for it as if it were a piano and don't take the trouble to find out what actually works on the harp and what doesn't, which greatly complicates the lives of the harpists, who must "unravel" incorrect notation to make it fit the harp.

———————

As the 1935–36 season rolled on, the peace treaty between Stokowski and the board of directors, so hard won the year before, seemed to be holding, but Stoki's restlessness was becoming more apparent. He had been Philadelphia's music director for twenty-four years at that point, an eternity for such a visionary man to stay in one place, especially in a place that didn't offer him the outlets to the wider world that he longed for. From little hints that Sam dropped, Phillips knew that negotiations were in progress over the maestro's future role with the orchestra, so she wasn't totally surprised on January 2, 1936, when Stokowski announced at the end of a rehearsal that he would no longer serve as the orchestra's primary conductor. Instead, he would take on the role of co-conductor, leading the orchestra for only a third of the concerts in the coming year, while Eugene Ormandy would be the resident conductor for the bulk of the season.

Although the players knew that such a change was inevitable, almost all greeted the news with sadness. Few of the players could call the maestro their friend; he was much too formal and remote for that. But he was a mesmerizing leader with whom they made magnificent music that filled them with joy and pride. It distressed them to think of his sharing control of the orchestra with another conductor. They were used to having visiting conductors come and go, but Stokowski had always been their primary leader. This change in status left them with an unpleasant sense of uncertainty.

By the time of the Friday and Saturday concerts that week, the newspapers had broken the news of Stoki's decision. In a podium speech after each concert, Stoki sought to reassure the audience that as co-conductor he would still play an active role in the life of the orchestra. He explained that he needed to cut back on the time he spent in Philadelphia in order to have more time to pursue the musical and technological "researches" he was involved in, which he hoped would someday benefit the orchestra and all those who loved music. Then, just as he was about to leave the stage, he paused a moment to thank the audience for their years of support and ask them to forgive him for all his shortcomings—just as he forgave them for all their coughs! It was a bittersweet reminder of the long history that Stoki and the Philadelphia audiences had shared.

Since it was clear that this was Stokowski's wish and not something the board had driven him to, the public outcry over this announcement was less than it had been when he tendered his resignation in 1934. His youthful supporters were heartbroken, of course. They cried and wrote impassioned letters asking the maestro to say it wasn't so, but the orchestra's older followers were more resigned to his decision. They had known that this day would come eventually.

It helped that Eugene Ormandy was chosen for the co-conductor position. Since he had come to Philadelphia to fill in for Toscanini five years before, he had led the orchestra as guest conductor in several regular season concerts and at Robin Hood Dell in the summers. The orchestra knew him well, and he was popular with audiences. At thirty-seven, he was young to take on such a prestigious position, but everyone recognized that this slight, young man with thinning red hair was an excellent conductor.

Born in Hungary in 1899, Ormandy, whose birth name was Jenö Blau, reached Philadelphia through a web of fateful coincidences and improbable connections. A child prodigy, he had distinguished himself as a virtuoso violinist, graduated from the Royal State Academy of Music in Budapest, and been made head of the Academy's violin department—all by the time he was twenty-one. One year later, in 1921, he sailed to the United States, planning to make a grand tour of the country as a violin virtuoso. Unfortunately, when he arrived, he found that the managers charged with arranging his tour had dissipated all the money that had been raised for it. Alone and broke in New York City, Ormandy took the only job he could find, in the last chair in the second violin section of the orchestra of the Capitol Theater, a famous movie palace like the Roxy Theatre.[5]

It took only one week for Ormandy's superior talent to be recognized and for the Capitol's conductors to move him from the back of the second violins into the concertmaster's chair. From there, he stepped onto a path that would eventually lead him to the Philadelphia Orchestra. It began in 1924, when the Capitol's chief conductor Erno Rapée fell ill shortly before a concert. Although the orchestra had another conductor on staff, he was also indisposed. It was up to Ormandy, as concertmaster, to fill in. Although he had never conducted an orchestra before, the young concertmaster rose to the occasion, taking up the baton and performing admirably, so much so that he earned enthusiastic praise all around. After that, the Capitol's leaders saw to it that he had frequent conducting opportunities, and Ormandy worked hard to master the art of leading an orchestra. Whenever he could, he slipped away to attend rehearsals of the New York Philharmonic to study the technique of its conductors.

Then, in 1927, Rapée gave up his position to follow the Capitol's former impresario, Samuel L. Rothafel—old Roxy himself—over to the newly built Roxy Theatre. That left an opening in the Capitol's conducting staff for Ormandy. With his natural gifts and on-the-job training, he quickly developed into a fine conductor—so good that he caught the attention of the ubiquitous Arthur Judson (this time wearing his artist representative's hat and scouting talent as president of Columbia Concerts Corporation). Judson was so impressed with Ormandy when he heard the young man conduct that he hired him to direct the studio orchestras that played for the Judson Radio Corporation's *Dutch Masters Hour* and *Jack Frost Melody Moments*.

Of course, Ormandy's biggest break came in 1931 when Judson brought him in as a last-minute substitute for Toscanini, whose technique he had studied in Philharmonic rehearsals. After covering himself with stars in his Philadelphia debut, Ormandy had been named conductor of the Minneapolis Symphony. Now after five years, he was returning to Philadelphia, still a young man, to share the job of conducting one of the world's leading orchestras with one of the world's leading maestros.[6]

Before the time came for Ormandy to step into his new position, the orchestra played under several outstanding conductors to close out the 1935–36 season. Among them was the redoubtable British conductor Sir Thomas Beecham. Having heard about the many amusing things that happened when Beecham had come to town in the past, Phillips was looking forward to having him lead the orchestra. He was famous among the men for his witticisms, she said, such as asking a player who wasn't paying attention, "Would you mind keeping in touch?" or meeting a man named Mr. Samuel Ball and commenting, "How singular." Once he fell off the podium into the strings. The players thoroughly enjoyed having Beecham conduct, not only for his clever remarks and the funny incidents that happened when he was there, she said, but also because he was a splendid conductor.

Phillips was particularly happy to be playing under Beecham because he had selected as the first work on his program Dvorak's *Slavonic Rhapsody No. 3*, which opens with a harp solo that tells the story of the piece and is later developed by the other instruments. It isn't often that the harp gets to begin a program in such a prominent way, so this was a special treat for Phillips.

However, that week King George V of England died, and Sir Thomas, a loyal British subject, arranged for a black box to appear in the Friday afternoon program announcing that the orchestra would begin the concert by playing Edvard Grieg's *Elegie* in memoriam. On Friday afternoon, Sir Thomas, a short, round man full of good cheer, walked jauntily onto the stage, hopped onto the podium, and, forgetting all about the Grieg, turned to Phillips and signaled her to begin the Dvorak.

What was she to do? Should she let him stand there waving his baton at her? "There was no Emily Post for this kind of thing," she said. She decided that she couldn't just leave him there, so she grabbed her harp and started the Dvorak, which was in a minor key and sounded rather like a dirge. With that, the entire audience rose to their feet to show respect for the departed king, thinking it was the memorial piece listed in the program.

Hearing the rustling behind him, Sir Thomas hissed at the first violist, sitting just below the podium, "What the hell's going on?"

"They think it's the *Elegie*," violist Samuel Lifschey hissed back.

"Oh God, I hope she doesn't get scared and quit," Sir Thomas replied.

He needn't have worried. Phillips knew enough to finish the opening phrase. She only hoped he would come to his senses in time to show her what to do next. And he did. After she finished, he gave her a rueful smile and, turning to the strings, gave the downbeat for the Grieg, which the musicians played with as much seriousness as they could while trying to stifle their amusement. When the *Elegie* was finished, Sir Thomas, with great aplomb, turned to Phillips and signaled her to play the opening of the Dvorak once again.

After the concert, she retired to her dressing room, feeling sulky because the harp's opening section hadn't worked out as smoothly as she had hoped. She was putting on her hat to go home when a knock sounded on the door. Thinking it must be a friend come back to commiserate, she opened it, and "there stood Sir Thomas with his hands folded over his tummy and his head bowed."

"My dear," he said, "they thought we were playing 'God Save the King' in a minor key, didn't they?"

Phillips found his remark absolutely charming. He didn't have to go to the trouble to apologize to her. After all, as a member of the orchestra, she was just one key in the conductor's piano, so to speak, but he was gracious enough to do it, and she was touched and amused by the way he acknowledged his mistake.

The incident threw the critics into a tizzy. They poured backstage at the intermission to find out what had happened, but one fellow never caught on. In fact, the next day he wrote that Phillips had played a very appropriate interlude for the king—"a revealing commentary on his musical discernment," she noted.

The orchestra performed the program three more times after that, one of them in Carnegie Hall. Each time, the players had all they could do to keep straight faces when Phillips began the Dvorak. Even Sir Thomas had to smile.

Years later, after Phillips had retired from the orchestra, Beecham returned to Philadelphia to conduct there for the last time. Old and frail by now, he shuffled onto the stage, looking dangerously as if he might not make it, but he conducted a wonderful Mozart concert, Phillips said. Afterward, she decided to go back to his dressing room, wondering whether he would remember her. The minute she walked into the room, he whistled the opening bars of the Dvorak rhapsody and gave her a warm greeting, thoroughly captivating her once again.

Edna Phillips in 1927.
(*Reading Times*,
Oct. 1, 1927)

Carlos Salzedo.
(Photo by Underwood
& Underwood Studios,
New York. Courtesy of
the Curtis Institute of
Music)

Salzedo leading a harp class at the Curtis Institute of Music. (Casper Reardon, 3rd from left; Florence Wightman standing behind harp; Edna Phillips seated next to her; Salzedo seated in front of group). (*Musical Courier*, April 21, 1927. Courtesy of the Curtis Institute of Music)

Edna Phillips. (Photographer unknown. Family collection)

Portrait of Leopold Stokowski by Edward Steichen, 1928. (Used by permission of the estate of Edward Steichen. Courtesy Rare Book & Manuscript Library, University of Pennsylvania.)

Philadelphia Orchestra, 1931–32. (The Philadelphia Orchestra Association Archives. Courtesy of the Print and Picture Collection, Free Library of Philadelphia.)

Marshall Betz, the Philadelphia Orchestra's longtime librarian and Stokowski's right-hand man. (Adrian Siegel Collection/the Philadelphia Orchestra Association Archives)

Stokowski and the Philadelphia Orchestra, 1935–36. (The Philadelphia Orchestra Association Archives. Courtesy of the Print and Picture Collection, Free Library of Philadelphia.)

Stokowski conduct-
ing. (Photo by Moss
Photos, N.Y. Courtesy
of the Rare Book and
Manuscript Library,
University of
Pennsylvania.)

Eugene Ormandy
conducting. (Photo
by Richard T. Dooner.
Courtesy of the Print
and Picture Collection,
Free Library of
Philadelphia.)

Edna Phillips at the harp. (Photo by Emil Rhodes. Family collection.)

"Leopold Stokowski. . . . giving a special concert for the benefit of unemployed musicians and gaping crowds near City Hall." (*Fortune* magazine, June 1936. Courtesy Print and Picture Collection, Free Library of Philadelphia.)

"Presenting the Orchestra's Mascot: Joan Rosenbaum to Make Transcontinental Tour in Basket." (*Philadelphia Record*, Feb. 16, 1936. Philadelphia Orchestra Association Archives)

Stokowski's Upside Down Orchestra, 1938. (Philadelphia Orchestra Association Archives. Courtesy of Rare Book and Manuscript Library, University of Pennsylvania.)

Women's Committee leaders who kept watch over Phillips, Frances Anne Wister (standing left) and Mrs. William Arnett (seated). (Jules Schick, photographer. Courtesy the Philadelphia Orchestra Association Archives.)

Phillips in 1941. (Photo by Richard T. Dooner, photographer. Family collection.)

Phillips and her children with composer Harl McDonald in 1940.
(Robert M. Lewis, photographer. Family collection.)

Edna and Sam
Rosenbaum, 1942.
(Adrian Siegel,
photographer. Family
collection.)

Sam Rosenbaum home on leave with his family, 1943. (Family collection)

Colonel Samuel R. Rosenbaum. (Family collection)

Marcel Tabuteau and Arturo Toscanini, 1944. (Adrian Siegel Collection/
the Philadelphia Orchestra Association Archives)

Sergei Rachmaninoff and Eugene Ormandy, 1938. (Adrian Siegel Collection/
the Philadelphia Orchestra Association Archives)

The Philadelphia
Flute, Harp,
and Viola Trio:
William Kincaid,
Edna Phillips, and
Samuel Lifschey,
1942. (Adrian Sie-
gel Collection/the
Philadelphia Or-
chestra Associa-
tion Archives)

Composer Alberto Ginastera, Eugene Ormandy, Edna Phillips, and harpist
Nicanor Zabaleta, 1965. (Adrian Siegel Collection/the Philadelphia Orchestra
Association Archives)

Edna Phillips at eighty. (Courtesy of the Settlement Music School)

## CHAPTER 11

# A Month Out
## of School

At the end of the regular season in 1936, the orchestra had a date with RCA Victor and the Pennsylvania Railroad that would fulfill a long-held dream of Stokowski's. Finally, the Philadelphians were to embark on a transcontinental tour, the first ever taken by a symphony orchestra. Thanks to generous funding from RCA Victor, they would visit twenty-seven cities across the United States and into Canada in an undertaking that Stokowski, who longed to share his great orchestra with the world, had worked many years to achieve.

It wasn't the grand tour to Europe or Russia that he once envisioned, but it was a start, the first of numerous far-reaching tours that carried and still carry the music of the Philadelphians around the world. It took years of campaigning by the maestro to launch his idea, but from that point on other tours followed, and the orchestra, as Stokowski had predicted, developed into the city's best ambassador, as well as its own best advocate, to the rest of the country and the world, making it "Philadelphia's most successful envoy to the world since Benjamin Franklin."[1]

Over a thousand well-wishers jammed into Philadelphia's old Broad Street Station at Broad and Market Streets on April 13, 1936, to bid bon voyage to the 107 men and three women (Edna Phillips, Elsa Hilger, and Marjorie Tyre) of the orchestra. The players, with cameras around their necks and big smiles on their faces, were filled with anticipation as they boarded the ten-car, maroon-colored train with the words "The Philadelphia Orchestra–RCA Victor Tour" emblazoned on its side. In a ceremony preceding the train's departure, Mayor Samuel Davis Wilson along with other dignitaries made speeches, and the orchestra's great supporter Miss Frances Wister presented Stokowski with a fox terrier representing Nipper, the RCA mascot who was pictured in advertisements at the time listening to "his master's voice" coming through an old-fashioned gramophone.

The usually detached maestro looked as excited as a boy throwing his hat into the air on the last day of school, Phillips said, and he maintained that level of zeal throughout the five-week tour. Before that he had maintained a distant relationship with the players, rarely sitting down to talk or joke with them, but now his reserve evaporated. Swept up in the general feeling of ebullience, the maestro began the trip by stopping by the compartments of various players after the train left the station, visiting the drawing room Phillips shared with Tyre, where he seemed as excited and happy to talk about the upcoming adventure as they were.

"It was a month out of school for everyone," Phillips said. Off on their great adventure, the players basked in the rolling luxury of the train's Pullman cars with their plush appointments as well as its elegant dining car with white linens and formal service and the more casual club car. Usually, the long stretches of travel occurred at night, while the orchestra members slept to the agreeable clackety-clack of the wheels on the tracks. When they arrived at the next tour stop the following day, the players would be taken to a hotel and assigned private rooms, where they could take proper baths and rest or go sightseeing until it was time for a rehearsal or a concert.

The first stop in the orchestra's odyssey was Hartford, Connecticut. By the time they arrived, the excitement was so intense that everyone was feeling pretty jittery, Phillips said, but they pulled themselves together to give a performance that started the tour off on a high note. After Hartford, they continued to Boston, where the audience that packed Symphony Hall seemed skeptical at first. This was the home of their beloved Boston Symphony, after all, and they weren't about to show too much enthusiasm for its foremost rival, but over the course of the evening they warmed to the Philadelphians and ended up cheering enthusiastically and calling for four encores. Stokowski, never shy to address an audience, gave one of his podium speeches on the occasion, this time expressing his extreme admiration for Boston's conductor Sergei Koussevitzky and his great orchestra.[2]

"Stoki just loved having us play those encores throughout the tour," Phillips said. "Being on the road and away from the union, he got away with having us play many more than he could have at home, but no one complained about going over time on that tour. We were all too caught up in the adventure of the thing."

*Time* magazine's coverage of the tour lavished praise on the orchestra, but even more on Stokowski. "Rightful hero of the tour is the conductor who built up the Philadelphia Orchestra to be one of the greatest in the world," it reported. "Last week's audiences were fascinated by Stokowski: his swift graceful dash for the podium, the svelte back he turned, the fine graceful hands which seem to mold every phrase of the music that is played."[3]

As the train rolled into each rail station along the way, a loudspeaker in the observation car announced the arrival of the Philadelphia Orchestra by blasting out its recording of the César Franck Symphony, the Brahms First, or the Beethoven Fifth, and crowds of locals would gather around to welcome Stokowski and his players. One day as they pulled into a station, Phillips heard women's voices outside the window of her car.

"Do you think she'll bring the baby out now?" one of them asked.

"Oh, no, it's breakfast time. She's probably giving the little one her orange juice," the other answered.

Phillips had to laugh. Publicity circulated before the tour featured photographs of her settling her daughter Joan into a basket in her harp case, preparing her to travel as the orchestra's "mascot" on the train. Phillips didn't expect anyone to take those stories seriously, but apparently some did. Speaking of Joan, it was hard for Phillips to leave her for five long weeks, especially because her first birthday fell in the middle of the tour. Stokowski got wind of that fact and had the orchestra play "Rock-a-Bye Baby" at a rehearsal on Joan's birthday. It was kind of him, Phillips remembered, but she still missed her little girl.

Being on tour and having to play concert after concert meant that many works had to be repeated at close intervals. To ensure that the players didn't get into a rut, Stoki devised different strategies to keep them alert. For example, when they were playing the maestro's synthesis of *Tristan* on one occasion, he surprised the cellos by suddenly signaling them to play at an unchanging level in a place where he usually called for a *diminuendo*. Another time he would give them a *subito piano* when they weren't expecting it. There was no getting into a routine with this maestro, Phillips said. He always kept his players on their toes.

After the orchestra played in Little Rock, Arkansas, the train headed west, stopping in Dallas and El Paso, then Phoenix, on its way to Los Angeles. That was the most uncomfortable leg of the trip, Phillips said.

Relentless heat dogged them all the way. Without air conditioning, they kept the train's windows open to try to keep cool, and since there were no screens, the players had to contend with flakes of soot flying in their faces. Phillips tried going out onto the observation platform once, only to be almost overcome by stifling billows of heat and soot. "Those weren't the days of comfort," she said.

The players endured the hardships with barely a complaint; their adventurous spirit prevailed throughout. Many players crossed the Mexican border to Juárez after the El Paso concert, returning with piles of sombreros and serapes to add to the cowboy hats and tourist paraphernalia they had already purchased in Dallas. In Phoenix, Kincaid, who was athletic and an excellent rider, decided he would take a horseback ride. Then Tabuteau, who was not in Kincaid's league in the riding department, decided to join him. All went well for a few moments until Tabuteau's horse suddenly took off at full gallop with Tabuteau struggling to hang on. Luckily, Big Beel, as Tabuteau called Kincaid, and some of the local cowhands managed to catch the out-of-control horse before Tabuteau incurred damage to more than his pride.[4]

Finally, on April 27, the company arrived in Los Angeles, which was Stokowski's main goal of the trip, and a place they were all curious to visit. Stoki's sights had been fixed on Hollywood for some time. He saw motion pictures as the way to bring classical music to more people than could ever be reached in concert halls or even through the radio or recordings. During previous visits to Hollywood, he had made many friends among the stars, some of whom formed a committee headed by Joan Crawford and her then-husband Franchot Tone to turn the Philadelphia concert into a gala event. Before the concert, Stoki showed the players just how much that particular performance meant to him by gathering them together and giving a pep talk just like a football coach, which was something he didn't normally do, Phillips said.

"You always play well," he told them. "But now you must excel even yourselves."

When it was time to tune her harp, Phillips went out onto the stage of the Pan Pacific Auditorium, where they were to perform. It was a wooden indoor-outdoor structure with cinder paths and bench seating for thirteen thousand people. She leaned over her harp to begin the process, but she found it hard to concentrate on tuning with so many famous movie stars coming down the aisles to take their seats. She couldn't help scanning the audience to see who was with whom and who was wearing what until she had to finally force herself to pay attention to the job at hand.

Just before the concert was to begin, the first cellist, Isadore Gusikoff, leaned over to her. "Harpo Marx wants to talk to you," he said. "He's a friend of mine, and he's going to come down to the stage at intermission. OK?"

Of course, Phillips agreed to his request. She would be delighted to meet Harpo.

Then a rustle of electricity spread through the auditorium. Looking as glamorous and charismatic as anyone in the audience, Stokowski strode to the podium in full lion-tamer mode to lead the orchestra through a thoroughly electric performance. At intermission, Phillips waited for her visitor as she had promised, but she didn't recognize the dark-haired man walking toward her "with a blonde on his arm."

"Do you really belong ta this outfit?" the man asked in a heavy New York accent when he got to the foot of the stage.

"Yes, I do," Phillips answered rather stiffly, not realizing who he was.

"Then you don't wanna talk to me 'cuz you're one of those fancy classical types."

Finally catching on that he was Harpo without his trademark curly blond wig, she came to her senses and answered, "I didn't know you *could* talk."

They both smiled at her reference because Harpo was the one who never spoke in the Marx Brothers movies. The ice broken, they had a happy conversation about his genuine love of the harp. He told her he was planning to go to Brittany that summer to study with the famous French harpist, Henriette Renié. Phillips, who had heard that Mlle Renié was a demanding teacher and a devout Roman Catholic who required her students to attend Mass every day, wondered how Harpo would hold up to her rigorous teaching style and rigid routine. Whether he realized it or not, Harpo was in for a difficult summer, she thought. Evidently, it wasn't so harsh that it dimmed his love for the harp, she later learned, for he ended up giving a good deal of money to the harp community, funding competitions and prizes and being very generous where generosity was needed.

The next day the orchestra performed before another audience of thirteen thousand in the Pan Pacific Auditorium and then headed up the California coast for a concert in Santa Barbara, where Stokowski had a home with his wife Evangeline and their daughters. After the Santa Barbara concert, a few of the principal players were invited to join the maestro and Evangeline at a party at the home of Henry Eichheim, a composer friend of the maestro. It was one of those wonderful dinner parties, Phillips said, "where the wine is chilled to just the right degree and everything is perfection." Eichheim, like Stokowski, was fascinated by exotic musical instruments. He had recently traveled to Bali and brought back a roomful of Balinese gongs, which he urged the guests to test.

The train wasn't ready to depart when they returned to the station, so Kincaid and Tabuteau turned on the RCA Victor machine that was in the club car and took turns dancing with Phillips on the pavement outside. She said it was great fun dancing with them and savoring the beautiful night air. Tabuteau, she laughed on remembering, had a most unusual way of dancing. He gauged his step completely to the phrase of the music. It was a little hard to follow him at first, she said, but once she caught on, it was lots of fun. "I was spoiled with luxuries like that," she said, "and I loved it."

The Philadelphians then returned to Los Angeles to appear in a coast-to-coast radio broadcast of the Kraft Music Hall Revue. Bing Crosby hosted the broadcast with his easy folksiness, asking Stokowski to play his favorite piece, Debussy's "Afternoon on the Farm."

While all this was going on in California, Sam gave a party in Philadelphia for the orchestra wives, who had remained at home while the orchestra toured the country. As the only husband among the orchestral spouses, he invited the wives to have cocktails in his garden and to listen to the Crosby show on the radio. "Come and be consoled," his invitation read. "Your husband and my wife have gone off to California."

After the broadcast, the orchestra left Los Angeles and headed north to San Francisco. Stokowski had accomplished much during his time in Hollywood. He had been able to firm up plans for the orchestra to perform the music for a new movie, *The Big Broadcast of 1937*, and for another to follow that, *One Hundred Men and a Girl*. He had also sown the seeds that would later grow into the Walt Disney–Leopold Stokowski–Philadelphia Orchestra masterpiece *Fantasia*. In all three cases, the Philadelphia Orchestra would record the music for the movie at home in Philadelphia, while dummy orchestras would stand in for the Philadelphians during the filming in Hollywood.

Those plans didn't meet with much approval back in Philadelphia. Phillips thought Stoki's goal of using the vast appeal of movies to awaken a love of music in the masses was commendable, but the orchestra's board of directors took a more jaundiced view of the maestro's attraction to Hollywood. Most thought Stokowski's love of the spotlight drew him there, not to mention his interest in the beautiful starlets.

After their heady days in Hollywood and its environs, it was time for the Philadelphians' train to turn homeward. The players thought they would be heading straight to Salt Lake City as planned after their concerts in San Francisco. But a last-minute change in the schedule called for a stop in Reno, Nevada, which, according to Phillips, was a pretty primitive place in those days, muddy and full of shabby gambling casinos. It was also temporary home to women waiting for quick divorces, which were legal in Nevada after a six-week residence. Upon hearing of the orchestra's arrival in Reno, one of those waiting-for-a-divorce wives, an acquaintance of Phillips's, asked her to a luncheon at a "fancy restaurant in the desert." Much to Phillips's surprise, Stokowski was also invited. Needless to say, he was the center of attention at the luncheon, she said, an interesting change for the women from the cowboys they usually encountered during their six-week residencies.

When the players assembled for a short rehearsal before the concert that evening, Tabuteau slouched in with a very long face. Everyone could tell he must have had a bad day at Reno's casinos. Next to the oboe, cooking, and his wife, Phillips said, gambling was Tabuteau's great passion. A regular visitor to the gaming tables in Nice and Monte Carlo when he went home to France for the summers, he often boasted about his system for winning. Apparently, his system along with his vaunted *pokeaire* face must have failed him in Reno, for he arrived at the rehearsal looking extremely glum. Seeing his stellar oboist looking so doleful, Stoki proposed opening that evening's program with Bach's "Come Sweet Death" in commiseration.

From the gambling halls of Reno, the Philadelphia Orchestra–RCA Victor Tour traveled onward and at least spiritually upward to Salt Lake City and the Mormon Tabernacle for the next concert. Following her usual practice, Phillips went to the performance area before most of the others to tune her harp and soon discovered that the acoustics in the Tabernacle were so fine that the least vibration of a string, something that normally wouldn't be noticed, rang out with startling clarity. Just to tune her harp in that exciting space was inspiring. By that time in her career, she considered herself a seasoned veteran, but her hair stood on end, she said, when Stokowski led the Hallelujah Chorus from *Messiah* with the Mormon Tabernacle Choir.

After their appearance in Salt Lake City, the Philadelphians headed for Denver, where, as had happened all along the way, the mayor and dignitaries of the city stood waiting when the train pulled into the station.

This time the governor of Colorado also joined the welcoming party, but a glitch spoiled the orchestra's usual grand entrance. Instead of Beethoven or Brahms blasting out of the train's loudspeaker to the delight of the local welcoming party, only the straining of the train's brakes could be heard as they pulled into the station. What was wrong? Finally, word got around that Kincaid had mistakenly unplugged the electrical cord for the speakers when he plugged in his electric shaver!

Continuing eastward after the Denver concert, the train made another unexpected stop in the tiny Nebraska town of Holdrege, which Stokowski, with his souped-up accent, pronounced "Holedraygee." It was just a dot in the middle of vast farmlands, and Phillips never learned why they stopped there. She theorized that Stoki must have been responding to his mystical belief that people everywhere were longing to hear great music. He was at his hyperbolic best on that topic throughout the tour, she said, seeing a splendid future for music in America everywhere he looked. In an interview given to the *New York Times* after the tour, he summed up his message: "Everywhere . . . there appears to be a thirst for music—not only a desire to enjoy the purely sensory pleasure of listening to beautiful tone or to revel in sound woven into organic design, but to treat music as a channel leading to cultural growth."[5]

On a less exalted note, when the train arrived in Holdrege at about 2:30 in the afternoon, Phillips decided to take a walk to look over the town. She had been walking for about ten minutes when a sharp wind came up and hailstones the size of golf balls suddenly began bombarding her. They were so big and hard they made temporary dents in her head and almost knocked her down, she said. To her relief, the storm only lasted a few minutes, and she scurried back to the train to restore herself for the concert in the high school auditorium that night.

While Phillips was walking that afternoon and other players were relaxing as they saw fit, Stokowski was busy conducting the local high school orchestra after Holdrege's mayor met the train and told him the youngsters had rehearsed a new work for the maestro. Would he lead it? Later Stoki explained the session to a *New York Times* reporter. "The youngsters were very enthusiastic," he said. "We went through the piece and had a lot of fun."[6] Impromptu encounters with young musicians were not uncommon for Stoki on the tour, Phillips said, which was understandable considering his belief in the generative power of youth.

As the players boarded the bus for the high school that evening, Phillips was happy to note that the weather was once again perfectly calm with no trace of hail or rain, which was good because some in the audience had come from as far away as three hundred miles to attend the concert. Considering that the huge orchestra had to cram itself onto a stage much too small for its numbers, things proceeded fairly well during the concert, and the crowd gave the music its rapt attention.

Then, in the middle of the last piece on the program, a thunderous pounding sounded on the roof. When the audience noticed it, Phillips said, they leapt out of their chairs and began whooping, yelling, and cheering so loudly that they drowned out the orchestra. Bewildered, Stokowski stopped the playing and looked around to see what was going on. It turned out that the sound on the roof was a rainstorm, and there hadn't been rain in that farm country for six weeks. At that point, the audience didn't give a hoot whether the magnificent Philadelphia Orchestra was playing for them or not. Rain had finally come! The drought was over! They were so happy they couldn't contain themselves.

The players had heard tumultuous cheering for their performances before, but nothing like the triumphant roar that arose from those farming people when the rains finally came, Phillips said, laughing. It certainly gave them a sense of perspective. Stoki might have been right about people's thirst for music, but at that moment their thirst for rain was undeniably stronger.

Then Phillips felt drops falling on her head from the ceiling above. As the rest of the orchestra swarmed off the stage, she grabbed her harp and pulled it onto the tiny bit of a wing that was available. Fortunately, the stagehands slapped it into its case and took it right back to the train, for the players learned later that the roof over the stage collapsed under the weight of the downpour soon after they left.

From Holdrege, the orchestra continued to Omaha, St. Louis, Minneapolis, Milwaukee, Cleveland, and then to the May Festival in Ann Arbor, Michigan, where it presented six concerts in four days as the resident orchestra of the festival, and where Stoki led college songs from atop a bar stool for three hundred students who had crowded into Ann Arbor's famous Pretzel Bell bar.[7]

After that the train started on its run to New York, stopping in Harrisburg, Pennsylvania, to pick up a railcar bearing a large sign that read "ORCHESTRA WIVES, ETC." Sam, the ETC., was on the car along with the other spouses, and they all traveled together into New York, where the orchestra played its final concert for fourteen thousand people in Madison Square Garden on May 17, 1936, after playing thirty-three concerts in thirty-five days in twenty-seven cities.

"Late that night, a watcher at North Philadelphia Station would have seen a strange spectacle," an orchestra program noted the next fall. "A long dusty train pulled in and commenced disgorging the most extraordinary things and people. Mexican wine in wicker bottles, gaudy gourds hanging in strings from the necks of very [tired-looking] individuals, dazzling sombreros, rainbow-hued *serapes*, cameras, boxes, bottles, bags, more boxes. This, in the wee small hours of Monday morning, May 18th, was the conclusion of the transcontinental tour."[8]

The players were happy to be home, Phillips said, but there was also a bittersweet feeling in the air. This was the end of their exclusive relationship with Stokowski. From now on, this proud band of travelers would operate under a new regime. Of course, Stoki would be back to lead them for certain periods in the fall and spring, but they knew that change lay ahead.

## CHAPTER 12

# On to *Fantasia*

A formidable lineup greeted Eugene Ormandy when he stepped into his role as co-conductor of the Philadelphia Orchestra in the fall of 1936. The players were a proud group who had been with Stokowski for years. They included virtuosos like Tabuteau, Kincaid, concertmaster Alexander Hilsberg, principal trumpet Saul Caston, the great timpanist Oscar Schwar, principal bass Anton Torello, and many others who had served the charismatic, bigger-than-life Stokowski long and well and who had risen to great heights under his leadership. The challenge of presiding over such a mighty lineup could easily have overwhelmed the young conductor.

But if Ormandy, who was to lead the orchestra for twenty-two weeks that season while Stokowski would be there for only six, felt overwhelmed, he didn't show it, Phillips said. Outwardly unbowed by Stoki's renown or the excellence of the players, he picked up the reins in a direct, unassuming, but very professional manner. Willing to work terrifically hard, he combined an impeccable sense of intonation with a powerful memory that enabled him to memorize scores in record time. His evident abilities calmed the fears of those in the orchestra who worried that he might not be up to the job, and the players responded well to his leadership, at least for a while.

"Stoki was so appassionato all the time," Phillips said. "To tell the truth, we were getting pretty damn sick of doing Wagner every morning at ten thirty. So much love and death and passion—it can wear on you after awhile. Ormandy was like a drink of cool water in comparison."

Ormandy's exquisitely sensitive ear was especially impressive to the players. He could ferret out from anywhere in the orchestra the least deviation from the correct pitch, which didn't surprise Phillips. In the Rosenbaum household, Ormandy's aural acuity was a legend. As a board member, Sam had been scouting out possible candidates for the conductor's job for a number of years to prepare for Stokowski's inevitable departure. Ormandy was one of the possibilities who interested him. In the summer of 1933, when Ormandy came to Philadelphia to conduct at Robin Hood Dell during a heat wave, Sam invited him to stay at his home on School House Lane, rather than taking a room in the city.

Sam offered Ormandy the sleeping porch since it was much cooler than inside the stuffy house. After one night, Ormandy told him he would rather sleep inside. The birds chirping in the early morning bothered him, he explained. They chirped out of tune! "With an ear that sharp," Sam said later, laughing, "imagine what Ormandy could do with the Philadelphia Orchestra!"

Still, while the players appreciated Ormandy's musical gifts and enjoyed the relief he provided from Stoki's intensity, they couldn't help missing the excitement and inspiration their former leader had brought into their lives. They did their best as professionals to accept and follow Ormandy, but some of them became disaffected. Now and then, Phillips would see a player raise an eyebrow over something Ormandy would do or snicker at his tangled syntax and frequent malapropisms, but she was loath to criticize his verbal slip-ups. After all, Ormandy had a *real* language barrier to overcome as he moved from speaking Hungarian to English, not the made-up one Stoki adopted.

Some of the players—Tabuteau in particular—just didn't like the repertoire Ormandy favored. When another *Rosenkavalier* waltz or something in that vein would come up, Tabuteau would scowl throughout the rehearsal. Viennese music seemed to disagree with his French constitution, Phillips said, and the more Ormandy chose to program it, the more Tabuteau glowered. That *pokeaire* face he bragged about never hid a thing, she chuckled.

The players also missed Stoki's style of rehearsing, which was so intense and fast-paced that it required their total concentration. His habit of pinpointing problems to work on while skipping over less difficult sections left much of the responsibility for a performance on their shoulders. The veterans were used to that and proud of their ability to excel under demanding circumstances.

Ormandy's style was quite different. He progressed more painstakingly through the different pieces on a program, which made things easier for newcomers, but boring for those who had been there longer. Phillips could see the value in Ormandy's approach. It had been hard for her to keep her head above water in her first seasons when Stoki skipped over sections in rehearsals and she wasn't sure how all the parts of a piece would fit together. Back then she often felt so confused she had to take a miniature score into a performance to know where she was. Playing all the way through a work as Ormandy did would have made her life as an orchestra novice much easier, but of course, Stoki would consider it a waste of time.

Under Ormandy, the veterans resented having to go through an entire Mendelssohn symphony they knew perfectly well for the greenhorns in the group. They also missed the occasional Friday mornings that Stoki would let them take off after four days of intense rehearsing "to think about what we were playing that afternoon," Phillips said. Ormandy rehearsed them painstakingly five days a week every week, and that didn't sit so well with the established players.

On the other hand, Philadelphia audiences accepted Ormandy as a replacement for their beloved Stoki surprisingly well. Although he lacked his predecessor's charisma and wasn't a dashing figure on the podium, the young maestro did have an alert, energetic, graceful platform presence. He also conducted concerts without a score, à la Stokowski and Toscanini, and he seemed intent on preserving the unique qualities that Stokowski had developed in the orchestra rather than imposing his own ideas on it. All who revered the Philadelphia Orchestra appreciated that. Most importantly, Ormandy was happy to focus on the traditional repertoire rather than the modern compositions Stoki favored. That made the majority of his audience—and the board of directors—very happy.

Ormandy had big shoes to fill in following Stokowski. Very big shoes. As Herbert Kupferberg writes, "Few symphonic conductors anywhere have ever made concert-going the exciting, exhilarating experience that Stokowski did for twenty years in Philadelphia."[1] Such a maestro was a hard act to follow. But, to everyone's relief, the Philadelphia Orchestra kept on a strong course with its new co-conductor. It gradually became apparent that Stokowski's partial withdrawal might not be the end of the story, as some had feared, but only another chapter in the orchestra's continuing development.[2]

Ormandy surpassed Stokowski in one area, Phillips said. He was a "made-in-heaven accompanist" who put a cushion of support under soloists, giving them a sense of security and comfort they rarely felt with other conductors. Rachmaninoff, Rubinstein, Heifetz, all the important soloists loved to perform with Ormandy. "He surrounded them like a good dining room steward on a ship—always watching for what they might need and ever ready to give it to them," she said. "If a soloist got lost or had a memory lapse, Ormandy was so flexible and sensitive he could propel the fellow along until he got his bearings again. I saw him get soloists out of difficulties I thought they'd never get through."

One Friday afternoon Phillips, freed from her duty on stage because the harp was not needed, sat in the audience to listen to the world-famous Yehudi Menuhin play the Brahms Violin Concerto. Apparently Menuhin was having a very bad day. She said her heart was in her mouth as she watched him struggle in certain sections. Sometimes he would play beautifully, but at other times she could tell he was in trouble. She held onto her chair, wondering if the revered violinist would fall into a humiliating tailspin. "Thank heavens for Ormandy's excellent memory," she said. "He knew every note of that concerto, and he pushed and pulled Menuhin through it so sensitively that most of the audience never knew there was a problem."

Phillips was reluctant to criticize Menuhin, who had been a child prodigy, a true phenomenon whose musical gifts were lavishly praised and who served the musical world in many ways. She said he deserved the highest accolades for all he had done in his career, but she didn't know what he would have done that afternoon without Ormandy to help him through the concerto.

After the concert she went backstage and found Ormandy standing by himself in a corner of the reception room, looking exhausted, while a group of admirers (who obviously didn't understand what had happened) clustered worshipfully around Menuhin. Phillips avoided that crowd and sought out Ormandy in the corner.

"Maestro, you deserve five extra stars in your crown for what you did this afternoon," she told him. Ormandy didn't say a word. He just wiped his brow and gave a sigh of relief.

Not only did Ormandy have to cover for faltering soloists; he also had to deal with slipups from within the orchestra, Phillips revealed. Once she made a big mistake herself, one that shocked him and everyone in the orchestra. They were playing George Enescu's *Romanian Rhapsody No. 1*, when she crashed in at completely the wrong spot with perhaps the loudest chord she ever played. It was in a different key from what the score called for at that point, and it was all wrong, the worst mistake she ever made, she said. Ormandy was shocked. He pivoted abruptly toward her and actually jumped a few inches up from the podium.

"Oh, Lord," Phillips thought, "I've really done it now." Trying to salvage the situation, she put her hands down as calmly as possible and pretended that she was supposed to bang in there just once. That left the clarinet and oboe free to carry on with what they were supposed to be doing all along. When they finished, Phillips played her part in its proper place. Afterward, ashamed of herself, she prepared for a scolding from Ormandy and everyone else in the orchestra. She knew she deserved it, but Ormandy just looked amused, and the other players actually complimented her.

"You played it with such violent conviction," one of them told her. "We have to forgive you!"

Another area where Ormandy might have bettered Stokowski, Phillips said, was in working with the orchestra on new music. Although Stoki deserved much credit for introducing so many new works to the orchestral repertoire, according to Phillips, he tended to rush through them without giving them the extra attention that such unfamiliar and unusual works might have needed. Ormandy spent more time working on challenging new pieces, she said, which definitely made it easier for the players to make their way through them.

However helpful Ormandy was to soloists and to his players trying to master new compositions, Phillips said, he was not the trainer of players that Stokowski was. "He couldn't take someone like me, a true greenhorn, and develop the qualities of that player," she said. "He had to have his players ready on a gold platter to fit right into the orchestra, and he bought them with a long purse."

---

At the close of Ormandy's first season, he led the second Philadelphia Orchestra–RCA Victor Transcontinental Tour. Just as it had the year before, the tour got off to a celebratory start from Philadelphia's Broad Street Station, which has since been torn down, with festivities presided over by the mayor and other dignitaries, accompanied this time by the rousing marches of the official police band. Stoki, who was in Philadelphia conducting the final concerts of the season but who would not be going on the tour, joined in the farewell celebration.

There was only one glitch. Oscar Schwar, the orchestra's beloved timpanist, affectionately known as Poppy, got himself entangled in the crowd and failed to get on the train before it left the station. Somehow word got through to the engineer, and the train held up at the Thirtieth Street Station until he could be found and put aboard.

Poppy Schwar's near miss gave everyone a good laugh, but as the trip went forward, Phillips said more than a few of the players wished they had missed the train altogether. After leaving Philadelphia, they traveled straight to Atlanta for two concerts the next day, where they found themselves deep in a heat wave that they didn't escape from for what seemed like ages. With no air conditioning on the train and only one shower stall per car, it was rough, Phillips said. "We had private hotel rooms with full baths available to us when we spent enough time in a city to make use of them, but sometimes we got off the train just long enough to play a concert under hot stage lights before speeding on through the night to our next destination."

Finally, they left the heat behind when they headed west toward California, which was pleasant, but then they ended the tour engulfed by rain at every stop from Ann Arbor all the way back to Philadelphia. Phillips said that weather woes and a certain amount of drudgery accounted for her major memories of that tour, except for a few after-concert parties she attended with the other orchestra principals along the way. She especially enjoyed a happy post concert party in Toronto with a group of people who sang Gilbert and Sullivan long into the night with Sir Ernest Macmillan, the Toronto Philharmonic's conductor, at the piano. As the guests sang their way through the *Mikado*, Ormandy joined in with gusto. He knew all the words, Phillips said, having learned them directing the orchestra in the pit of the Capitol Theater.

Apparently, those after-concert parties attended by the principal players didn't sit well with some in the orchestra who weren't included. After the orchestra returned to Philadelphia, one of the excluded cellists gave Phillips's friend Kit Wright an earful, which, when Phillips heard what was said, opened her eyes to the resentment felt by the players who didn't get to participate in the extra advantages enjoyed by the principals. There wasn't anything she could do about it, though, except decline the invitations, and that she didn't want to do. She did enjoy those parties.

All in all, the second tour lacked the sense of excitement and adventure of the first tour, at least in Phillips's opinion. Stokowski was more spontaneous than Ormandy and often surprised the players with unexpected stops or variations in the programs, she said. With Ormandy, things went along pretty much as planned. Fewer memorable incidents happened along the way, and the players came back far less enthused than they had been the year before.

After the orchestra's return to Philadelphia and before Marcel Tabuteau and his wife departed for their usual summer sojourn in France, they invited the Rosenbaums to dinner at their Center City apartment. Not only was Tabuteau a star in the orchestra, he was also a star in the kitchen, so much so that *Time* magazine wrote an appreciation of his culinary prowess as well as his musical achievements, claiming that "the Philadelphia Orchestra without Marcel Tabuteau would be like soup without salt."[3]

Talking about their recently completed tour that evening, Phillips remembered Tabuteau using the language of gastronomy to express what many of the players felt about it. "Stokowski's tour was like butter made from the finest cream," he said. "Ormandy's was like oleomargarine."

––·––

Freed from having to spend so much of his time in Philadelphia, Stokowski set about pursuing his mission of delivering great music—and himself—to the masses via Hollywood.

"My ultimate aim is to bring the beauty of music to the greatest number of men, women, and children all over the world," he told the *Philadelphia Public Ledger* on July 6, 1937. "Motion pictures are an ideal medium for this. . . . That is why I am planning to work in Hollywood for a third of each year, and the rest of the time to conduct concerts and radio."[4]

He made his initial foray into the movies right after the orchestra's first transcontinental tour. After traveling back to the East Coast with the orchestra, Stoki turned around and went straight back to Hollywood to make *The Big Broadcast of 1937* with Jack Benny, Martha Raye, and Benny Goodman. For that movie, which was basically a variety show, the Philadelphia Orchestra recorded two of Stoki's Bach transcriptions in Philadelphia, with a dummy orchestra standing in for them in Hollywood.

The next year Stoki took on a starring role in the movie *One Hundred Men and a Girl*, in which Deanna Durbin, playing the daughter of an unemployed musician, tries to convince a famous conductor, played, of course, by Stokowski, to hire her father and his orchestra. To make sure the music in the movie met his standards, Stoki brought his Hollywood recording engineer plus Deanna Durbin and her family, as well as an assistant director and several other figures involved in the film, to Philadelphia, where the orchestra again recorded the music heard in the film. Among the works the orchestra performed were the finale of Tchaikovsky's Fifth Symphony, an excerpt from *Lohengrin*, and Liszt's Hungarian Rhapsody No. 2. Once again, a dummy orchestra staffed by Hollywood musicians stood in for the players during the filming. But Stoki was right up there in all his glory. Actually, Phillips confided, she didn't think he was a very good actor.

To answer charges from outraged critics who huffed and puffed that he was degrading classical music by presenting it in such a common forum, Stoki wrote the following in *Musical America*:

> I want to explain . . . not why we are now appearing and playing on the screen but why we did not do so before. With my orchestra, I pioneered in recording symphonic music for the phonograph. I believe our constant willingness to experiment with the science of sound aided materially in the great technical improvement in the fidelity of music reproduced from the familiar black disks. Later we plunged into the new field of radio broadcast and learned more about microphones. . . . Naturally such serious study of acoustics made me anticipate the point at which the sound screen would become a fit vehicle for that richest and most subtle of all musical mediums—the full symphony orchestra. That point has arrived. But I was determined that our Hollywood debut would wait until all conditions were right. Music has been my life work, so I was not—and am not—willing to conduct frothy or inferior music just because it has the name of being popular or familiar.[5]

His explanations didn't do much to assuage the perturbation of the highbrows, but the public responded well to the movies, and many people were exposed to great music for the first time.

In the midst of Stoki's musical endeavors in Hollywood, he also took on a role he had often played in Philadelphia—that of ladies' man. This time he created special consternation in the boardroom, for the woman he became involved with was one of the biggest movie stars of the era—Greta Garbo. Stoki was somewhat of a matinee idol himself, but his fame paled before that of the glamorous Garbo. Her beauty and alluring screen personality fascinated rich and poor, highbrows and lowbrows everywhere. In the gossip industry, the romance of the gorgeous movie star and the illustrious conductor set off a frantic hunt for information about the pair.

Spies zeroed in on the two lovers from everywhere, trying to ferret out the tiniest bits of news, and gossip columnists breathlessly reported the briefest of sightings and the wildest of rumors. *Modern Screen*, one movie magazine among many, appeared on newsstands with a picture of the couple on the cover under a headline proclaiming "Garbo Finds Love."[6] "Has Garbo a chance at happiness?" asked Martha Kerr, author of the article. Yes, Kerr claimed, she had indeed "found love . . . and it is our wish that she will find continued happiness in the companionship of the man she loves—Leopold Stokowski!"

Tales about Stoki and Garbo circulated widely, including reports that they sunbathed together in the nude. Rumor had it that marriage was just around the corner, but Philadelphians knew that couldn't be true. Stoki was still married to Evangeline. Then Hollywood gossip columnist Louella Parsons reported that Evangeline had taken up residence in Nevada, and everyone knew what that meant. She was there to get a divorce.

It was all very titillating, and Phillips was as intrigued as anyone about the rumors, especially when stories started circulating that Garbo was coming to Philadelphia to hear Stoki's orchestra in its own home. Dying to know whether the stories were true, she decided to ask Marshall. She stopped at his post in the green room on a Thursday morning after rehearsal as he was putting music parts together at a large table.

"Marshall, I hear that Greta Garbo's in town. Is it true?"

His face took on a peculiar look, but he didn't answer right away. Puzzled, Phillips asked again, stepping forward a bit to let a man in a dark hat pass behind her. "Do you know whether she's here?"

Hesitating a while longer, Marshall finally answered, after nodding to the man as he went out the door. "You just let her by," he said.

"What do you mean?" Phillips asked.

"Dat was her."

Phillips zipped out the door and spotted Garbo just getting into a car. Of course, that was the way Garbo dressed to disguise herself, in a mannish suit and a wide-brimmed hat. "Darn," she said, "I should have known."

That Saturday night, the Academy of Music sparkled with anticipation. The audience, dressed formally as usual for Saturday, seemed especially alert and excited. Of course, they had heard the rumors about Garbo and were busy trying to spot her. Phillips couldn't tell where she was, but she knew she was there because at the end of the concert, Stoki surprised the audience—and the orchestra—by announcing that they would play a special encore. Then he led the players through a rendition of *Prelude to the Afternoon of a Faun* that was so burning hot that electricity seemed to be coursing through the floorboards and everything and everyone on the stage. When they finished the piece, the players felt completely drained. Stoki had inspired them to pour their hearts and souls into their playing. Whether Garbo was there or not, Phillips said, a fire burned onstage that night.

That summer, the famous couple apparently thought they could escape the constant scrutiny they faced in the United States by traveling separately to Europe and then reconvening. They quickly found that didn't work, either. Crowds of stargazers and paparazzi quickly found them and surrounded them, just as they had at home. The mobs in Italy were so aggressive Stoki had to enlist the carabinieri to stave them off. Wherever the pair went, they attracted nosy onlookers, and, of course, news of their adventures made it quickly back to Philadelphia. *Time* reported that Stokowski had rented the Villa Cimbrone in Ravello for a month, where Garbo joined him, and "soon romantic villagers were clacking of arm-in-arm walks in twilight, unabashed embraces. . . . [Once] correspondents cornered Stokowski in the Hotel Caruso, where he had gone to telephone. . . . Next day the beleaguered Villa Cimbrone was guarded by four carabineers, [and] three police dogs. On the locked gate hung a 'keep out' sign."[7]

Predictably, the orchestra's board of directors was not amused by the notoriety surrounding their troublesome conductor, even if he wasn't full-time anymore. Perhaps Stoki sensed that and wanted to let it be known that he was hard at work on musical matters and not just flitting around Europe with the glamorous Miss Garbo, for he sent Phillips a letter on stationery from the Grand Hotel in Stockholm addressed in his distinctive handwriting to "Mrs. Samuel Rosenbaum." He had written a few brief notes to her about musical matters over the years, asking her to play a solo or some such thing, but he had always addressed her as Miss Phillips or Edna. However, this time Phillips speculated, he used "Mrs. Rosenbaum" to get Sam's attention as well as hers.

The letter itself contained a perfectly serious discussion of the harp and its technical limitations. Interested in the tone of all the instruments in the orchestra, Stoki inquired whether Phillips might have time "to experiment with [the harp's] problems of high and low register at the Bell Laboratories," and went on to say, "I should be so glad to have your co-operation because the harp is so important to the total sound of the orchestra—thru its rapid, intense rhythms it is the only instrument that can express the voluptuous and emotional quality of some music, and yet it is sometimes drowned because of its own weakness of low and high register."

After a short paragraph about "his wonderful summer up in the arctic zone in Lapland . . . Norway . . . Sweden," he ended the letter with what Phillips knew was a message for the board of directors. "Now I am ready to work again and will reach Philadelphia on September 8," he wrote. Then he signed the letter with a big, bold *Maestro*.[8]

The ploy didn't work.

On September 29, 1938, the board issued the following pronounce-ment: "Eugene Ormandy has been appointed musical director of the Philadelphia Orchestra, and Leopold Stokowski's participation in the affairs of the Orchestra, except for appearances as conductor for some of its concerts, is at an end. The post of music director, formerly held by Mr. Stokowski . . . gives Mr. Ormandy full authority over the orchestra's personnel, the content of programs, and the selection of soloists and guest conductors."[9]

Whether board members were punishing Stoki for his escapades or not, their abrupt announcement actually didn't change things very much from the point of view of the orchestra, Phillips said. Stokowski contin-ued to lead the orchestra for his usual fall and spring intervals for three more years, and he and Ormandy seemed to have a good relationship. They each held the interests of the orchestra uppermost and behaved with dignity and respect toward one another. That didn't stop them from doing things their own way, however.

During his stints on the Philadelphia podium, Stoki kept on experi-menting with the orchestra's seating plan in his restless search for the best way to project sound, and Ormandy kept on putting it back the way it had been after Stoki left town. After Stoki turned the whole orchestra upside down in 1938, putting the woodwinds in the front and stacking the rest of the players up and back from them on risers that rose high above the stage, Ormandy immediately changed them back after he was gone. In that case, Phillips was happy to get back to ground level after she and her harp had spent the Stoki weeks teetering on the edge of one of the highest risers.

The two maestros also supported each other on personnel changes, in spite of rumors to the contrary. At one point, Stoki got the blame when eight players, some of them longtime orchestra members, were let go, but the truth was that he and Ormandy had made that decision together. (They were later forced to rescind the firing of four of the players under pressure from the American Federation of Musicians.)[10] In addition, the two maestros seemed to have no problem deciding which works each of them would conduct, thus avoiding clashes over repertoire.

As for the Stokowski-Garbo romance, after the summer of 1938, it had run its course, and the two went their separate ways. Evangeline did get her divorce, and Stoki did not marry again until he wed Gloria Vanderbilt in 1945. He went on working in Hollywood, this time on a project that would have lasting import—*Fantasia*. But the orchestra wouldn't get involved in that for another year. In the meantime, Phillips had much to occupy her time in Philadelphia.

—•—

Edna and Sam's second child, a son, David Hugh, was born in April 1938. This time, when Phillips realized she was pregnant, she didn't take the chance of asking for a prolonged leave from the orchestra. Since she was such a healthy character, she said, she saw no reason to take as much time off as the doctors had made her do during her first pregnancy. "I just wore an enormous black cape with a big rhinestone buckle that covered the situation pretty well and kept on playing until a month before David was born, which was at the end of the season anyway."

And happy she was that she had stayed on, for a milestone for the Philadelphia Orchestra occurred on March 10, 1938, when a woman was given the opportunity to conduct a pair of regular season concerts. The distinguished Frenchwoman Nadia Boulanger, one of the twentieth century's most influential teachers of composition and a highly respected composer and conductor, earned that honor. In spite of Boulanger's fine musical pedigree, Phillips was dismayed to see the men of the orchestra making it obvious that they did not want to play under a female conductor. She could feel the intense hostility flowing toward Boulanger from the men at their first rehearsal together. It was shocking, even worse than the hostility Phillips had felt when she first joined the orchestra.

Boulanger must have felt it too, Phillips said. It was so obvious. But she took the podium with quiet self-assurance and great dignity. Looking every inch a nineteenth-century Frenchwoman in a long black bombazine skirt and a long-sleeved, high-collared black blouse with a small gold watch pinned to it, Boulanger surveyed the orchestra quietly before she began. She spoke without raising her voice, but there was a sense of authority about her that immediately caught everyone's attention. She had planned a program that fit the Stokowski mode in that it contained recently composed works, one of them by her deceased sister Lili Boulanger, *Pour les funérailles d'un soldat*, as well as older pieces that were new to modern ears. Like Stokowski, who had resurrected Bach for modern audiences, Boulanger focused on another composer from the distant past, Renaissance master Claudio Monteverdi.

Her program wasn't designed to win favor with the bulk of the orchestra, Phillips said. In fact, it probably added to their resistance. However, none of that mattered once Boulanger began to work with them. There was no self-consciousness about her and no special cordiality, but in two minutes, Phillips said, she had the men behaving like obedient little boys in school. Suddenly, complete musical rapport arose between the conductor and the orchestra. Boulanger knew her business, and the players recognized her abilities and were completely ready to follow her.

After rehearsal, Phillips overheard a remark from timpanist Poppy Schwar, one of the orchestra's most beloved players who had been with the orchestra almost since its inception: "I [would] like to play Brahms with that one!"

That was the highest compliment he could pay, Phillips said. Seeing the transformation from disdain to respect within the orchestra gratified her. She thought it a beautiful piece of quiet triumph for Boulanger, who had proven that a woman could command the attention and respect of the orchestra just as well as a man.

Unfortunately, the orchestra's management had allotted only half of the concert's program to Boulanger. Saul Caston, who had taken up conducting under Stokowski, led the other half. As propitious as Boulanger's start was, it took fifty years before another woman, Catherine Comet in 1988, had the opportunity to conduct a full concert with the Philadelphia Orchestra.

Another woman who made a significant appearance with the orchestra in 1938 was contralto Marian Anderson. Her performance in the Brahms Rhapsody for Alto Voice and Male Chorus and Orchestra won resounding praise for her beautifully modulated voice. She also performed a group of spirituals that moved listeners deeply. Phillips saw tears glistening on Kincaid's face as he listened to her haunting rendition of "Sometimes I Feel Like a Motherless Child."

During the years that Stokowski and Ormandy shared the podium, the players had many opportunities to compare their different approaches to conducting. Phillips discovered rather accidentally a big difference between the two in the 1938–39 season.

After nearly ten years in the orchestra, she had grown tired of wearing black all the time. It seemed she had played a thousand concerts wearing nothing but black. Wanting a change, she looked around to see if she could come up with something to vary the menu without being too outrageous. In the process, she noticed that the color of the cellos next to her on the stage fluctuated from one to the other quite attractively. Some had very dark, almost red, varnish. Others were lighter and more blond or tan. She looked for a color that would blend with those cellos, perhaps a deep garnet. It would provide a subtle change from the ever-present black, she decided.

She located a bolt of garnet-colored, silk-backed velvet at Stapler's fabric store on Fourth Street and had it made into a gown. Very dark, almost the color of a raisin, the color blended beautifully, Phillips thought, and it made up into a gorgeous dress. Based on the same pattern she and her dressmaker had developed for her basic performance dress, it featured a sweetheart neckline (which plunged deeper than the decorous V that had bothered the ladies of the women's committee years before), and its skirt contained twelve yards of material, as did all the gowns she wore with the orchestra. She had devised a trick with a large hatpin, which she used to secure the folds of material above her ankles when she sat down and still shield from view her feet as they worked the pedals of her harp.

Phillips was pleased with the dress. However, when the time came to actually wear it for a concert, she had second thoughts. Perhaps it might be best to wait until a guest conductor was on the podium to break it in, she decided. Little did she know that Ormandy had decided to check up on the orchestra when the next guest conductor took over and had seated himself in the back row of the family circle to listen to the concert. At intermission, he came flying backstage in search of his wayward harpist.

"Edna, what have you done?" he demanded. "You have departed from tradition! Everyone wears black in the orchestra, as you well know. How could you have done such a thing?"

"I thought it would blend with the cellos and give a nice look to the orchestra," Phillips answered, unwilling to apologize.

"That's not the thought at all. You must wear black!"

Oh well, she thought, I guess that's that. And she put the dress away.

Then Stokowski came back for his late spring concerts. "It was damn hot to be wearing that heavy velvet dress," she said, "but I decided to give it one more try. Stoki had just transcribed *Clair de Lune*, for orchestra, and the harp was all over the place in his transcription. After the first Friday concert, he called me to the podium to make some changes, but before he began, he took a look at my dress and exclaimed, 'What a perfect color! You must wear it all the time.'"

"And there you have the difference between our two conductors," Phillips said. "Ormandy wanted to shoot me, but Stoki liked the color because it embellished the orchestra. One was conventional, the other an artist."

---

*Fantasia*—or *Fanta-zee-ah* as the maestro called it—was Stokowski's last big experiment with the Philadelphia Orchestra, and once again he raised the ire of the board of directors. What was this rubbish? they sputtered.

Pairing the Philadelphia Orchestra with Walt Disney and his cartoons? What an utterly shocking idea! But however strong the outrage among the board members, Stoki wasn't to be deterred.

*Fantasia* had grown out of a chance meeting between Stokowski and Walt Disney when the maestro had journeyed back to Hollywood in 1937 following the orchestra's transcontinental tour. Disney, who had been making a series of "Silly Symphony" short films since 1929, "began to toy with the idea of doing a film using classical music, but one that had an implied story." Seeing Stokowski in a restaurant one night, Disney asked if he might be interested in working with him on making a short film using Dukas's *The Sorcerer's Apprentice*. "Would you like to do the music and I'll do the pictorial part?" he asked."[11]

Of course, Stokowski said yes. What better way could he find to spread his gospel of great music to the masses than by doing it through the Disney Studios? Then, after completing *The Sorcerer's Apprentice*, Disney, partly for financial reasons because making it had turned out to be so expensive, "decided to discuss with Stoki the possibility of expanding the idea into a concert project by adding many additional segments."[12] In that form, it would presumably spread out the costs and reap greater returns as a full-length movie. Once again, Stokowski leaped at the chance.

Speaking of the Stokowski-Disney relationship, a Disney biographer, Neal Gabler, writes that

> They made an odd pair—the epitome of the classical artist and the epitome of the commercial artist—which may have been part of the personal attraction, just as it was part of the artistic partnership. Stokowski seemed to love the free-spiritedness of the Disney studio; Walt seemed to love the highbrow legitimization that Stokowski bestowed. At times they could sit together, usually with [composer and music critic] Deems Taylor, and listen to music for hours. . . . But for all the comity and real friendship between them, sometimes the cultures clashed. At one session Walt kept turning up the volume when the music was soft and turning it down when the music was loud, prompting Stokowski to explode, "What is loud should be loud, and what is soft should be soft!"[13]

The science of reproducing highly complex sounds and coordinating them with film images had finally reached a stage where it was possible to go ahead with a pioneering project like *Fantasia*. Fascinated as always with technology, Stoki was ready to put the new science to the test in his ongoing quest to make classical music accessible to the larger public.

"When Stokowski arrived back in Los Angeles in September 1938 along with Deems Taylor, Walt couldn't wait to start listening to and selecting the music. The three of them spent virtually the entire month in Room 232 [at Disney Studios] listening to records of classical pieces, dozens of them, and pondering possible visualizations."[14]

After they had settled on the music, it was Stoki's job to record the music in Philadelphia. In April 1939, the Academy of Music was transformed into a giant recording studio, with wires winding all over the stage, crawling down the steps to a big studio set up in the basement, and stretching out to a trailer parked on Locust Street. In all, thirty-three microphones were set up to feed into nine different tracks in the ad hoc studio in the Academy basement. The stage was littered with strange contraptions for capturing sound that looked to Phillips like aquariums. Sound technicians kept poking around, she said, measuring this and that, setting up microphones, getting ready to record the music the maestro had chosen for the film. "He had so many wires on that stage it was worth your life just to walk around," she told a reporter from the *Philadelphia Inquirer* at a celebration for the reissue of the movie on its fiftieth anniversary.[15]

At the time, sound engineers were close to producing stereophonic sound. Disney's Fantasound system wasn't quite there, but it was close. Its intent was to catch and reproduce the dynamic balance of a full orchestra by recording the sound on different tracks and playing it back from speakers situated in various positions in the theaters that showed the film.

On April 6, 1939, the orchestra began recording the music for *Fantasia*, working through Saturday and Sunday of that Easter weekend, stopping for two programs on Saturday and a radio broadcast on Sunday, and holding another session later in the week. As they so often did with Stokowski, the orchestra worked intensively. With barely a break between pieces, they plowed through Stoki's selections from Bach's *Toccata and Fugue in D minor*, Tchaikovsky's *Nutcracker Suite*, Stravinsky's *Rite of Spring*, Mussorgsky's *Night on Bald Mountain*, Schubert's *Ave Maria*, that old warhorse *Dance of the Hours* by Ponchielli, and Beethoven's *Pastoral Symphony*. Of course, the players grumbled about having to work over Easter weekend, but they were used to that kind of thing with Stoki.

"The holiday sessions were very difficult but not that unusual," David Madison, a violinist who would later become associate concertmaster, said on the occasion of the film's fiftieth anniversary. "We were used to anything from him. We recorded on Thanksgiving Day. Our regular recording sessions sometimes lasted ten hours, deep into the night, until the musicians would complain and the union would be called in. But anything Stoki did was fine by me. He was my hero."[16]

"Sometimes he would push us too hard," Phillips said, "and the union would complain on our behalf, but attitudes were different then, and the players complained far less under Stoki than they might have under another conductor. So we worked our heads off and threaded our way through the wires that snaked around the stage, dodged microphones, and stepped over those sound boxes, but most of us didn't really understand what he was trying to do. All that apparatus struck us as being much too complicated for its own good."

Sol Schoenbach, the orchestra's principal bassoonist felt the same way. "The whole thing was a mess from beginning to end," he said at a symposium on Stokowski. "We had no idea what it was about. We were strewn around with wires stretching everywhere around us. We were all mixed up."[17]

Phillips also had her battles with the electrical paraphernalia. Apparently, the men listening to the recordings down in the basement heard a scratching sound every time she pulled her harp back to play. As a result, she was banished to the pit, where she had to crane her neck to see Stoki above her on the podium, which made it difficult for her to be sure that her playing was blending with that of the rest of the orchestra. "I felt like I was way out at Nineteenth and Chestnut," she said, "blocks away from the players above me. I worried the whole time that I might sound out of step with them, but everything seemed to work well enough. In the finished movie, the harp blends in just as if I were sitting in my usual place."

Even Stoki had his problems. "The maestro," Gabler writes, "chafed at some of the restrictions [imposed by the Hollywood technicians]—he had to station different sections of the orchestra between partitions for better sound reproduction and had to listen to a 'click track' as he conducted to keep the tempo for the animation."[18]

In spite of the rush to complete the recordings, Stoki stopped everything at one point to work with Schoenbach, who was a relatively new principal, having joined the orchestra in 1937. The maestro kept after him relentlessly to get the opening solo of the *Rite of Spring* just right. Phillips said it required Schoenbach to play way up in "the most dangerous part" of the bassoon. Stoki wanted him to produce an unearthly, eerie sound to bring out the poetry and drama of the musical story, and he wouldn't let up until the young bassoonist got it right. Before the maestro was satisfied, Schoenbach had played the passage more than forty times.

Phillips felt sorry for him because the pressure was so intense, but the truth was, most of the first-desk players had been through similar tortures under Stokowski, she said, and they had emerged much the better for it. "There was something indescribable when you knew that you had gotten what he was aiming at," she explained. "Other conductors just wanted everything in its place, but Stoki wanted so much more. That's what gave us so much more color in our tone."

When *Fantasia* appeared in movie theaters in 1940, Phillips watched with amusement the Hollywood musicians who stood in for the Philadelphia Orchestra on screen, especially her stand-in, who played the high harp passage in the opening of the *Toccata and Fugue* on the low strings! Aside from that, she found *Fantasia* delightful, but some stuffy critics—appalled to see hippos in tutus dancing to music made by the Philadelphia Orchestra—complained loudly that the movie was an affront to classical music. The worst offense in their opinion was Stokowski shaking hands with Mickey Mouse. Where was his dignity?

A leading critic of the day, Virgil Thomson, noted in his review of *Fantasia* in the *New York Herald Tribune* on November 14, 1940, that there were indeed lapses in musical taste in the movie. But he wrote, "Leopold Stokowski, whatever one might think of his musical taste, is unquestionably the man who has best watched over the upbringing of Hollywood's stepchild, musical recording and reproduction. Alone among successful symphonic conductors, he has given himself the trouble to find out something about musical reproduction techniques and to adapt these to the problems of orchestral execution. . . . Musicians will thank him and bless his name."[19]

*Fantasia* was not a box-office success when it first came out, but over the years it has grown in stature and is now considered a masterpiece. Rereleased numerous times and distributed through recordings, videotape, CDs, DVDs, Blu-ray, and Netflix, it has now been seen by vast numbers of people, more than Stokowski at his most grandiose might ever have imagined. It has awakened an interest in classical music in many who may never have been exposed to it otherwise and inspired countless talented young people to make their careers in music.

However *Fantasia* would be viewed in the future, the orchestra's board of directors reacted with anger at Stokowski when it was released in 1940. Relations between the maestro and the board had now deteriorated to their lowest ebb, and Stoki's association with the orchestra was nearing its end. Ormandy got along famously with the board and never gave them any trouble. With him there to take on full responsibility for the orchestra, the board's more conservative members were less and less inclined to countenance Stokowski's experimentation.

No immediate break occurred that season, but rumors of insults and slights between board members and the maestro circulated widely, and the orchestra's players waited for the final shoe to drop. Before it did, thirteen of those players, including Phillips, would find themselves embarking on one more adventure with Stokowski.

## CHAPTER 13

# A Silent Exit

Ever the teacher and developer of young talent, Stokowski had long dreamed of gathering together a group of highly qualified young people and forming them into a first-rate orchestra. But it wasn't until war began to overtake Europe in 1939, and German and Italian influence threatened to take hold in South America that Stoki's All-American Youth Orchestra finally got its start. The Berlin Philharmonic Orchestra and performers from La Scala had recently made tours through South America, winning friends for their respective countries. Alarmed, the Roosevelt administration wanted to counter those successes by sending U.S. cultural emissaries to Latin America. However, little government money was available to finance such projects.[1]

Stokowski stepped up to offer one solution to the dilemma. What better way to challenge the cultural impact that the Berlin Philharmonic and La Scala made on South America and counter the propaganda then circulating about the Hitler Youth Movement than by forming an orchestra of fresh-faced and highly talented young Americans as goodwill emissaries? To do this, he proposed to form an orchestra of young people from all over the United States. It would forge cultural ties with South Americans through the universal language of music and the charm of youth, and he would find a way to pay for it.

He found that way by contacting RCA, the company that recorded the Philadelphia Orchestra and had underwritten the orchestra's two transcontinental tours, and securing a pledge from it to underwrite the South American tour. The concept was embraced by all involved, and Stokowski embarked on the project with the help of the National Youth

Administration, which set up rounds of auditions throughout the country to help Stoki winnow out applicants and choose players from among ten thousand instrumentalists between the ages of sixteen and twenty-five who tried out for the orchestra's one hundred positions.

Then a change of heart by RCA stopped progress on the project. Toscanini, an early and vociferous opponent of fascism, had latched onto the idea of traveling to South America to fight Nazi propaganda with *his* orchestra, which by then was the NBC Orchestra. Since RCA president David Sarnoff had created the NBC Orchestra especially for Toscanini, that ended RCA's backing for Stokowski's enterprise and left Stoki without the funding he had counted on.[2]

That might have ended the whole undertaking, but once Stoki had a vision, his commitment to it was not easily diverted. He and his aides scrambled to secure new backing, turning to Columbia Records, which eventually agreed to underwrite the tour. Now Stoki was able to continue choosing and assembling a group of highly talented young instrumentalists from across the States. Unfortunately, the break in the schedule had set the timing back, which meant that Stokowski had less than a month to work with his youthful musicians to weld them into a legitimate symphony orchestra before setting forth on the Good Neighbor Tour of Latin America with the All-American Youth Orchestra (AAYO). *Time* magazine reported on June 10, 1940: "Last week, chins up, the Stokowski outfit insisted that its South American tour would begin in mid-July."[3] And so it did.

Perhaps an orchestra made up of a hundred talented young people with shiny faces and big smiles would have been an appealing ambassador for the United States if it had played only reasonably well, but that wasn't good enough for Stokowski. In the short time he had to work with the youthful instrumentalists, he managed to create an orchestra so noteworthy that even the most demanding of critics agreed that its playing equaled that of the finest professional orchestras—even the vaunted Philadelphia Orchestra.[4]

Relying on his strong organizational skills, Stoki chose thirteen players from the Philadelphia Orchestra and set them strategically within his new ensemble to provide a backbone of expertise for the final product so that it could be brought together quickly. "One of these was the splendid harpist Edna Phillips," wrote Oliver Daniel. "She explained that Stoki wanted to have . . . a nucleus of Philadelphians with him, so everyone who had hair went along!"[5]

At first when Stoki asked her to join the tour, Phillips demurred, uneasy about leaving her children for two months, but Sam urged her to go. Concerned about the early successes of the Axis armies in Europe, he supported the project. If the All-American Youth Orchestra could play a positive role in tamping down Axis influence, he was all for it. In that he differed with most of his fellow board members, who resented all the attention Stokowski's latest enterprise was getting in the press, viewing it as a distraction from news about the Philadelphia Orchestra.

Sam also saw the tour as an opportunity for Phillips to see something more of the world. As usual, he promised to supervise the household while she was gone, as he had done so well when she had been away on orchestra tours. "You'd better go now," he told her, "or you won't have a chance for a long time. We're going to get into this war sooner or later."

When Phillips signed on with the AAYO, Stoki gave her two jobs. First, she would be principal harpist, helping to train Lynne Wainwright, the talented young woman he had chosen as second harpist. Next, she would be the *consejera superiora*, or chief chaperone, which meant that she was to supervise the young people to see that they observed the social proprieties and stayed out of trouble. Since he had chosen twenty young women to play in the AAYO (by far the largest number of women ever yet included in a traditional U.S. orchestra), he knew he needed to have them accompanied by a chaperone so as not to offend the proprieties of the South American countries they would be visiting. It also occurred to him that he had better set some parameters for the behavior of his young charges.

About an hour after they left New York Harbor on the SS *Uruguay* on July 31, 1940, Stoki called everyone together in the ship's grand ballroom. Standing straight and stern before the happy young people, who could barely contain their excitement over the adventure that lay before them, he solemnly presented Phillips to them as their *consejera superiora*. "I expect you to observe the highest standards of behavior," he told them. "As your chaperone, Miss Phillips will be watching to make sure that you behave in a manner befitting the fine young men and women that you are." Then he laid out general rules for their behavior and signed off with a final pronouncement, "I don't want you to drink anything stronger than milk on this voyage."

Chaperoning wasn't a job Phillips had ever considered before. But how hard could it be? Although she was thirty-three at the time, only eight years older than the oldest of the youths, she felt confident that chaperoning them wouldn't present problems; they were such a fresh-faced, wholesome-looking group. It wasn't until the end of the trip that she learned to her embarrassment how deceiving looks could be.

En route to Rio de Janeiro, the first official stop on the tour, the orchestra rehearsed every day at ten A.M. in the ship's ballroom, much to the delight of the other passengers on board. They loved to gather their deck chairs around the portholes at rehearsal time, Phillips said, and the orchestra became quite the attraction on the voyage. The passengers followed the comings and goings of the young people with fascination and rarely complained when Stoki got the captain to order the ship's engines and even air conditioning turned off to cut down on noise when the orchestra was rehearsing or recording for Columbia Records, which happened often throughout the tour. They didn't even mind when Stoki asked the captain to make an unscheduled stop in Barbados so that he could carry out another of his great goals for the trip, which was to find and record music native to various locales in Latin America for research purposes and, ultimately, for the rest of the world to hear.

The maestro had sought out the best places to find authentic native music along the ship's route, but his advance research turned out to be off base in Barbados. After disembarking from the ship with his Columbia recording crew, he followed the tips he had been given to locate the island's best music but found nothing worth recording. Finally, the group thought they might have discovered the right place, but when they went inside, all they heard was a player piano pounding out "I Can't Give You Anything But Love, Baby." Their sure tip turned out to be "a house of joy!" Phillips exclaimed, laughing. Crestfallen, the recording crew and Stokowski returned to ship, which set sail posthaste.

Stoki's temporary disappointment did little to dampen the happy spirits on board the SS *Uruguay*, however. Everyone was having a wonderful time, Phillips said, most of it spent in joyous absorption in music making. In the snatches of time between rehearsals and individual practicing, the young people occupied themselves with table tennis, sunbathing, and chamber music concerts. In the evenings, they danced, played cards, or strolled about the decks. Everyone appeared to be well-behaved. In fact, Phillips thought she was the only one she knew of who got caught drinking. One evening a few days out, she felt queasy from the rolling of the ship. She had heard that brandy might calm things down, so she ordered a snifter from the bartender and was sipping it in a small room off the bar when Stoki strolled through. She said he just smiled when he saw her and continued on. She wasn't so sure he didn't stop to get one himself.

The young people drifted off to their quarters at quite reasonable hours every evening, bidding their chaperone good night with perfect manners, so Phillips didn't worry about them, although she did notice one morning that the English horn player looked a little the worse for wear at their ten o'clock rehearsal. They were working on Bach's "Little" G Minor Fugue, and he was supposed to make the second entrance alone, but he couldn't because he was sound asleep in his chair. Now what was the maestro to do? Phillips wondered. They were on the high seas, and he couldn't throw the fellow out and get a replacement.

"How could you do this to yourself?" Stoki asked the young man in a disgusted tone. "Don't you realize how you're deteriorating every minute you do something like this?"

The dressing-down seemed to take care of the situation. The young man never flagged again, and neither did any of the other players. They tackled the difficult music Stoki chose for them with wonderful verve, whether it was the Shostakovich Fifth Symphony, the Brahms Fourth, Dvorak's Ninth, or any other of the complicated works on Stoki's agenda, and they played beautifully, Phillips said.

One afternoon Stoki invited some of the Philadelphia Orchestra members to his cabin for tea. In the midst of a lively discussion about the talented young people in their midst, he stopped mid-sentence and turned to Phillips.

"You know, Edna," he said, "when a slightly off-color comment is made in the midst of the young ladies in this orchestra, they just laugh it off. They don't freeze up and pretend they didn't hear it."

Ah-ha, was he harking back to her response to his foolish virgins reference in that long-ago rehearsal? Phillips wondered. He must have been.

"But, Maestro, it's different when there are twenty of them," she answered. "They can take care of each other, but when there's only one, she has to take care of herself."

He looked as if he finally understood, she later said, but he didn't acknowledge it. Still, she knew he got the point, and that was enough.

As a consequence of Stoki having halted the ship's progress several times during the voyage, they arrived in Rio de Janeiro's spectacular harbor for their first concert not in the morning as planned but at sunset, which was a glorious time to come upon one of the most beautiful sights in the world, Phillips said, but only a few hours before the concert.

The ship anchored out in the harbor at some distance from shore, and a flat-bottomed tender came alongside. The players clambered down to it as quickly as possible. Trying to keep their balance aboard the tender, which was rolling with the waves, they stood among the cases that held the harps, double basses, timpani, and other instruments, clinging to each other while Stokowski stood at the bow with the wind blowing through his hair. It made a wonderful picture, Phillips said. The maestro looked like George Washington crossing the Delaware, and they were the soldiers huddled behind him.

When the tender pulled up to a steep stone staircase that descended down to the water, the players stepped onto it and climbed to street level. From there, they walked shakily, still on their "sea-legs" after being on board ship for eleven days, the three blocks to the beautiful Teatro Municipal to prepare for their first performance.

"Oh, my, how the stage of that theater swayed as I bent over to tune my harp! I felt like I was still at sea on a rocky day. On top of that, the perfume of the ladies in the audience, all dressed so elegantly for the evening, wafted up to us," Phillips said. "I was really green about the gills, and I'm sure the others were, too. But Stoki somehow kept us in line. We made it through the concert and got a wonderful, warm reception from the audience."

After the concert, the players were taken to their hotels in Rio. Happily for the women, Phillips said, they were lodged in the finest hotel in town. It was wonderfully luxurious, and they enjoyed similar treatment throughout South America. In deference to local standards of decorum, the tour sponsors always put the women and men in different hotels, and, Phillips said, the women received the most lavish and watchful care.

Phillips's name was given to the concierge at each stop as the *consejera superiora*. She was tasked with seeing that the girls were properly accompanied when they went out in the evenings and such. Nothing the girls did ever gave her pause, she said, except once in Buenos Aires, where they stayed in a veritable palace. After rehearsal one morning, Phillips had returned to her room to freshen up before lunch, when the concierge called with an urgent request that she come down to the lobby. The dining room steward was terribly upset: a young woman was trying to enter the dining room wearing slacks.

Phillips had a hard time making the young and independent cellist she found at the door to the dining room see that she was offending the Latin American sense of propriety. Searching for a way to change the young woman's mind, she finally asked her if she would go into the dining room in her pajamas.

"Oh no!" she replied, apparently shocked at the idea.

"Well, this seems as bad as that to them."

Finally, to the relief of the dining room staff, the young woman accepted Phillips's argument and agreed to change into a skirt.

At each stop—from Rio to São Paulo to Montevideo to Buenos Aires and smaller cities and towns that they reached by rail—the youth orchestra met with warm and enthusiastic receptions and loved the adventure of seeing so many beautiful cities and concert halls. Along the way, Phillips had the good fortune of being invited to the homes of people who had sailed on the SS *Uruguay* with the orchestra. In Buenos Aires, a lovely woman gave a dinner party in her honor. Looking for a gift for her hostess that day, Phillips found a record shop and asked the proprietor if he had any recordings of Stokowski conducting the Philadelphia Orchestra.

"No Tokoki," the shopkeeper answered. "Only Tokanini."

Poor Stokowski. Toscanini kept trumping him, especially in Argentina, where he was extremely popular. Phillips told Stokowski about the shopkeeper's comment at an after-concert reception the next night and then wished she had kept her mouth shut. He laughed heartily, but it must have stung, she said. The Italian colony in Buenos Aires was full of Toscanini aficionados who seemed to have it in for Stokowski. But Stoki made light of their catcalls and even adopted the nickname "Tokoki" for the rest of the trip.

In spite of his failure to find authentically native music in Barbados, Stoki had much success with his mission to find and record native music at other stops on the tour. He had an especially fruitful experience in Brazil, where he had the help of the noted composer and native son Heitor Villa-Lobos, whose works Stoki had often played with the Philadelphia Orchestra. Villa-Lobos gathered together some of Brazil's most popular musicians and brought them to the SS *Uruguay*, where Stoki spent all of one night and the next morning overseeing the recording of forty pieces, including sambas, macumbas, batucadas, and emboladas. The result was a 78 rpm album, *Native Brazilian Music*, released in 1942 by Columbia Records. In 2006, it was among the twenty-five culturally important recordings chosen for the National Recording Registry by the National Recording Preservation Board of the Library of Congress. In addition to recording native music, the maestro also made the goodwill gesture of playing works by native composers throughout the tour.

The group sailed home from South America on the SS *Argentine* with Stoki working the AAYO hard to prepare for their final concerts in the United States. Phillips found it awe-inspiring to watch him with his young players. They were so open to the joy of music, she said, they seemed to become extensions of his arms and eyes, instantly responding to the slightest nuance in his conducting. Stoki had always had a mysterious way of communicating with his players that brought out the best in them, she said, but he wrought a real miracle with those youngsters. They started out as a group of disparate amateurs and ended up as a superbly blended group of professionals. "There was a sense of discovery and enthusiasm in their playing that made it utterly compelling," she said.

On the homeward voyage, yet another reminder of support for Toscanini occurred. One evening the chef served a dessert that Stoki thought was so good he made a big fuss over it. He called the chef out of the kitchen to thank him and asked him what the name of the dessert was. To the embarrassment of all, the chef answered, "Coupe Toscanini."

That really was too much, Phillips said. Once again Stoki laughed off the slight, but she thought it was a shame that he kept getting squelched like that.

As the ship steamed homeward, Phillips discovered to her dismay that her chaperoning skills were not as sharp as she had thought them to be. On their last night out, the sea was churning and the ship was rocking so much that she decided to sit out in the fresh air on a deck chair rather than retiring to her stateroom below decks. In the chair next to hers sat Teddy, a property man who had labored to transport instruments and players to the twenty-seven concerts in the six countries that had made up the tour. The two were reminiscing about the events they had witnessed, when a young girl walked by.

"As chaperone, I must say I admired that young woman very much," Phillips told Teddy. "She's such a clean-cut young woman and has such nice manners."

"Oh, Miss Phillips," Teddy said, "One week it was the violas. The next the second violins!"

And then he told her about all the shenanigans that went on during the voyage "right under my nose!" she said. "It seems those innocent-looking young people had worked out elaborate ways to fool me, and I had been their perfect patsy. I'd overheard them ordering Cokes with lots of ice from the bartender but had never given it any thought. Well, 'lots of ice' turned out to be their code for rum. And the 'Ginger-Ale-with-a-straw' orders they gave the bartender meant that they wanted Scotch and soda. But that wasn't all. When I thought the darlings were going off to their cabins after they bid me goodnight, they were actually heading to the lifeboats to carry on with the evening's festivities!

"Some chaperone I was!" she continued. "Just before we disembarked the next day, the young people gathered around me and gave me a rousing cheer. They said I was the best *consejera superiora* they could ever have wanted. It was very funny, and Stoki clapped and cheered right along with them. He was probably in on the joke from the beginning!"

When the ship arrived in New York, Eleanor Roosevelt and her son Franklin Jr. met the youthful ambassadors at the dock with a citation from Secretary of State Cordell Hull praising their goodwill efforts on behalf of the nation.[6] Later the orchestra gave concerts in New York, Baltimore, and Washington, D.C. that received rapturous applause and rave reviews. Of their Carnegie Hall performance, Howard Taubman, of the *New York Times*, wrote: "The audience heard why the hometown boys and girls made good in South America. Mr. Stokowski, whose creation this orchestra is, left with a wonderfully talented body of young instrumentalists in his charge. He brought them back a major orchestra, ready to meet the best ensembles in America on virtually an equal footing."[7]

The accolades that must have given Stokowski the greatest pleasure came from the audience in Philadelphia's Academy of Music. Wild applause, cheers, and stamping of feet erupted at the end of the AAYO performance there, and the maestro had to wait through many bows to have his say. When he got the chance, he aimed his words squarely at the Philadelphia Orchestra board of directors.

"It is wonderful to be here," he said. "But I am a little sad because I have long wanted to make such a tour with the Philadelphia Orchestra. When I suggested it, I was told it was impossible, but I can't understand that because we've done it."[8]

————•————

Rehearsals for the opening of the Philadelphia Orchestra's 1940–41 season began a week after Phillips returned from the AAYO odyssey in mid-September. "It was difficult," she said, "because it seemed so hard on the children. There was a wistfulness about them that tugged at my heart." She knew Joan and David had been well cared for by everybody at home, but she couldn't help feeling she was asking too much of her family by having to be away from the children so much. However, there was little she could do. Ormandy and the Philadelphia Orchestra needed her serious attention right away, and she had to give it.

As the season opened, Phillips and the other players who had participated in Stokowski's tour found the atmosphere inside the orchestra more than a bit frosty. They came back flushed with excitement from the enthusiastic receptions the AAYO had received throughout the tour, but they soon realized that Ormandy did not appreciate the exuberant praise his co-conductor was receiving, and he seemed to resent the role that they, as Philadelphia Orchestra players, had taken in the AAYO. It was best, Phillips decided, to proceed cautiously as the season got under way.

And then there was Sam, who had always been so supportive of her career. He didn't make things easier for her that fall. On the contrary, he made them more difficult. He had developed objections to Ormandy's conducting style, and he wasn't hiding them. Much to Phillips's chagrin, he was making his doubts increasingly clear. He had long taken an interest in Ormandy's career and had supported his appointment to the co-conductor position, but as time went on, unlike most of his colleagues on the board of directors, he began to see things he didn't like. Backstage after concerts, he was heard several times remarking about things that needed improvement. When Ormandy heard about Sam's comments, he went to Phillips with fire in his eyes to complain.

"Stoki would have dealt with Sam himself," she said, "but Ormandy never seemed to understand that my role as a member of the orchestra should be kept separate from my role as the wife of a board member. He was trying to make me a go-between."

One day, she exploded to Sam: "You've got to talk to Ormandy directly and stop this random criticism. I'm right in the middle here. You're putting me in an untenable position."

So Sam talked to Ormandy himself and reported back to her what was said.

"I told him that the brasses were overpowering the strings, and the orchestra sounded like a goddamn band in the park," Sam said. "And he told me that Harl [Harl McDonald, manager of the orchestra at that time] said the brasses sounded fine to him. And I told him Harl was just kissing his ass to keep his job."

Another time, Sam told Ormandy that he didn't like the atmosphere of informality that prevailed at his rehearsals. He thought the maestro needed to maintain his ascendance over the orchestra by keeping the players at arm's length as Stoki did. A conductor needed respect from the orchestra, Sam told him, not affection.

"Friendship ends at the stage door," he told Ormandy one day. "Be like Zarathustra. When you go to the orchestra, go with a whip!"

Half bemused at Sam's remarks and half annoyed at him for making them, Phillips soldiered on.

While Sam was busy berating Ormandy, most of his fellow board members were perfectly happy with the young conductor, who was so much more amenable to their wishes than Stoki had ever been. They felt confident that he would never go off and create anything like the All-American Youth Orchestra to take attention—and record sales—away from the Philadelphia Orchestra.

In fact, to show its appreciation of Ormandy, the board voted that fall to give him a new five-year contract with the title Conductor and Music Director—and announced its decision to the newspapers the day before Stoki arrived for his stint with the orchestra in late November of 1940.[9] By that time, the recordings Stoki had made with the AAYO for Columbia Records were outselling the Philadelphia Orchestra's RCA recordings, and the board members were furious. They counted on revenue from record sales and resented a challenge to it. As the board began deliberations on Stoki's contract for the next year, the atmosphere was sour.

Statements attributed to anonymous board members appeared in the newspapers charging Stoki with being an opportunist only interested in money and fame for himself and claiming that he had demanded an increase in his fee and insisted on performing new works that would be far too costly for the orchestra's budget. Stokowski vociferously denied the charges and countered with another of his open letters to the board, which also appeared in the newspapers. Saying that his fee in Philadelphia was less than he received when he conducted in other U.S. and European cities and less than half of what Toscanini received when he conducted the Philadelphia, he demanded that the anonymous attacks on him be stopped.[10]

"I am sure it is a small minority, possibly only one member of the board, who is giving out these false rumors and withholding his name," he wrote. "Do you not think it would be more fair if the individual members of the board signed their names in future to all statements they make, just as I am signing mine to this letter?"[11]

Once again, the gauntlet had been thrown down. Stokowski and the board had resumed their battle stations. Stoki readied the premieres of two new works in his series of concerts. The first was the Shostakovich Sixth Symphony, which, surprisingly, was accepted with few objections by audiences and even the board. The next work did not get such a dispassionate reception. It was the world premiere of the Schoenberg Violin Concerto, and it caused a giant uproar. Trying to prevent Stokowski from presenting the piece in the first place, the board refused to pay the fee for the violinist he had engaged to play it, Louis Krasner. But that didn't stop Stokowski. He paid Krasner's fee himself (although Krasner offered to forgo it, an offer that Stoki did not accept) and went right ahead with the performance.[12]

"It was like the good old days after performances of Varèse and some of the more cacophonous Russians," the *Philadelphia Evening Bulletin* reported.[13] Just as they had in earlier years, people got up from their seats and walked noisily out of the auditorium while the concerto was being played. Afterward, those remaining cheered Krasner for his performance of the difficult work but booed Stokowski for choosing to inflict it on them. One critic said that listening to the work was like being in "a hen yard at feeding time."[14]

Yes, it was like old times, but somehow it wasn't. The boisterous interchange that used to occur when Stokowski presented new works lacked the esprit it once had. The zestful give and take was missing.

After his three-week concert stint, Stoki left Philadelphia with the question of his contract for the 1941–42 season still unresolved. Offers and counteroffers were exchanged. The *New York Times* ran a special dispatch from Philadelphia on December 12, 1940, stating that manager Harl McDonald had "been empowered to negotiate a contract" with Stokowski. However, "certain limitations had been set . . . and [Stokowski's] financial proposal" was criticized.

"The temper of board members," the dispatch continued, "left the impression that Mr. Stokowski either would be back for a short period next fall as guest conductor and at terms somewhat less than he is asking, or he would not be found directing the Philadelphia Orchestra at all next season."[15]

In March, Stokowski responded to the board with an elliptical letter: "I would like to conduct the concerts you have suggested for next season, but in view of the national emergency, which daily is becoming more serious, I feel I should for a period keep myself free and available to serve our country and government."[16]

On behalf of the board, Harl McDonald wrote back asking Stokowski to reconsider.

A telegram came back—"My letter was final."

The board had gotten what it wanted. It was happy with Eugene Ormandy. And Stokowski had also gotten what he wanted—freedom to take on challenges in wider circles. "His restless soul could no longer be contained in Philadelphia," Phillips said. "It had been a long and remarkably fruitful relationship, but now it was over."

In March 1941, Stokowski came back to Philadelphia for his final concerts as co-conductor of its orchestra. In observation of Easter, which fell within that period, he had programmed Bach's *St. Matthew Passion*. Tradition held that there be no applause at its conclusion, due to the religious nature of the work. Thus, after twenty-nine years of creating transcendent joy, controversy, consternation, and pure pleasure in the Academy of Music, Stokowski left its stage in silence.

"But wait!" writes Oliver Daniel in his huge tome about the maestro, "There is a happy epilogue. There was one more concert to come, a children's concert. Here there were no melancholy recollections, no emotional farewells. Stoki, enjoying himself immensely, wanted only to have his young audience enjoy the concert, too."[17]

Still, he would not return to Philadelphia for nineteen years.

## CHAPTER 14

# Cajoling and
# Seducing Composers

With Stokowski gone and Ormandy completely in charge, the Philadel-phia players carried on as the professionals they were, still committed to performing at the highest levels and still proud to be members of a great orchestra. It was what professionals did.

Phillips took on another project at this time in addition to her orches-tra duties. Over the years, she had grown frustrated by the scarcity of works written for the harp, especially when she performed as a soloist with the orchestra and found that the number of suitable works she had to choose from was limited. Finally, in 1940, she decided to do something about the problem. With her husband's generous support, she set out to expand the repertoire by commissioning new works for the harp from the best composers she could find. But finding and pinning down those composers turned out to be much harder than she had imagined.

"Few composers at the time understood what to do with the harp," she explained. "They thought it was too complex and felt intimidated, so it became my job to cajole and seduce different ones to write for us. I had to fight against the mistaken idea that the harp is a limited instrument. It's not limited in the slightest if it's handled the right way, and it has so many tone colors that it lends itself well to modern music.

"If a composer is sensitive and knowledgeable enough to create a texture that lets the harp's true colors shine out," she stated, "it won't get lost even against a full orchestra. Salzedo said that the limitations of the harp exist in the minds of limited composers and ill-informed critics, and he was right."

She began her quest by asking Manuel de Falla, whom she met during the AAYO tour, to write a work for her. The Spanish Civil War had forced the great composer into exile in Argentina, and he had visited Stokowski when the AAYO was in Rosario, near Buenos Aires. Phillips loved his writing for the harp and thought he understood the instrument and used it well. "I tried my best to get him to write something for me, but he felt too weary to tackle a project at that time."

Another disappointment in her quest was Sergei Prokofiev, whose writing for the harp Phillips thought was extremely effective. She longed to have a concerto for harp written by him. At a reception in Washington hosted by their former School House Lane neighbor, Francis Biddle, who was then attorney general in the Roosevelt administration, Edna and Sam tried to get a letter with their offer of a commission to Prokofiev through the Soviet ambassador. They asked the ambassador to put their letter in the diplomatic pouch for delivery to the composer, and he agreed to do it, Phillips said, but they found out later that their letter probably never reached Prokofiev, for Moscow issued an edict soon afterward that no works could be commissioned from outside the Soviet Union.

"And that was that," she said. "We never heard from Prokofiev."

Always sociable and outgoing even if she spent hours alone with her music, Phillips enjoyed herself at the attorney general's reception and delighted in meeting the various dignitaries he had assembled. However, she did make a bit of a faux pas. "I was introduced to a Mr. Hoover, and I asked him very politely, I thought, what he did in Washington. Somehow I didn't catch on that I was talking to J. Edgar Hoover. Sam almost choked on his drink at that point as he jumped in to try to smooth things over before I offended the poor man further."

Still trying to talk prestigious composers—"They needed to be important so the works would get attention"—into writing for the harp, Phillips next targeted Benjamin Britten. He agreed to meet with her in New York, where she spent a pleasant afternoon playing for him and discussing the technical requirements of the harp, but when she asked him to write a work for her, he declined. At the time, he was preparing to return to England to stand with his countrymen against the German bombardment. He was too distracted to think of accepting a commission, he told her.

She lost that chance, but she always wondered whether she had prompted Britten to think about the harp. "He composed the *Ceremony of Carols* on the ship taking him back to England and used the harp in such an original and wonderful way in it," she said. "It really doesn't matter that he didn't accept our commission. That is a great work for the harp."

Another important composer of the day that Sam and Edna hoped would produce a harp concerto for them was Carlos Chavez. Although he accepted an advance on a commission, things went awry and the promised work never materialized.[1] Even Phillips's Curtis Institute schoolmate Samuel Barber turned her down.

At times, the search seemed doomed, but in the end, Edna's "seducing and cajoling" succeeded in attracting a number of excellent composers to write works for the harp.[2] She quickly discovered that was only the beginning. Once a composer agreed to accept a commission, there was still much work to do. "Composers today seem to be well-versed in the harp," she explained. "The schools are doing their job, but back then I had to work with them to show them what could and couldn't be done. I had to make sure that their finished compositions would lie well under the fingers and feet of the harpist, that the pieces could be played without the harpist having to do a lot of rearranging."

Harpists often complain that compositions for the harp seem to have been written for the piano, which complicates the situation greatly since the mechanics of the two instruments are entirely different. For example, a harpist can use only four fingers on each hand, rather than five as a pianist does. The little finger is too short to provide enough force when plucking a string. There are also no black keys for sharps and flats on the harp as there are on the piano, only pedals that must be raised or lowered to change the pitch. If a composer doesn't understand those technicalities and others that are more subtle and complex, harpists have to spend hours unraveling compositions to make them playable.

"Many interesting effects can be achieved on the harp," Phillips said. "I was constantly introducing them to the composers of my day. The harp goes all the way back to the Queen of Sheba, yet it lends itself marvelously to contemporary music because of its many tone colors and the wonderful effects you can make on it. Salzedo created a system of symbols for those effects, but most composers just use their own today."

Edna's first commission happened almost by accident. One day Edna was playing and singing English nursery rhymes with her children in their home on School House Lane. Joan and David loved tunes like *Oranges and Lemons, Lavender Blue, Dilly Dilly*, and *I Saw Three Ships Come Sailing By*, and she would improvise accompaniments for them on the harp. Harl McDonald, a noted composer as well as the manager of the

Philadelphia Orchestra, happened to come to Roxboro House that afternoon to meet with Sam. He heard Phillips playing in the music room and commented on how lovely the pieces sounded on the harp.

"Why don't we string some of the tunes together in a suite?" he suggested. Edna and Sam immediately liked the idea. It reminded them of Robert Schumann's *Kinderszenen* (Scenes from Childhood), which they both knew and liked, and so they commissioned McDonald to write his suite *From Childhood*, a concerto for harp and orchestra, a lovely piece that became especially popular in the war years. Its warmth and good cheer seemed to lighten the bleakness of those grim days, Phillips said.

After that, Sam and Edna commissioned a variety of works, including harp concertos for chamber orchestra as well as for full orchestra; pieces for harp and string quartet; pieces for harp and chorus, and other combinations.

"Several of our commissions have turned out to have real meat on their bones," Phillips said, "especially Alberto Ginastera's *Harp Concerto, opus 25*, which ranks as one of the most important works for the harp written in the twentieth century. It's a true masterpiece. I'm very proud of that."

Ginastera seemed to take to composing for the harp naturally, she said. From the beginning, he knew what he wanted, and she didn't have to teach him what to do. But it took so many years for him to complete the work that she had stopped playing professionally by the time the piece was ready to be premiered in 1965, so Nicanor Zabaleta was the soloist when the work was premiered by Eugene Ormandy and the Philadelphia Orchestra that year.

"After Ginastera accepted our commission in 1956, we hoped it would be ready in time for the 1958 International American Music Festival in Washington, D.C. But as we neared that date, I started getting letters from Argentina—he was Argentinean—telling me about problems with Peron and his troubles with an opera he was writing and other difficulties. The harp concerto kept getting put off. It took forever, but what a triumph it turned out to be! It was well worth the wait."

The terms of a commission when Phillips was still performing stated that she would have exclusive performance rights for the first year after the completion of a work. After that, full rights for the work would go back to the composer. Phillips began presenting the premieres of her commissions in 1941, when she played Harl McDonald's *From Childhood* with the Philadelphia Orchestra. Critic Samuel L. Laciar called it "one of the best things that Mr. McDonald has yet done," and said, "Miss Phillips, one of the finest American harpists, played the solo part superbly. A thorough master of the technique of the instrument, she revealed a surprising number of tone colors through the use of harmonics, by plucking the strings at various distances from the lower attachment on the instrument and in many other ways known only to an expert harpist."[3] The piece got such a happy reception that the orchestra featured it with Phillips as soloist in thirteen concerts on tour that year.

In addition to the McDonald suite, Phillips gave the first performance of two other works she had commissioned with the Philadelphia Orchestra: *Concerto for Harp and Orchestra* by Nicolai Berezowsky, and *Concerto for Harp and Chamber Orchestra* by Ernst Krenek. She also played the premieres of six additional commissions that she and Sam commissioned. One of those, which Phillips premiered with the Juilliard String Quartet at the Library of Congress in 1958, was *Concertino antico* for harp and string quartet by Peggy Glanville-Hicks, one of the first women to win an international reputation as a composer of distinction. Australian by birth, Glanville-Hicks studied with composers Fritz Hart, Ralph Vaughan Williams, and Nadia Boulanger. Among her best-known works are two operas, *Transposed Heads* and *Nausicaa*.

Although Phillips didn't commission Vincent Persichetti's *Serenade no. 10, opus 79*, for flute and harp, she worked very hard with him to perfect it and played its premiere performance. She also worked with him on another piece for the harp. "Vincent was a busy man," she said. "He came over at five o'clock in the morning for what seemed like weeks to work out his compositions with me. I was bleary eyed by the end. It had to be between five and six in the morning because he was so busy. He taught three days a week in New York at Juilliard. Then he had other jobs in Philadelphia." In the end, although Phillips didn't commission Persichetti's compositions, the harp repertoire benefitted once again from her efforts on its behalf.

---

Even though Stokowski with his sometimes impetuous demands was no longer commanding the orchestra, the players found that the demands on their time were greater than ever during the 1940–41 season. The orchestra's touring schedule had evolved from the big transcontinental expeditions of 1936 and 1937 into more tours within the regular season. Until 1936, the players had traveled to New York, Washington, Baltimore, and sometimes Hartford on short-run tours, but now the orchestra began to expand its orbit to include cities that were farther away. During the

1940–41 season, the orchestra traveled to thirty-three cities in three-, four-, and five-day jaunts. That kind of touring forced Phillips to be away from home more than she had ever been during regular seasons in the past.

"Even with Sam's total support, that much time away from home was taking a toll on my family," she said. "All that traveling added on to the regular season concerts taxed all of us. At night I would lie awake on the train or in a hotel room worrying about Joan and David. I was leading such a gypsy life, while they were left at home without me. Sam was overseeing them, and we had a wonderful governess, but saying good-bye to the children got harder and harder each time I had to go away."

In the past, thoughts of leaving the orchestra and pursuing a solo career had flickered through her mind. Now she wondered if that path might give her more flexibility and fulfill an ambition put into her head years before by Salzedo, who maintained an impressive solo career and wouldn't consider confining himself to one orchestra, even as principal harp. As much as she loved her role in the Philadelphia Orchestra, she was finding the touring obligations then in force extremely onerous.

"One day Joan asked me why I couldn't be like the mothers of her friends who waited at the fence gate with chocolate chip cookies for them to come home from school," Phillips said. "I doubt they really did that, but she looked so wistful telling me. It was the final straw that convinced me that it was time for me to leave the orchestra."

"All that traveling was just too much. I needed to step back," she said, and so she wrote a solemn letter of resignation, stating that she would be leaving the orchestra at the end of the season, part of which appeared in the *Public Ledger*: "Membership in our orchestra is a privilege that requires complete subordination of every other activity. It is more than an engagement. It is a way of life."[4]

Sam had a lighter way of stating the case when he was asked what he thought about his wife's resignation. "As vice president of the Philadelphia Orchestra," he said, "I greatly regret that Edna Phillips has resigned as solo harpist. As vice president of the family firm of Phillips and Rosenbaum, there is something to be said for it."[5]

Circumstances would later conspire to make Phillips's resignation short-lived, but while it lasted, it allowed her to hold her head high among the mothers of her children's classmates. As a woman with a career, Phillips often felt uncomfortable among the women she encountered who didn't work outside of the home. She felt an undercurrent of disapproval in their relations with her. "I was out of step with their way of life," she said, "and a lot of them acted like I was doing something I shouldn't be doing."

During the long economic depression of the 1930s, women who had careers were rare indeed. There was such a desperate need for men to find jobs to support families that newspapers often portrayed women with careers in a negative light, while stories praising women who relinquished their careers to become homemakers were plentiful. "The issue of whether married women should work was chewed over constantly in the newspapers and women's magazines, with the consensus coming down on the side of not," writes Gail Collins.[6]

One such story that damned the idea of "career mothers" with faint praise appeared in the Philadelphia *Evening Bulletin* in 1939, accompanied by a glamorous photograph of Phillips. Opening with the tale of a "onetime screen star [Mae Murray]," suing for custody of her son, the article emphasizes the problems that families of working mothers faced and says that successful working women "are the first to point out the cost it requires." A college professor, one of the successes the article mentions, acknowledged that a mother involved in interesting work brings something positive to her family. "But, she warned, it's a difficult job, and she's had to sacrifice bridge and some of the things many women dote on." Another successful woman cited was an architect, who said: "If papa is agreeable and cooperative, a woman can do both, but she must be healthy because it takes lots of energy." Other than her glamorous photo, Phillips is only briefly mentioned: "Edna Phillips, Philadelphia Orchestra harpist, wife of Samuel Rosenbaum, real estate and radio executive, is another with kiddies and a career."[7]

At the end of the season, when Phillips left the orchestra, the *Public Ledger* marked the occasion with the headline "First Harpist's Harp Now Takes Second Place." The article quotes Phillips and praises her devotion to home and family with these words: "'At a certain period I felt it was safe to leave my children,' said the gold[en]-haired harpist. 'But now I feel that this is a new era—I'm making THIS more my profession.' She indicated the house, built in 1799 [*sic*], the lawn that dips down to a box-scented, brick-pathed garden, and the sound of laughing children. In place of her customary routine of daily rehearsals, 87 out-of-town concerts and 125 local concerts . . . she has 'moved from remote to direct control' of her home."[8]

Phillips said she had to laugh at the mother-returning-to-the hearth tone of the article, for even though she left the orchestra, she didn't take up bridge and settle into the socially acceptable role of the wife of a prosperous man. Her professional life had too tight a hold on her. Without the hectic schedule she had been forced to maintain with the orchestra, she was able to devote more time to her children, and she was glad for that. "But I was like a trained horse," she said. "Music was still the stall I returned to. I still practiced five hours every day, taught my students at the Philadelphia Conservatory, and sought out and worked with the composers who were writing works for me."

She also began to build a solo career by playing the premiere of a work she and Sam had commissioned, *Sea Chanty* by Paul White, with the Rochester Symphony Orchestra under José Iturbi. Later she made a recording of the work for Columbia Records with the first chair players of the Philadelphia Orchestra's string sections under the direction of Ormandy.

In this period Phillips and William Kincaid formed a harp and flute duo that appeared frequently in the Philadelphia area and as far away as South Carolina. Later they added Samuel Lifschey, the orchestra's principal violist, to their duo to create the Philadelphia Flute, Harp, and Viola Trio.

As always, Phillips said, Kincaid was an indefatigable worker. Playing his beloved platinum flute, he never stinted on giving of himself in performance or at a rehearsal. The duo and later the trio often rehearsed in Phillips's barn-studio on School House Lane, a favorite spot for many of her musical friends who loved it for its bucolic setting. "Sometimes when we finished rehearsing and the weather was good," Phillips said, "Kincaid, a big, ruddy man, would sit cross-legged under a huge maple tree that shaded the barn to play his flute, letting the sound float out into the breeze, and my children and their friends would gather around to listen."

Her separation from the orchestra didn't prevent her from being called back from time to time. Although Ormandy had hired Lynne Wainwright, the excellent second harpist from the AAYO, as her replacement, he often called Phillips back to play for special occasions. One of those occasions occurred when Toscanini came to town after he argued with the managers of his NBC Symphony Orchestra and tempestuously walked away from his position as its conductor. That gave him time to make a series of recordings with the Philadelphia Orchestra. Remembering Phillips from the times he conducted the orchestra in the 1930s, he insisted that she be his principal harpist, so back she went to do Strauss's *Death and Transfiguration*, and Debussy's *Iberia* and *La Mer* with Il Maestro.

Phillips was struck with Toscanini's intense concentration during the recording sessions. "Immediately after we finished each section, he stood—never sitting down once—on the podium, listening intently to the playback," she said. "He was in his midseventies by then, but he never relaxed for a second in his drive to assure himself that the playing was perfect before he gave his OK." Amusingly, one of the main problems that turned up in the early playbacks was a strange rumbling sound that could be heard underneath the music. "It turned out to be Toscanini singing under his breath! He would get so carried away he didn't realize he was doing it."

Remastered and reissued in 2007, those recordings, plus others made in the following years, received much praise from music critics. One wrote, "Every Toscanini fan will want this set. It is recommendable to Toscanini skeptics as well—because the Philadelphia recordings show the maestro at his very best—and the Philadelphians are the lushest, suavest, most beautiful orchestra in the world. The combination of Philadelphia beauty and Toscanini rigor is formidable."[9]

Whenever Toscanini came to town, Eugene and Steffi Ormandy would host small get-togethers for him in their apartment on Rittenhouse Square. One evening Edna and Sam were invited. After supper, they walked Toscanini back to the Warwick Hotel, a block away at Seventeenth and Locust Streets, where he was staying. The Kincaids also came along. The marvelous flutist was always one of Toscanini's favorite players, Phillips said. "Caro Kincaid," he called him.

Before saying good night, the group decided to have a nightcap in the hotel bar, where a small band was playing Tommy Dorsey's hit song, "And the Music Goes Round and Round." Pretty soon, the tune got into Toscanini's ears, Phillips said, and he couldn't get it out. As he headed across the lobby to the elevators at the end of the evening, they could hear him still humming it.

Another time, Ormandy gathered the orchestra's principals together with Toscanini at his apartment to listen to a Sunday afternoon radio broadcast of the NBC Symphony Orchestra led by Stokowski, who took over as conductor of the NBC Symphony after Toscanini resigned. It was a painful affair, Phillips said.

"I still wonder what Ormandy was thinking when he asked us to sit together and listen to Stokowski conduct Toscanini's former orchestra. Toscanini was sure to speak out," Phillips said. And he did.

From almost the first note, Toscanini railed against Stoki's interpretation of the Brahms Fourth Symphony. His anger grew as the broadcast progressed, and, just as it always did when he got angry, his face began to flush until it turned bright red.

"Carla, his long-suffering wife, was there with us," Phillips said. "Oh my, what a terrible autocrat he was to her! The more she tried to calm him down, the more fiercely he snapped at her. Finally, in an absolute tizzy, he jumped up and demanded that the radio be turned off."

Of course, the party was ruined. For Phillips, who had played for ten years under Stokowski, Toscanini's fiery criticism was hard to endure. She knew that Stokowski had his flaws. His ego was immense and he was inclined to go overboard at times, but she still had the highest respect for his artistry. At the same time, she also admired Toscanini as a superb conductor, a master of masters. His outburst distressed her, but what bothered her more was seeing her former colleagues seeming to take Toscanini's side. Were they just fawning over the great man, or did they really agree with him? She couldn't say. All she knew was that it was an altogether upsetting episode.

# CHAPTER 15

# War Stories

Sam had been right when he urged Edna to take advantage of Stokowski's offer to join the AAYO for the South American tour. "We're going to get into this war sooner or later," he had said, and, of course, the United States did get into the war. The Japanese attacked Pearl Harbor on December 7, 1941, and Hitler and Mussolini declared war on the United States four days later. The U.S. government rushed to put itself on a war footing, but the situation was grim. Losses on the battlefront piled up and the prospects for winning appeared dim.

Finally, Sam could stand no more. He had learned a lot in life, he told Edna. Maybe some of that could be put to use in the war effort. In World War I he had served under the judge advocate general as legislative draftsman. Now it was time for him to offer his services to the country once again, and so in the summer of 1942, he entered the army as a major.

Not long before Sam left, Phillips received a call from Eugene Ormandy. Lynne Wainwright, her replacement as first harpist in the orchestra, had suddenly resigned her position, leaving Ormandy with little time to find a replacement. Would Phillips consider coming back to the orchestra? Surprised by the call, she hesitated. How could she return to that hectic life without Sam there to help her watch over the children and run their home?

Sam offered another perspective. He knew that a lonely life lay ahead for Edna with him overseas and urged her to accept Ormandy's offer. "Time will pass more quickly if you're occupied with the orchestra," he said. He also informed her that she wouldn't have to worry about the orchestra's heavy touring schedule taking her away from home. As a member of the board of directors, he knew that the orchestra would soon announce that it had to curtail its touring because the trains were needed to transport troops.

That meant Phillips would have a much easier time balancing her home and orchestral life. Freed from the need to travel, and with the governess still at Roxboro House, Phillips saw that "the children would be pretty well surrounded," so she accepted her old position as principal harpist. "In those bleak times," she said, "it seemed the best thing to do."

"When a door closes," Ormandy had told her, "it rarely opens again." She knew he was right. Positions such as hers did not open up often. She was fortunate to have the opportunity to resume her life in the orchestra once again.

—— · ——

After training at several stateside bases, first in military government and then in psychological warfare, Sam was assigned to the west of England, where he was quickly promoted to lieutenant colonel, and Edna took up the reins of the household. With Sam away and the news from overseas discouraging, loneliness and worry plagued Edna and the children during the war years, as they did all those left behind on the home front. "It was bleak," she said. But they had friends to rely on for companionship, and school and work to keep them busy, which helped. Sam had been right when he told Edna to take on a challenge. Her life in the orchestra did make the time pass more quickly.

However, there was one problem Sam had not foreseen, and that was Eugene Ormandy. Very soon after Sam left, the maestro began, in Phillips's words, "to lay siege" to her, sending passionate looks in her direction during rehearsals, offering her special favors, and generally embarrassing her with his ill-disguised ardor. It was obvious to the whole orchestra what he was up to. One of his ploys was to tell her in front of the full orchestra that she needn't come in for rehearsal the next day if no music that required the harp was on the schedule. That had never been the orchestra's policy, Phillips said. The protocol was that the harpist must check in at the beginning of each rehearsal, even if the works on the program didn't call for the harp. A soloist might fall ill or some other problem might arise that would require a substitution, and the harpist had to be on hand for that possibility. Ormandy's fawning favors made Phillips squirm. She felt exposed and compromised.

As his blandishments grew more insistent, rumors began to spread, and observers started assuming that Phillips and Ormandy were having an affair. What other explanation could there be for his favoritism and longing gazes? The rumors spread so far that Sam's brother Paul heard the gossip and asked Phillips what was going on. After that, she said, she confronted Ormandy and "put a stop to it."

That, at least, is Phillips's explanation of what happened. Upon being asked for this book whether she and Ormandy actually did have an affair, she exclaimed, "That worm! You think I'd give in to him after resisting the glamorous one?"

Still, several members of the orchestra as well as others who knew her at the time thought the rumors could be true. Marilyn Costello, who eventually followed Phillips as the orchestra's principal harpist, could understand why onlookers thought that. "Ormandy could be horribly persistent," she said.[1] After Costello resisted his overtures in her first year with the orchestra, she explained, he made her life truly unpleasant for a time, frequently belittling her playing in rehearsals and causing her great embarrassment.

Whether the rumors about an affair between Ormandy and Phillips were based purely on speculation provoked by Ormandy's flagrant wooing of her or not is difficult to ascertain today. Whatever the reader chooses to believe, Phillips called it "a cheap trick" by Ormandy, and apparently by other men she declined to name, to make passes at her while Sam was overseas. She resented those overtures greatly.

Along with the thousands of wives left to manage their households while their husbands were at war, Phillips had many responsibilities at that time in addition to her orchestral duties. The first thing she had to do was learn to drive. The gardener, who had doubled as the family driver, also went to war soon after Sam did, so Phillips had no choice. "Someone had to get to the drugstore when a prescription was needed," she said. Apparently, not everyone enjoyed the ride. "From the stories about my driving that have come down the years, one would think I was a madwoman behind the wheel! But I don't think I was *that* bad. Anyway, I couldn't go too far. Gas rationing kept everyone's trips to a minimum."

Friends helped take up the slack left by Sam's absence, especially Kit Wright and her husband Sidney, who lived in a farmhouse in Wyncote on the outskirts of Philadelphia and often invited Edna and the children to stay with them. Their home was filled to the rafters, Edna said, with the Wrights' four children plus four nieces and nephews from England who had been sent over to escape the bombings. "With all those children about plus plenty of cats and dogs and chickens, Joan and David and I were well-occupied when we might otherwise have been feeling desolate."

Kit and Edna had a special bond. They had met in 1931, when Edna, a new member of the orchestra and a bit of a celebrity, had merited an invitation to the Sunday evening singing parties given by Henry and Sophie Drinker for music lovers they knew and approved of. Kit, a granddaughter of prominent industrialist Joseph Wharton, was among the attendees. The friendship between Kit and Edna lasted for more than fifty years until Kit's death in 1988. An accomplished painter and poet, Kit published a book of poems in 1957 dedicated to "My fellow explorer in the wilderness of art and daily living, Edna Phillips."[2]

During the war years, Phillips joined her orchestra colleagues in performing for servicemen stationed at Fort Dix, New Jersey, and other nearby bases. The players also contributed their services for a nationwide broadcast that inaugurated America's Community War Chest Drive, and volunteered to play at USO concerts and at the Philadelphia Naval Hospital. As painful as it was to see the suffering of the wounded men at the hospital, Phillips said, she was gratified to be able to offer some lighter moments. When she and her colleagues performed Paul White's *Sea Chanty*, "It never failed to get an enthusiastic response," she said, "and it often inspired sing-alongs that were lots of fun."

Inside the orchestra, Phillips once again made the most of the opportunities her position gave her to observe preeminent artists at work conducting and performing. She wasn't so pleased with Bruno Walter, when he came to town. Although he was the idol of many music lovers and a handsome, distinguished-looking man, she said, he talked too much for her. Stokowski, Toscanini, and most of the other conductors she favored conveyed their intentions much more economically without long explanations, but Walter talked and talked and talked. Phillips said he dragged on like Thomas Mann's *Buddenbrooks*.

"One paragraph would become a chapter and on and on as he described every vestige of a work. It was endless. He caught me yawning once and glared at me, but he kept right on talking. The surprise of it all was that in concert, everything would unfold just as the maestro had explained. He got exactly what he wanted, and the concerts were excellent. But he bored me to death. I thought I was the only one who felt that way, but one day I was talking to [concertmaster Alexander] Hilsberg, and he said Walter's rehearsals put him to sleep, too!"

Another memorable musician Phillips enjoyed seeing was the splendid pianist Artur Rubinstein, who appeared often in Philadelphia. He was a friend of Sam's and had often dined with them when he was performing in Philadelphia.

"Feature by feature, Rubinstein was rather homely," Phillips said, "but he had enormous charm that overrode his unimposing appearance." One day in the fall of 1944, after Rubinstein and Phillips had each finished rehearsing in the Academy of Music, their paths crossed at the stage door.

"I'm about to have a wonderful feast," Rubinstein announced, rubbing his hands together as if he were anticipating a fine meal. He was on his way to see the famous art collection of Dr. Albert Barnes in Merion, a suburb of Philadelphia. To be invited to see the Barnes collection of impressionist and modernist masters was a true distinction, for the irascible doctor guarded the doors of his museum ferociously, keeping out all those whom he deemed unacceptable. It didn't matter how important a person was. Barnes was notorious for slamming the door in the faces of those he considered unworthy, the richer and more socially prominent the better. It was they whom Barnes blamed for pillorying his collection of European art when he first displayed it at the Pennsylvania Academy of the Fine Arts in 1923. Rubinstein, unlike the hated socialites, had apparently impressed Barnes with the sincerity of his interest in seeing the artworks. He had a notable art collection himself and was quite knowledgeable.

On the spur of the moment, Rubinstein asked Phillips to go along with him, and she accepted, "although in the back of my mind, I knew there might be some trouble when we arrived since I wasn't officially invited," she said. "It turned out that I should have listened to my misgivings. As soon as we got to the door, Barnes let it be known that he didn't care whether I was the Philadelphia Orchestra's solo harp or Sam Rosenbaum's wife or anything: I was an intruder and I didn't belong there. For awhile, it looked as if I'd have to wait outside in the taxi while Barnes entertained his invited guest, but eventually he relented under Rubinstein's charm, and I was allowed in."

As they walked through the unique museum Barnes had built to hold his collection, the doctor showed the pianist works by Renoir, Cezanne, Matisse, Picasso, and others he had collected, along with pieces of African sculpture, American cabinetry, and metalwork, which he displayed alongside the paintings. Phillips trailed behind, fascinated. Afterward, Mrs. Barnes served tea. Somewhere in the conversation that ensued, it came out that she had moved a piece of sculpture so that she could see it better.

"My goodness, how Barnes yelled at her!" Phillips recalled. "Apparently, she had committed a mortal sin by moving a work from its assigned place. Barnes rivaled Toscanini at his most furious with that outburst! But however cantankerous he was, that afternoon was a happy interlude in a very dark period."

---

It seemed to Phillips that her spur-of-the-moment visit to the Barnes collection might be a harbinger of better times ahead. She had watched the war in Europe take a better turn after D-Day. Since then, in battle after battle, the Allies had succeeded in pushing back Hitler's armies from land they occupied. After liberating Paris, the U.S. army advanced to Luxembourg, and on September 10, 1944, the Fifth Armored Division liberated that country.

Under special orders from General Omar Bradley, the army took over a small villa and a radio station in Luxembourg City. Sam was sent there in October by the Psychological Warfare Division of the Supreme Headquarters Allied Expeditionary Force to take charge of Radio Luxembourg, which had one of the strongest transmitters in Europe and which the Germans had been using to broadcast propaganda. The Allies planned to use it for the same purpose.

As commanding officer of the Radio Luxembourg Detachment, Sam had a staff of international experts, among them the Austrian novelist and expatriate Hans Habe, who led the propaganda operations of the station for the Allies, and Stefan Heym, who had fled his native Germany to escape the Gestapo in the early 1930s.[3] Both Habe and Heym had become U.S. citizens. There were also several BBC broadcasters and Oxford dons on the staff. The team was known as the Second Mobile Radio Broadcasting Company. Its job was to create broadcasts that would influence German soldiers and civilians to surrender, while at the same time bolstering the morale of allied prisoners held by the Germans.

The station broadcast musical performances during the daytime hours, which, without Edna knowing it at first, turned out to be an even more meaningful way to communicate with Sam than by letter. Among the musical offerings Radio Luxembourg played were recordings made by the Philadelphia Orchestra, including her *Sea Chanty* album. Although Edna wrote to Sam nearly every day, their correspondence had to go through military censorship, which robbed it of some of its personality, she said, but Sam later told her that hearing her play evoked the atmosphere of home more intensely and poignantly than anything else and helped ease the pain of separation.

By December 1944, the Allied cause seemed destined for victory. Surely, peace was just around the corner, at least in Europe. With the Allies advancing inexorably on Germany, many thought Hitler would soon be forced to surrender.

In that spirit, Phillips and her old friend and mentor Carlos Salzedo accepted an invitation to another impromptu party at the Ormandys' apartment. She had been working with Salzedo on a new work she and Sam had commissioned—*Concerto for Harp and Orchestra* by Nicolai Berezowsky—which she was planning to premiere with the orchestra in late January. Salzedo was advising her on how to approach the complicated piece when the telephone rang. It was Steffi Ormandy calling to invite Edna to a party she and Eugene were having for Jascha Heifetz that evening. When she heard that Salzedo was working with Phillips, Steffi asked him to come along, happy to have another harpist at a party that promised to contain mostly violinists.

"Ah, Ed-naa, my beloved accomplice!" Salzedo exclaimed, delighted to be included in such a gathering. *Accomplice* was the right word, Phillips said, for the two of them often acted as accomplices over the years, conspiring to secure jobs for harpists they thought worthy and cooking up other intrigues to further their various causes.

The orchestra's concertmaster Alexander Hilsberg attended the party along with noted violinist Lea Luboshutz, a prominent teacher at the Curtis Institute, and several others. Heifetz had a reputation for being a cold fish, Phillips said, but that evening he was relaxed and convivial. At one point, Steffi played a recording of the *Nutcracker Suite*, and Hilsberg and Luboshutz, both Russian émigrés, danced to the "Waltz of the Flowers," swooping around the Ormandys' apartment with its Biedermeier chairs and tables hastily backed up to the walls as if they were in a ballroom. "It was a wonderful party," Phillips said, "filled with colorful characters, music, and dance." She left the party buoyed by its good cheer.

Unfortunately, that feeling was short-lived. On December 16, Hitler sent three powerful German armies—a quarter of a million men—crashing into southern Belgium. The onrush caught the U.S. commanders totally by surprise, with their troops exhausted from months of steady combat, ill equipped, low on food, and even short on winter clothing. Hitler's audacious strategy succeeded in driving a wedge into U.S. lines that came to be known as the "bulge." The Nazis quickly advanced to the middle of Luxembourg in a massive final effort to turn back the Allied tide, and for six bitterly cold, snow-filled weeks in the rugged forests of the Ardennes, the Battle of the Bulge raged on. It has been described as "the single biggest and bloodiest battle American soldiers ever fought. Over 76,000 Americans [were] killed, wounded or captured."[4]

Caught in the onslaught, across a river no wider than the Potomac from thousands of German troops, Sam and his Radio Luxembourg crew faced almost certain capture or worse. The Germans got so close, Phillips later learned, that when a U.S. officer burst into the station where Sam and his staff were still going about their duties and asked where the Germans were, Sam replied, "Spit and you'll hit one."

"At this point," Stefan Heym's biographer writes, "the Second Mobile Radio Broadcasting Company was engaged in transmissions from the powerful Radio Luxembourg. . . . It was an obvious target of enemy attack . . . [and it was] an act of considerable bravery to stay at the transmitter as the enemy's advance continued and the capture of Luxembourg began to seem likely."[5]

Finally, General Bradley ordered the Radio Luxembourg team to go off the air, burn their files, and prepare to retreat. Edna learned afterward that Hans Habe heard Sam whistling as he was pitching papers into the furnace in the basement. "How can you be so nonchalant?" Habe asked him.

"I'm fifty-five years old," Sam answered. "I've seen the most beautiful places. I've eaten the best meals, drunk the best wines, and made love to the most beautiful women. I don't give a damn."

Fortunately, as desperate as the situation was, Sam didn't have to abandon his post at Radio Luxembourg after all. Hitler's armies did not succeed in their last-gasp invasion. Generals Eisenhower and Patton ultimately rallied to bring together huge counter forces, and after six weeks of fierce fighting, the Germans were pushed back to where they had begun. The "bulge" in the Allied lines was closed, and the loss marked the beginning of the end for the Germans.

But it was a terrible time. Sam knew that back at home Edna and the children were filled with anxiety. News of the dire situation was sure to have frightened them. When the Battle of the Bulge finally ended in late January, he made a tape recording to reassure his family and sent it home. (On the tape he calls Phillips by her middle name, Megan, which he used often, knowing that she preferred it to the less euphonious Edna.)

Dearest Megan and Joan and David, and you, too, Peg and Heather, if you are all together when I turn up like this and make talky-talk out of a machine.

It is just a year since I last drove away from the Lane, but it was many months before that I really stepped out of our quiet little world into a different one. Trains and ships and planes and motors have carried me into many places. I have slept in Michigan and Virginia and Washington and New Jersey and New York and Scotland and England and France and Belgium and Holland and Germany. Now here I am living in another little country on the German border where big guns and tanks and planes and men are slugging it out to decide who goes where and when. There seems no prospect of an early decision, so there is nothing to be done meanwhile but carry on.

Are you wondering if I am very homesick and miserable at this prospect of a still longer separation from you all? You know I have never had you out of my mind. If the postman has been as faithful as I have, you must know pretty much everything I have done and thought. Every day of all these months, I have written you without a single break.

Yet, odd as it may seem, I cannot find it in me to wish to be anywhere else at this moment than just where I am. It seems to me so much more important to share in this great enterprise, in however small a way, than to indulge any personal wishes for comfort or reunion. Much as I want to be with all of you, and to share your fun and help with your problems, yet I am so convinced I can do more for you here that it just never enters my head to want to walk away from this task before my part of it is done.

Fortunately, these last four months have been among the most interesting and exciting of my life. I really feel we are doing something worthwhile here, and you too must believe that whatever you are doing without me you must try to do a little better than before, even if it is harder, because that is the way you do your share for the same great cause.

One of our programs here is called "Letters that never arrived." We read out letters that we find in the mailbags when we capture a German command post. These are from soldiers to their families and friends, or the other way. They are full of the tender messages and personal accounts that pass on paper between those who love each other. Whether they are Germans or Britons or Americans, men and women think pretty much the same thoughts and feel pretty much the same emotions, except that it is tragic to see how the German believes he has the right to practice cruelties by command of his State that I doubt he would commit in his private life. But what impresses me most is how fortunate we are in the kind of lives you and I lead, free to think and say what we like and to live as we please. And how little we have suffered even from the war, compared to the privations and sacrifices of all Europe in the sixth year of continuous destruction. Against these, the temporary trial of our separation can be borne with cheerful fortitude.

So let's all keep on doing what we are doing as merrily as we can. You, Megan, dear, pluck your famous harmonics and shed your glow over your enraptured audiences. You, Joan and David, study your books and your music and keep your possessions neat and tidy. And you, Peg and Heather, start out with your wits and your charm to convince a skeptic world that it can use you. Here, at my outpost, I shall continue to adore all of you while I scribble and gabble at the enemy and dodge his occasional missiles.

Don't have any concern about our creature comforts. It is amazing how comfortably we are housed and how adequately we are fed. Even during the recent German advance, daily life went on regularly except in the places actually evacuated when they were to come under fire or were threatened by the enemy,

We had one amusing experience. For the Sunday when the German thrust began, we had arranged a special luncheon for a group of enlisted men in the Music section as a special reward for good work. It was at an inn some distance from here in the country. It turned out that all through lunch the boys were aware of an unusual amount of noise and explosions in the surrounding fields, but they went on with the food and the wine and the speeches, and the party was voted a great success. When they emerged from the inn, they discovered the place was right smack in the line of the German advance, and not only they but the rest of the village took to the trucks and came away in a hurry. They had to thread their way on the roads through long lines of our tanks and artillery going up to positions around the inn for defense. It gave them something to remember.

Now you can see why we have little time here for moping or movies. Every day is a show of its own. We are fortunate to have a detachment full of talented and cultivated individuals. There is always someone you can talk to intelligently about what O. Henry calls "subjects." You may be quite reassured about our habits. With an eight o'clock curfew, there is nothing to do of an evening but work.

Now there is all the gossip I can add to my platter of wisdom. Let me finish with God Bless You All and *Hasta Luego* and I know you are sending me the same.[6]

On May 7, 1945, Phillips was on tour with the orchestra, the first relatively long-distance tour the orchestra had embarked on since the war began. They arrived in Buffalo, New York, that day amid excited rumors that Germany had surrendered. No verification had come yet, but the feeling that it was about to happen was so strong that Ormandy changed the program the orchestra was to play that evening to feature Beethoven's Fifth Symphony rather than the Mendelssohn symphony printed in the program. Joyous buzzing filled the air when the audience arrived for the concert. The rumors had been confirmed. General Dwight Eisenhower had accepted Germany's unconditional surrender that day in Reims, France.

When the orchestra reached the triumphant last movement of Beethoven's Fifth, the audience could contain itself no longer. It rose to its feet spontaneously and remained silent until the final notes. Then it burst into exultant, unquenchable applause until Ormandy launched into John Philip Sousa's "The Stars and Stripes Forever." This time, it was the players' turn to rise to their feet. In their joy and excitement, they played standing up, and once again tumultuous applause, mixed with tears, hugs, and prayers, rang out in the auditorium at the end and continued on into the streets as the audience poured out the doors. It was a night to remember for all.[7]

Having been promoted again during the war, Colonel Rosenbaum arrived home six months later, in November 1945, after finishing his work with the Supreme Headquarters Allied Expeditionary Force in Paris. For his service, he received the U.S. Legion of Merit, the French Legion of Honor, and decorations from Luxembourg, Belgium, Czechoslovakia, Poland, Italy, and China. He was justifiably proud of those honors, and Edna and the children were justifiably proud of him and happy to resume their lives together on School House Lane. But picking up where he left off before the war wasn't so easy for Sam. He had to reassemble the threads of his career, and for someone who led as complicated a professional life as he did, that demanded much time and energy.

It didn't help that once the war was over, the orchestra intensified its touring schedule. That took Phillips off the premises just when Sam needed her support at home so that he could devote his attention to reestablishing his career. No longer a young man, his energies sometimes flagged a bit, and for the first time, Phillips said, he grumbled about the difficulties of supervising the household while she was away. It was time, Phillips decided, to close the door on her life in the orchestra once again, and this time she knew it would be for good. She had had a wonderful run in the orchestra, but she was ready to move on.

The orchestra announced Phillips's impending resignation in March 1946, and just as they did when she arrived at the orchestra sixteen years before, the newspapers made a big story of it. The *Philadelphia*

*Evening Bulletin* ran an especially fulsome article about her departure. "It was heart strings vs. harp strings for Edna Phillips, first lady of the Philadelphia Orchestra," the story began. "The distinguished musician has made her choice. Miss Phillips, only 39, is abandoning her position in a pre-eminent symphony orchestra, giving up those scintillating evenings at the Academy, the tours, the tumultuous acclaim, that exciting shoulder-rubbing with the world's leading musicians—leaving all this for a mother's simple role."[8]

"That was really too much! Even the children laughed at that," Phillips said. "It wasn't as if my life in music was over, just one phase of it. One can lead many lives in music, and it was time for me to move on."

———•———

After staying away for nineteen years, Leopold Stokowski returned to conduct the Philadelphia Orchestra in February 1960. Of course, Edna and Sam were at the Academy of Music to hear him. As they settled into their seats before the concert, they noticed that many of the seats around them were filled with very old people who must have commandeered the tickets of their sons and daughters for the evening. Edna smiled when she heard two elderly ladies talking to each other in the row behind her.

"Did you remember to bring your cough drops?" one asked, obviously thinking of Stokowski's many lectures from the podium on the evils of coughing during a performance.

"Oh yes," the other answered. "But it's hard to choose which ones to buy these days. The drugstore has so many new flavors."

Then Stokowski swept onto the stage and crossed to the podium. Almost eighty, he was no longer the Adonis that Edna once knew. His flaxen hair had grown a bit stringy and less radiant, and his pace was not so brisk as it once was. But when he stood before the orchestra, she could tell in a moment that the magnetism was still there. Once again the players' attention was riveted on him. They were ready to follow his slightest wish. As the music began to unfold, Phillips recalled the spell that Stokowski had cast over the orchestra when she was a member, and she thought of Tabuteau's words about the maestro from years before.

"With Stokowski," he had said, "I play seven concerts, and six are colorful and glamorous and fascinating and beautifully interpreted, but in the seventh concert, something strange happens. A kind of brush fire goes through the orchestra. It becomes incandescent, and the music goes to the stars."

What a glorious world they had known.

# AFTERWORD

Edna Phillips's original plan for her memoir was to keep its focus on her years in the orchestra, and I have stuck to that plan with her biography, but she and Sam accomplished so much in their lives that I would be derelict if I didn't give at least some attention to their many achievements later on.

———

Sam Rosenbaum did indeed pick up the strands of his career after he returned from the war, and his achievements in later life were impressive. At the end of 1948, the U.S. Secretary of Labor Maurice J. Tobin named him to the position of independent trustee of the Music Performance Trust Funds for the Recording Industries. The position was created as part of a collective bargaining agreement between the record companies of North America and the American Federation of Musicians to settle a national strike that prevented the making of records for most of 1948. The AFM had staged the strike because recordings had reduced the need for live performances by musicians and drastically cut the number of jobs available to them. In the strike settlement, an independent fund was created in accord with the provisions of the Taft-Hartley Act, which was passed by the U.S. Congress the year before. The record companies agreed to pay a small royalty on each record sold, which would then be kept in a nonprofit fund for the public good. It was Sam's responsibility to organize and administer the accumulated assets.

Long active in labor relations, Sam had served as chairman of the Labor Committee of the National Association of Broadcasters when he was president of radio station WFIL in Philadelphia in 1937. In that role, he negotiated the national plan of settlement with the AFM to avert a nationwide strike of network musicians. Following that, in 1941, the U.S. Department of Labor called him in to settle the differences between the National Symphony Orchestra of Washington, D.C., and its musicians in a strike that had caused the cancellation of the National Symphony's 1940–41 season.

The *New York Times* included the following in its announcement of Sam's appointment to the trustee position in 1948: "Expressing himself specifically on the matter of records, Mr. Rosenbaum said . . . it was not surprising that musicians should protest the loss of employment resulting from the use of disks which they themselves had made. He added that 'there is an economic and human problem here which must be approached with tolerance and understanding.'"[1]

Sam's appreciation of both the manufacturers' and the musicians' sides in the dispute led James Caesar Petrillo, president of the AFM, to endorse his appointment. Edna loved the way Petrillo gave his approval, which she characterized as "If he's alright wid youse guys, he's alright wid me."

In his role as trustee, Sam set up the operating structure of the Music Performance Trust Funds and, during his tenure, distributed over $100 million of royalty income to musicians across the United States and Canada who gave free concerts in schools, parks, and other public venues. "You wonder why I have so many friends?" he once asked Edna with a twinkle in his eye.

After retiring as trustee in 1967, Sam finally had time to devote to his lifelong fascination with languages. In the ensuing years, he completed three important translations: *Maurice Ravel: Variations on His Life and Work* by H. H. Stuckenschmidt (Calder and Boyers, 1969); *Theodora, Empress of Byzantium* by Charles Diehl (Ungar Publishing Co., 1972); and *Euripides*, by Siegfried Melchinger (Ungar Publishing Co., 1973). After that, he began to explore the possibility of writing a biography of his old associate and friend Arthur Judson. He was in the process of gathering information on Judson when he died on November 9, 1972, at the age of eighty-four.

Before Edna Phillips ever met Sam Rosenbaum, she told a reporter from the *Philadelphia Evening Bulletin* that she didn't see why she shouldn't marry as long as she chose the right husband.[2] One would have to say after observing their long, successful marriage that she chose well.

As Edna Phillips foresaw when she left the orchestra, she never did step out of the world of music. She continued to commission works for the harp and work with composers to polish them, an ongoing responsibility and commitment, and she performed the premieres of the compositions with orchestras and other ensembles. She also worked on developing a solo career, traveling to "Cuba and other lovely places to concertize," and gave chamber concerts with William Kincaid and Samuel Lifschey as part of the Philadelphia Flute, Harp, and Viola Trio. She had some success as a soloist but admitted that it wasn't as easy to get herself and her harp to her various destinations as a soloist as it had been as a member of the orchestra.

What absorbed Phillips for many years were two community projects involving children and music that she gave her heart to: Young Audiences and the Settlement Music School.

Young Audiences is a national organization with the goal of developing and inspiring an understanding of music in children by having professional musicians perform in schools and interact with students.[3] An early advocate of the Young Audience philosophy, Phillips founded the organization's second chapter—the first was in Baltimore—and developed the Philadelphia chapter into an impressive organization. "It was a big job to recruit the players, teach them how to communicate with school age audiences, locate schools, make schedules, find volunteers to accompany the musicians, and, of course, raise money for the whole undertaking. It took hours and years of my time, but every moment was worth it," she said, adding that her interest in the project "probably came from being part of Stokowski's concerts for young people and seeing youngsters take so readily to music when it was presented well." Whatever prompted her dedication, she said, "I just had a bee in my bonnet to make Young Audiences work."

In the same vein, Phillips also devoted herself to another worthy project—Philadelphia's Settlement Music School (SMS). Working with her friend Sol Schoenbach, who left his position as principal bassoonist in the Philadelphia Orchestra in 1957 to become executive director of SMS, she launched its first satellite branch in the Germantown section of Philadelphia, an important step that helped propel the growth of the school, which is now the nation's largest community arts school. She continued her involvement with SMS for years as its honorary president and artistic advisor, insisting always that it maintain the highest standards.

"Sam had a favorite saying—'Kids who blow horns don't blow safes, and kids who tote fiddle cases don't land in police stations,'" she laughed. "I guess that's one reason to introduce children to music!"

Young Audiences and Settlement Music School are only two of the musical enterprises that Phillips devoted herself to after she left the orchestra. She became a director of the Musical Fund Society, the oldest continuing musical organization in the United States, and served as cultural advisor on the board of the Philadelphia Foundation, a fund for the distribution of charitable trusts. She chaired the board of the Basically Bach Festival of Philadelphia, advising its founder Michael Korn on artistic matters and working hard to ensure the festival's success. In addition, she served as music advisor to the highly respected Philadelphia Chamber Music Society.

"Edna was not just an instigator and inspirer of people and programs, but a virtual force of nature," said Robert Capanna, who became executive director of SMS after Schoenbach's retirement, serving in that position from 1982 until 2009. "Her students became her projects, and her projects created a well-ordered universe of opportunities to expand the reach of music and the place of the harp in the musical firmament. Recognizing that not all of her students were destined for the concert stage, she was a true entrepreneur, creating situations that swept up people and programs and led them to new places that they frequently discovered were just where they wanted to go. Her aim was to get everyone in her orbit to collaborate on what was the grand project of her later life—the development of a musical culture with the harp on center stage."[4]

Surprisingly, Phillips turned down the position of head of the harp department at the Curtis Institute of Music when Efrem Zimbalist, then director of the conservatory, offered it to her in 1961 after Carlos Salzedo died. She knew that Salzedo had left in the Curtis files a letter naming her as his successor, but she was so deeply involved in Young Audiences and Settlement Music School at that time that she felt she couldn't take on a new responsibility. The position went to Marilyn Costello, her successor in the Philadelphia Orchestra.

But Phillips did not give up teaching. She continued as head of the harp department at the Philadelphia Conservatory until 1972. Saying she drew sustenance from teaching, she continued working with a few students even after her retirement from the conservatory. She also returned often to the Salzedo Harp Colony in Maine to help her friend Alice Chalifoux, who had taken over its management after Salzedo's death, and to serve as a coach and mentor to its students.

Deeply involved with the harp community, Phillips often took young harpists under her wing when they needed help, even opening her Philadelphia home to students who needed a place to stay. Margarita

Csonka Montanaro was one of those students. Sam and Edna took her into their home when she came to the United States from Cuba. After completing her studies at the Curtis Institute, Margarita joined the Philadelphia Orchestra, where she was named to the co-principal harp position in 1994.

As a female pioneer in the orchestral world, Phillips didn't have the luxury of support from other women when she began her career, but after she had achieved her place in that world, she worked hard to support the women who followed her and to open doors through which they could pass.

"It always gave me great pleasure to back a good horse," she said. "I loved to act as a catalyst and get behind a young person with promise." In the process she helped numerous "good horses" acquire harps, get scholarships, and, when possible, find positions in orchestras. "I can't resist—if I see someone worthwhile—giving them a push forward."

One such promising student was Ann Hobson Pilot, who was a student at Girls' High School in Philadelphia when Phillips heard her play. Instantly recognizing the young woman's talent, Phillips, in Hobson Pilot's words, "kept her eye on me" from then on, offering helpful advice and encouragement. "She did more than mentor me," Hobson Pilot said. "She arranged for me to get a full tuition scholarship from the Philadelphia Foundation to the Cleveland Institute of Music, where I studied with Alice Chalifoux."[5] One of the country's finest harpists, Hobson Pilot became the principal harpist of the Boston Symphony, retiring after forty years in 2009 with bountiful accolades to continue her life in music as a soloist and a mentor herself to other young musicians.

Judy Loman, who served as principal harp of the Toronto Symphony from 1960 to 2001, also got a valuable push from Phillips. "Edna paved the way for me to start my career by writing a letter and getting me an audition in Toronto," Loman explained. "She was one of my inspirations, an excellent musician and a wonderful model to aspire to. There was a real presence to her. Wherever she went, you knew she was there, charming, friendly, and supportive. I'm very grateful to her."[6]

She also found time to help out friends from the orchestra. "Eight years ago Edna Phillips retired as first harpist with the Philadelphia Orchestra—which then numbered Alexander Hilsberg as first violin," a columnist in the *Philadelphia Evening Bulletin* wrote in 1954. "Now he's conductor in New Orleans and for Monday night had scheduled a Wagner program with Eileen Farrell as soloist. But his first harp had taken sick—in desperation on Sunday night he long-distanced Edna to help him out. Like a fire horse she hopped a plane, arrived in N.O. at 4 A.M., and played that night."[7]

After her children begged her to accept the offer, Phillips even sat in on a recording session with Spike Jones and his City Slickers band when they came to Philadelphia. Famous for his humorous takes on the classics, Jones was touring the country with his "Musical Depreciation Review" at the time. "I played about twelve glissandos and not much else, and I was paid a fortune!" Phillips said. "Most importantly, I got some autographs that really impressed the kids and their friends."

When Jones asked her to recommend a harpist to tour with the band on the way back to California, "I asked him what the harpist would do in his band, and he said, 'She's supposed to sit there and knit and smoke a big black cigar.'"

"You know," she said, remembering the incident with a laugh, "that's just what it's like being a harpist at times. You sit there for what seems like hours while the orchestra plays all around you. But you'd better not smoke a big black cigar!"

Numerous honors and awards crowned Phillips's achievements as the years passed. One that she thoroughly enjoyed because of the glamour of the festivities that accompanied it came at the Philadelphia Art Festival in 1955, when, along with Grace Kelly, Marian Anderson, Alexander Calder, Eugene Ormandy, and Franklin Watkins, Phillips received an award from then-mayor Joseph Clark for bringing "glory to the city through pre-eminence in art."[8] She was later named a Distinguished Daughter of Pennsylvania and then Pennsylvania's Mother of the Year. "Can you believe it?" she laughed. "Me, the one who didn't bake cookies!" Among other awards she received, she remembered especially the Gimbel Philadelphia Award "for outstanding achievement in the field of music education," which was presented to her by Eleanor Roosevelt.

In one of our last interviews, Phillips said she took great pleasure in the many lives she led in music after she left the orchestra and was happy for the recognition her efforts received. "But," she added somewhat wistfully, "I've always missed the sound of the harp in the orchestra and the marvelous music that surrounded me there."

Edna Phillips Rosenbaum died on December 2, 2003.

# APPENDIX

## The Edna Phillips Harp Commissions

*Works commissioned by Edna Phillips Rosenbaum
and Samuel R. Rosenbaum*

MANUSCRIPT AND PUBLISHING DETAILS AS OF 2011

Compiled by Clinton F. Nieweg,
Philadelphia Orchestra Principal Librarian (ret.)

Edna Phillips's personal copies of the Phillips Rosenbaum commissions (along with other music for the harp) were donated to the University of Illinois Music and Performing Arts Library by the Rosenbaum's daughter, Joan Rosenbaum Solaun, in 2004. They are currently held in the "Edna Phillips Music, 1930–1970" collection, Sousa Archives and Center for American Music, University of Illinois, hereafter abbreviated as EPM-Ill.[1]

**BACARISSE, Salvador** (b. Madrid, Spain, September 12, 1898; d. Paris, France, August 5, 1963) Spanish composer
*Concierto para Arpa e instrumentos de viento* (*Concerto in E♭ Major for Harp and Wind Instruments*), op. 92
Composed: 1954
Dedicated "to Edna Phillips"
Repository: Manuscript copy cataloged in EPM-Ill. Box 1, Folder 8: Salvador Bacarisse, "*Concerto in E♭ Major for Harp and Wind Instruments*, op. 92, transcription for harp and piano" Score, undated. Ink manuscript on onionskin paper, 48 pp. Box 2, Folder 6: Salvador Bacarisse, "Concierto para Arpa e instrumentos de viento, op. 92" P, undated.
A handwritten list from Edna Phillips (which contains items up to 1970) notes about this work, "not performed as yet."[2]

**BEREZOWSKY, Nicolai** (b. St. Petersburg, Russia, May 17, 1900; d. New York, N.Y., Aug. 27, 1953) Russian-American composer
*Concerto for Harp and Orchestra* Op. 31
Composed: 1944
"Written for and dedicated to Miss Edna Phillips"
Mvts: I. Moderato. II. Adagio. III. Allegro non tanto.
Solo Harp—3[1.2.pic] 2 3 2—4 2 3 1—tmp+2perc—str$^3$
Duration: 22 minutes
World premiere: Jan. 26, 1945, Edna Phillips, harp, the Philadelphia Orchestra, Eugene Ormandy conductor, Academy of Music
Full score and parts on rental. With original harp cadenza [and editing] by Carlos Salzedo; edition for harp and piano, 42 pp.; 31 cm. Item no. 464-00031. Publisher: Elkan-Vogel, Inc. ©1947 Rental T. Presser Co., King of Prussia, Pa.
Repositories: 1) Manuscript score (59 pp.) and parts cataloged at the Edwin A. Fleisher Collection of Orchestral Music in the Free Library of Philadelphia, call no. 1073M. 2) Cataloged and held by the New York Public Library, Music Division: Folder 6 [Concertos, harp, orchestra, op. 31], [n.d.], holograph score (reproduction) [MAI-81]; Folder 7 [Concertos, harp, orchestra, op. 31], [n.d.], holograph sketches (some photocopies) [MAI-55624] <http://digilib.nypl.org/dynaweb/ead/nypl/musberezo/@Generic__BookView>. 3) Columbia University Rare Book and Manuscript Library, New York, N.Y.: Nicolai Berezowsky (1900–1953) Papers 1917–1956, Box 6, [correspondence with] Phillips, Edna 1946, and Box 6 [correspondence with] Rosenbaum, Samuel R. 1943–1947.4) Copy cataloged in EPM-Ill. Nicholas Berezowsky: "I. Salzedo, from Concerto for harp" solo harp part, undated Ozalid copy, 8 pp., with markings by Edna Phillips.

**CHÁVEZ, Carlos** (b. Mexico City, June 13, 1899; d. Mexico City, Aug. 2, 1978) Mexican composer
A concerto for harp was commissioned from Carlos Chávez, but it never materialized. Robert L. Parker researched the commission and explained its fate in "Carlos Chávez's Phantom Harp Concerto," for *American Music* 10, no. 2 (summer 1992): 203–16.[4]

**CSONKA, Paul** (b. Austria-Hungary [now Austria], October 24, 1905; d. Palm Beach, Fla., November 25, 1995) Austrian-American composer
*Concierto de Navidad*, Christmas concert for women's chorus and harp
Composed: August 1953
Mvts: I. *Amoroso Pastorcillo*; II. *Al Niño Jesús*; III. *La Nana*. *Amoroso Pastorcillo* (text by Dianisio Solis) encourages the shepherds in the field to sing

and dance in preparation of the birth of Christ (4:13); *Al Niño Jesús* (text by Ventura de la Vega), a hymn of praise to Jesus (5:07); *La Nana* (poem by R. S. Gomis), a lullaby to the newborn babe (5:54).

Duration: ca. 15 minutes

World premiere: Edna Phillips, harp, Mt. Holyoke College Chorus, Ruth Douglass conductor, Town Hall, New York City, 1954.

Publishers: 1) Washington, D.C.: Pan American Union; New York: (sole selling agent) Peer International, ©1958. Includes biographical note on the composer in Spanish and English. Publisher plate nos. 24–27 Pan American Union

Language: Spanish with parallel English translation; words also written as text with English translation following score.

2) Peer International Corp. (Peermusic Classical) *Concierto de Navidad* para arpa y coro femenino (Christmas Concert for Harp and Women's Choir), Paul Csonka. English translation by Catherine Morris Wright. 60247-118 choral score, SSAA chorus (with soprano solo) with harp. 60246-158 harp part.

Repositories: Manuscript copy cataloged in EPM-Ill., Box 1, Folder 6: Paul Csonka "*Concierto de Navidad* for harp and female chorus" score. Contains: 1) Ink manuscript on onionskin paper, 22 pp., "revised full score with both Spanish words & English, Catherine Wright translator, Havana." 2) Ink manuscript on onionskin paper, 16 pp. 3) Ozalid copy of manuscript. Text freely rendered by S. R. Rosenbaum posted at <http://www.northshorechoral.org/seasons/04–05/pgm12052004.pdf>

Sample recording: Elektra Women's Choir sings three Christmas works with harpist Rita Costanzi. <http://www.elektra.ca/index.php?lookup=repertoire&by=cd&val=2\>.

**DELLO JOIO, Norman** (b. [Nicodemo DeGioio] New York, N.Y., Jan. 24, 1913; d. East Hampton, N.Y., July 24, 2008) U.S. composer

*Concerto for Harp and Orchestra*

Composed: February 1 to April 26, 1943

Solo Harp—1 1 2[1.2/bcl]—2 0 0 0—3perc—str

Duration: 20 minutes

World premiere: October 3, 1947, Edna Phillips, harp, Little Orchestra Society, Thomas K. Scherman conductor, Town Hall, New York City

Publisher: Carl Fischer, 0223 ©1946, first published 1947. Rental agent: T. Presser Co., King of Prussia, Pa.

Sample recordings: 1) Edward Vito, harp, Little Orchestra Society, Thomas K. Scherman conductor, Columbia analog, 33 1/3 rpm, mono, 12 in. LP 1950. 2) Ann Hobson Pilot, Harp, New Zealand Symphony, James Sedares conductor, Koch International, 1993.

**DOHNANYI, Ernö** [Ernst von] (b. Pozsony, Hungary [now Bratislava, Slovakia], July 27, 1877; d. New York, N.Y., Feb. 9, 1960) Hungarian composer
*Concertino for Harp and Chamber Orchestra* op. 45
I. Andante. Allegro ma non troppo; II. Allegretto vivace; III. Adagio non troppo.
Completed: Aug. 17, 1952, Tallahassee, Fla.
Commissioned by Edna Phillips and Samuel Rosenbaum
Solo Harp—1 1 1—1 0 0 0—str
Duration: 15 to 16 minutes
World premiere: Jan. 16, 1963, Athens, Ohio, Lucile Jennings, Harp, Ohio University Symphony Orchestra, Karl Ahrendt, conductor
Publisher: Associated Music Publishers Inc. ©1952; Rental agent: G. Schirmer, Chester, N.Y. Piano reduction (36 pp.) + solo harp part (22 pp.); Solo harp part (22 pp.).
Publisher: Lyra Music Publications, Palm Bay, Fl. ©1981, http://www.lyramusic.com.
Repository: Manuscript: British Library, Add. Ms Mus. 10.803 (composing score)
Sample recordings: 1) Lucy Wakeford, Harp, English Sinfonia, John Farrer, conductor, ASV1107, 2000. 2) Sara Cutler, Harp, American Symphony Orchestra, Leon Botstein, conductor, Bridge 9160, 2001. 3) Clifford Lantaff, Harp, BBC Philharmonic Orchestra, Matthias Bamert conductor, Chandos 10245, 2004.

**GINASTERA, Alberto** (b. Buenos Aires, Argentina, April 11, 1916; d. Geneva, Switzerland, June 25, 1983) Argentine composer
*Concerto for Harp and Orchestra* op. 25 [*Concierto para arpa e orquestra*, op. 25] (1956–65)
Commissioned: 1956, completed 1964, revised 1968/1974
Commissioned by Edna Phillips and Samuel Rosenbaum for the Philadelphia Orchestra
"Composed for and dedicated to Edna Phillips"
Mvts: I. Allegro giusto (8'); II. Molto moderato (6'); III. Cadenza: Liberamente capriccioso—Vivace (9').
Solo Harp—2[1.2/pic] 2 2 2—2 2 0 0—tmp+4perc(tambn, tamtam, crot, claves, woodblk, sd, bd, guiro, td, whip, maracas, xyl, glock, field dr, 2 tri, 4 tom-toms, 4 cowbells, 3 sus cym, 3 bongos)—cel—str [8.8.6.6.4—maximum number of players]
Duration: ca. 23 minutes
World premiere: Feb. 18, 1965, Nicanor Zabaleta, Harp, the Philadelphia

Orchestra, Eugene Ormandy conductor, Philadelphia. [Miss Phillips had retired from playing by the time Ginastera finished the work.]

Publisher: Boosey & Hawkes ©1956, 1974. Harp and Piano Reduction by Meredith Davies M-051-38014-5. Harp Solo M-060-03100-7. Study Score ©1974, Hawkes Pocket Score 1185, M-060-09009-7. Large Full Score M-060-03099-4.

Repository: Manuscript copy cataloged in EPM-Ill., Box 1, Folder 1: Alberto Ginastera, *Concierto para arpa e orquestra*, op. 25, Solo harp part, undated Ozalid, 44 pp.

Sample Recordings: 1) *Concierto para harpa y Orquestra*. Soloist Nicanor Zabaleta, Harp. Conductor Jean Martinon. Orchestre National de l'ORTF Paris [French National Orchestra]. 1968 version. 1970 LP. (Includes works by Saint-Saens and Tailleferre.) Program notes by H. J. Zingel in German, English, and French. Deutsche Grammophon 2530 008. 2) *Concerto for Harp*. Soloist Ann Hobson Pilot, Harp. Conductor Isaiah Jackson. English Chamber Orchestra. June 15, 1994. Studio CD, Koch International Classics 3-7261-2H1. 3) *Concerto for Harp*. Soloist Nancy Allen. Conductor Enrique Bátiz. Ciudad Philharmonic/Orquesta Filarmonica de la Ciudad, Mexico. Recorded at the Sala Nezahualcoyotl, Mexico City. Program and biographical notes ([5] pp.: ports.) in container. 1989. Studio CD, ASV CD DCA 654.

**GLANVILLE-HICKS, Peggy** (b. Melbourne, Australia, Dec. 29, 1912; d. Darlinghurst, Sydney, Australia, June 25, 1990) Australian composer

*Concertino antico for Harp and String Quartet* "using an ancient mode set by Flavius Josephus in A.D. 1"

Composed: 1955

"Written for and dedicated to Edna Phillips, München 6.7.55. Commissioned by Judge [*sic*] Samuel Rosenbaum"

Mvts: I. Ceremony: *Maestoso*, Rag of Bilaval (C Major) Lydian Mode; II. Ritual, *Lento e molto misterioso* (Same as theme from Meditation for Orchestra, 1965); III. Roundelay, *Giocoso tranquillo*.

World premiere: Jan. 17, 1958, Edna Phillips, harp, and the Juilliard String Quartet, Library of Congress, Coolidge Auditorium, Washington, D.C.

Publisher: Lyon & Healy Publications ©1995. Harp part 702680-145. Harp part and string quartet parts 702680-150. Piano reduction with Harp, arr. Cheryl Dungan Cunningham 702680-155. (Allows for performances with piano instead of string quartet.)

Repository: Box 29, Mitchell Library, State Library of New South Wales, Australia, Peggy Glanville-Hicks papers.

Recording: Library of Congress, National Audio-Visual Conservation Center (Culpeper, Va.) holds the concert recording of the premier performance.

**GREEN, Ray** (b. Cavendish, Mo., Sept. 13, 1908; d. New York, N.Y., April 16, 1997) U.S. composer
*Rhapsody on Appalachian Folk Tunes* for harp and chamber orchestra, AKA *Lonesome Valley*
Composed: 1949–50
Solo Harp—2 1 2 2—2 2 1 0—tmp + perc—str
World premiere: 1953, Edna Phillips, Harp, with the Birmingham Symphony (now Alabama Symphony), Arthur Bennett Lipkin, conductor
Publisher: AME (American Music Edition, founded in 1951 by composer Ray Green)
Repositories: AME Archives: Northwestern University Library
Manuscript copy cataloged in EPM-Ill., Box 2, Over-sized scores and recordings, Folder 1, Ray Green "Rhapsody for Harp and Orchestra," July 25, 1950, Contains: score, Ozalid, with conductor's markings, 66 pp.; Solo harp part, ink manuscript, 16 pp., New York, with markings by Edna Phillips.

**HAIEFF, Alexei** (b. Blagoveshchensk, Siberia, Aug. 25, 1914; d. Rome, Italy, March 1, 1994) Russian-American composer
*Eclogue "La nouvelle Héloïse"* for harp and string quartet
Composed: manuscript score dated Rome, July 15, 1953
Commissioned through the League of Composers on its 30th Anniversary by Samuel Rosenbaum.
Dedication: "For Miss Phillips"
World premiere: May 9, 1954, Edna Phillips, harp, with the New Music String Quartet for the League of Composers, Carnegie Recital Hall, New York.
Publisher: Chappell & Co., New York, ©1963 as Eclogue "La Nouvelle Heloise" for harp and string orchestra
Repositories: 1) Composer archives: <http://www.nypl.org/ead/2553 #id3698044> The Alexei Haieff Papers, JPB 96-2, Music Division, New York Public Library, Astor, Lenox and Tilden Foundations. Box 1, Folder 5. New York: Chappell and Co., 1963. 1 [published] score (28 pp.) [MAI-43672] Emendations in pencil. Box 1, Folder 6. New York: Chappell and Co., 1963. 20 parts. [MAI-43678] Solo harp part, violin I, violin II, viola, violoncello and bass parts. Box 4, Folders 14 & 15. ms. score (16 pp.) [MAI-43209] Manuscript reproduction. 2) Copy cataloged in EPM-Ill., Box 2, Folder 5: Alexei Haieff, "Eclogue 'La Nouvelle Heloise' for Harp and String Orchestra," S and P, 1963. Published version, with handwritten annotations.

Published score and parts in 16 academic libraries: <http://www.worldcat.org/title/ecologue-for-harp-and-string-orchestra-la-nouvelle-heloise/oclc/4619446&referer=brief_results> [Haieff wrote a different *Eclogue* in 1945 for violoncello and piano]

Rehearsal tape: Library of Congress, Washington, D.C. OCLC no.: 50538771. American Harp Society no. 56 (Performers: Ann Hobson, harp; C. Glenn, violin; A. Jempelis, violin; F. Tursi, viola; A. Harris, cello). Recorded on June 28, 1969, during the American Harp Society National Conference in Rochester, N.Y. Cataloged from information supplied by the American Harp Society; actual tape contents may vary.

**KRENEK, Ernst** (b. Vienna, Austria, Aug. 23, 1900; d. Palm Springs, Calif., Dec. 22, 1991) U.S. composer born in Austria

*Concerto for Harp and Chamber Orchestra* op. 126

Composed for and dedicated "to Edna Phillips"

Mvts: I. Andante con molto; II. Allegretto; III. Adagio.

Work finished: February 17, 1951

Solo Harp—1 1 1—2 1 0 0—str

Duration: 19 to 20 minutes

World premiere: Dec. 12, 1952, Edna Phillips, harp, the Philadelphia Orchestra, Eugene Ormandy conductor, Academy of Music

Publisher: Vienna: Universal Edition ©1961, orchestra score and parts on rental. Rental agent: European American Music Distributors LLC. Harp and piano reduction ©1961 UE12434

Repositories: Parts masters from Sam Rosenbaum cataloged at the Edwin A. Fleisher Collection of Orchestral Music in the Free Library of Philadelphia, call no. 368M.

Sample recording: Krenek: *Concerto for Harp and Chamber Orchestra* and *The Ballad of the Railroads*, C24, conductor, Ernst Krenek, Vienna Radio Symphony Orchestra.

**McDONALD, Harl** (b. Boulder, Colo., July 27, 1899; d. Princeton, N.J., March 30, 1955) U.S. composer

Suite *From Childhood* for harp and orchestra

Work composed: 1940.

Dedication: "Composed for Edna Phillips."

Commissioned by Samuel R. Rosenbaum.

Mvts: I. Allegro moderato; II. Molto moderato; III. Allegro moderato vigorosamente. Cadenzas in mvts I and III, Carlos Salzedo.

"The work combines English nursery rhymes and everlasting folk-melodies."

Paraphrase on *I saw three ships* and *Lavender's blue* and *Oranges and Lemons*.
Solo Harp—2[1/pic. 2] 2 3 2—3 2 0 0—tmp—str
Duration: 24 minutes
World premiere: Jan. 17, 1941, Edna Phillips, harp, with the Philadelphia Orchestra, Eugene Ormandy conductor, Academy of Music
Publisher: Elkan-Vogel, Inc. Rental agent: T. Presser Co., King of Prussia, Pa.
Repositories: 1) Copy cataloged in EPM-Ill., Box 1, Folder 2: Harl McDonald "Concerto for Harp and Orchestra: 'Suite from Childhood,' third movement" Solo harp part, undated. Ozalid copy, with pasteovers, 7 pp. 2) Manuscript score (135 pp.) and parts, cataloged at the Edwin A. Fleisher Collection of Orchestral Music in the Free Library of Philadelphia, call no. 994M. 3)Cataloged in University of North Texas Library, Denton, TX 76203.
Recording: 1) RCA Victor, 1941. Edna Phillips, Harp; Harl McDonald, conductor. 2) Included on *Nostalgique* recording featuring twentieth-century works for solo harp and orchestra. Harp, Anna Mason Stockton, conductor, Felix Slatkin <www.harp.com>, 2994-05.

**NORDOFF, Paul** (b. Philadelphia, Pa., June 4, 1909; d. Herdecke, North Rhine–Westphalia, Germany, Jan. 18, 1977) U.S. composer
*Trio for Harp, Flute and Viola*
Work composed: 1942
Commissioned by Edna Phillips
World premiere: June 26, 2004, First movement only: Southampton Trio, flutist Nicole Lambert, violist James Day, and harpist Cheryl Dungan Cunningham, for the American Harp Society National Conference, Philadelphia, Pa.[5]

**WHITE, Paul** (b. Bangor, Maine, Aug. 22, 1895; d. Henrietta near Rochester, N.Y., May 31, 1973) U.S. composer
*Sea Chanty*, Quintet for harp and string quartet (string bass optional)
Mvts: I. Allegro non troppo, *Blow the Man Down*; II. Andante espressivo, *Tom's Gone to Hilo*; III. Allegro Giocoso, *When Johnny Comes to Hilo*.
Work composed: 1941–42
Dedicated "to Edna Phillips"
Duration: 15 minutes
World premiere: March 4, 1942, Edna Phillips, harp, with the Rochester Philharmonic Orchestra [strings], José Iturbi conductor, Rochester, N.Y. RPO program note: "This work was commissioned by Mr. Samuel R. Rosenbaum of Philadelphia, for his wife Edna Phillips for many years

harpist with the Philadelphia Orchestra. She is the soloist for the world premiere of the composition which we hear this evening."

Mr. White furnished the following notes concerning the score for the world premier: "Sonata Allegro form, using above chanty and a "somewhat" original tune of my own for the second theme. The chanty—a short development. The chanty in minor mode; repeated in major—short coda. Bits of the tune appear, the complete tune, harp cadenza, the tune in reverse, repetition of tune and short coda."

Publisher: Elkan-Vogel, Inc. ©1944 Rental: Theodore Presser Co., King of Prussia, Pa. Harp and Piano score 164-00208; two sets of cadenzas are incorporated in this work—one by the composer, the other by Edna Phillips. Harp part 164-00208H. Quintet parts 164-00208P.

Repositories: 1) Oversize manuscript score copy cataloged in EPM-Ill. Box 2, Folder 3: Paul White "Sea Chanty Quintet" score, 1941. Pencil manuscript, unpaged. Box 2, Folder 4: Paul White "Sea Chanty" sound recording (two 78 discs), undated. 2) Manuscript score (28 pp.) and parts; Large folio, cataloged at the Edwin A. Fleisher Collection of Orchestral Music in the Free Library of Philadelphia, call no. 981M. 3) Composer Manuscript archives: Paul White (000.48): Location: A3A 2, 3, Sibley Music Library at the Eastman School of Music, Rochester, N.Y.

Original recording: Paul White: *Sea Chanty for Harp and Strings* (Harpist Edna Phillips with string quintet, Eugene Ormandy conductor; Columbia Records). MX 259 Columbia Masterworks 1943. 2 analog, 78 rpm sound discs, 12 inch. 71713-D Columbia Masterworks and 71714-D Columbia Masterworks. Notes: "Under the musical direction of Eugene Ormandy." Program notes in album. Performer notes: Edna Phillips, harp; Alexander Hilsberg, Sol Ruden, violins; Samuel Roens, viola; Samuel Mayes, violoncello; Anton Torello, double bass.

# NOTES

## CHAPTER 1. IN THE LIONS' DEN

1. Laura Lee, *Philadelphia Evening Bulletin*, May 8, 1930, Free Library of Philadelphia Newspapers and Microfilm Center.

2. Quoted in Neuls-Bates, *Women in Music*, 202.

3. Ammer, *Unsung*, 118–38.

4. J. Michele Edwards, "North America since 1920," chapter 9 in Pendle, *Women and Music*, 359.

5. "Reading Musician Named Harpist in Orchestra at Roxy's Theatre, New York," *Reading (Pa.) Times*, October 1, 1927, family collection.

6. Hall, *Best Remaining Seats*, 71–91.

7. Mordaunt Hall, "New Roxy Theatre Has Gala Opening," *New York Times*, March 12, 1927.

8. Hall, *Best Remaining Seats*, 120–35.

9. Horowitz, *Classical Music in America*, 346.

10. Edwin H. Schloss, *Philadelphia Record*, February 26, 1931.

11. Daniel, *Stokowski*, 227.

12. "Angel's Disciple," *Time*, September 14, 1959, www.time.com/time/archive, accessed May 4, 2012.

13. Lawrence and Salzedo, *Method for the Harp*, 431–44.

14. Owens, *Carlos Salzedo*, 94–116.

## CHAPTER 2. A FORMIDABLE ARENA

1. Associated Press dispatch, January 12, 1929, quoted by Daniel in *Stokowski*, 300.

2. "Leopold Anton Stanislaw Boleslaw Stokowski," *Time*, cover story, April 28, 1930, www.Time.com/time/archives, accessed May 4, 2012.

3. Kupferberg, *Those Fabulous Philadelphians*, 22–29.

4. Horowitz, *Classical Music in America*, 181.

5. Lebrecht, *Maestro Myth*, 142.

6. Kupferberg, *Fabulous Philadelphians*, 34.

7. Ibid., 40.

8. Samuel Lacier, *Philadelphia Public Ledger*, March 3, 1916, Free Library of Philadelphia Newspapers and Microfilm Center.

9. "Vast Throng Hears Mahler Symphony," *New York Times*, April 10, 1916, New York Times Archives, www.NYTimes.com, accessed May 4, 2012.

10. Mueller, *American Symphony Orchestra*, 151.

11. Toff, *Monarch of the Flute*, 237.

12. Chasins, *Leopold Stokowski*, 89.

13. Joseph Horowitz, "A Window on Stokowski's Greatness," *New York Times*, March 5, 2000.

14. Ewen, *Music Comes to America*, 67.

15. Burt, *Perennial Philadelphians*, 473.

16. Olin Downes, "Stokowski Triumphs," *New York Times*, December 17, 1924, New York Times Archives, www.NYTimes.com, accessed May 4, 2012.

17. Harold C. Schonberg, "An Audience's Conductor," *New York Times*, September 14, 1977.

18. Ardoin, *Philadelphia Orchestra*, appendix.

19. Kupferberg, *Fabulous Philadelphians*, 54.

20. "Stokowski's Satire," *Time*, April 26, 1926, Free Library of Philadelphia Newspapers and Microfilm Center.

21. Kupferberg, *Fabulous Philadelphians*, 91–93.

22. Story told to the author many years later by Viola Brehm (a member of the Chestnut Hill Women's Committee for the Philadelphia Orchestra, who was the young lady in question).

23. Henry Prunières, "A French Music Critic Hears American Orchestras," *New York Times*, December 7, 1930, New York Times Archives, www.NYTimes. com, accessed May 4, 2012.

24. Ammer, *Unsung*, 249–54.

### CHAPTER 3. THE LITTLE GOAT

1. Shanet, *Philharmonic*, 249.

2. Daniel, *Stokowski*, 315–16.

### CHAPTER 4. KEEPING UP WITH THE SPEED KINGS

1. "Solo Harpist to Be First Girl in Philadelphia Orchestra," *Philadelphia Public Ledger*, September 14, 1930. "Woman Harpist for Phila. Orchestra," *Philadelphia Record,* September 14, 1930, Free Library of Philadelphia Newspapers and Microfilm Center.
2. Robinson, *Stokowski*, 22.
3. Daniel, *Stokowski*, 194.
4. Kupferberg, *Fabulous Philadelphians*, 59.

### CHAPTER 5. ONE STEP AHEAD OF THE SHERIFF

1. Samuel L. Laciar, *Philadelphia Public Ledger*, October 4, 1930, Free Library of Philadelphia Newspapers and Microfilm Center.
2. Ibid.
3. Wister, *Twenty-Five Years of the Philadelphia Orchestra*, 48–58.
4. "Stokowski in New Studio," *New York Times*, October 13, 1930, New York Times Archives, www.NYTimes.com, accessed May 6, 2012.
5. Hans Fantel, "Stokowski, an Audio Prophet," *New York Times*, May 30, 1982.
6. Sergei Rachmaninoff, quoted in "In Their Own Words: The Artist and the Gramophone," *Gramophone*, April 1931, 8–11.
7. Burt, *Perennial Philadelphians*, 475.

### CHAPTER 6. A SEASON OF FIRSTS

1. Stokowski's seating plan was eventually adopted by most orchestras and is currently in general use.
2. Daniel, *Stokowski*, 316.
3. Kupferberg, *Fabulous Philadelphians*, 81.
4. Anecdote Salzedo told to Phillips.
5. "Stokowski Offers Music from Ether," *New York Times*, December 18, 1930.
6. Daniel, *Stokowski*, 263.
7. Chasins, *Leopold Stokowski*, 130–31.
8. Daniel, *Stokowski*, 266.
9. Chasins, *Leopold Stokowski*, 130.
10. David Patrick Stearns, "Remembering Stoky," *Philadelphia Inquirer*, April 15, 2007.
11. Daniel, *Stokowski*, 280–82.

## CHAPTER 7. "ANSWER YES OR NO"

1. Samuel R. Rosenbaum, "The Philadelphia Orchestra and Robin Hood Dell," *Tempo*, no. 8 (September 1944): 10–12.

2. "Open-Air Concerts for Philadelphia," *New York Times*, June 1, 1930.

3. Kupferberg, *Fabulous Philadelphians*, 87.

4. Roger Dettmer, *Fanfare* 9, no. 1 (September/October 1985): 58.

5. Quoted in Kupferberg, *Fabulous Philadelphians*, 88.

6. Carles painted the portrait that appears as the frontispiece of this book. Phillips did not know him at the time and was unaware that he was sketching her for a painting that would eventually be titled *The Harpist*.

7. "Stokowski in a Blue Shirt Conducts Jobless Band," *Philadelphia Public Ledger*, May 4, 1932, Free Library of Philadelphia Newspapers and Microfilm Center.

8. Norman Abbott, "Stokowski's $200,000," *Philadelphia Record*, April 17, 1932, Free Library of Philadelphia Newspapers and Microfilm Center.

9. Kupferberg, *Fabulous Philadelphians*, 89, and Daniel, *Stokowski*, 236–37. Original sources: *Philadelphia Evening Bulletin*, September 28–30, 1932; *Philadelphia Public Ledger*, October 9, 1932.

10. Quoted in the *Philadelphia Public Ledger*, October 9, 1932, and the *New York Times*, October 16, 1932.

11. David Patrick Stearns, "I Remember Stoky," *Philadelphia Inquirer*, April 15, 2007.

12. Storch, *Marcel Tabuteau*, 130.

## CHAPTER 8. "MORTALLY WOUNDED"

1. Seib, *Player*, 173.

2. Ibid.

3. Allen Barra, "They Didn't Get Much Better than Matty," *Philadelphia Inquirer*, September 23, 2003.

4. "Christy Mathewson Dies Unexpectedly," *New York Times*, October 8, 1925, New York Times Archives, www.NYTimes.com, accessed April 28, 2012.

5. Seib, *Player*, 173.

6. Special to the *New York Times*, Jan. 9, 1933, Free Library of Philadelphia Newspapers and Microfilm Center.

7. "Plane Crash Kills Mathewson's Bride," *New York Times*, January 9, 1933, Free Library of Philadelphia Newspapers and Microfilm Center.

8. Bylaws, Cosmopolitan Club of Philadelphia.

9. "Phila. Orchestra Harpist to Wed Patron of Music," *Philadelphia Inquirer*, May 7, 1933, Free Library of Philadelphia Newspapers and Microfilm Center.

10. Laura Lee, *Philadelphia Evening Bulletin*, May 8, 1930, Free Library of Philadelphia Newspapers and Microfilm Center.

### CHAPTER 9. WAR ON BROAD STREET

1. Hans Fantel, "Stokowski, an Audio Prophet," *New York Times*, May 30, 1982, New York Times Archives, www.NYTimes.com, accessed May 7, 2012.

2. *A Musical Galaxy*, Victor Talking Machine Co., Camden, N.J., 1927.

3. Daniel, *Stokowski*, 318.

4. Using the surname of her second husband, Rosamond Bernier co-founded the prestigious art magazine *L'œil* in 1950 in Paris. Returning to the United States in 1970, she became a much sought-after lecturer, appearing at the Metropolitan Museum of Art more than two hundred times as well as at numerous other venues. Calvin Tompkins, in the March 13, 2008, *New Yorker*, called her "the world's most glamorous lecturer on art and high culture." She has published a second book, *Some of My Lives: A Scrapbook Memoir*.

5. "Stokowski Denies He's a Communist," *Philadelphia Evening Bulletin*, December 9, 1933, Free Library of Philadelphia Newspapers and Microfilm Center.

6. Chasins, *Leopold Stokowski*, 142.

7. Ibid., 126.

8. "Manager Resigns in Stokowski Rift," *New York Times*, October 24, 1934, New York Times Archives, www.NYTimes.com, accessed May 7, 2012.

9. Kupferberg, *Fabulous Philadelphians*, 97.

10. Daniel, *Stokowski*, 335.

11. *Philadelphia Evening Bulletin*, December 9, 1934, Free Library of Philadelphia Newspapers and Microfilm Center.

12. *Philadelphia Record*, December 13, 1934.

13. *Philadelphia Inquirer*, December 14, 1934.

14. *Philadelphia Inquirer*, December 11, 1934.

15. *Philadelphia Inquirer*, December 14, 1934.

16. January 6, 1935, *Philadelphia Record*, Free Library of Philadelphia Newspapers and Microfilm Center.

17. Leopold Stokowski to Flora Greenwood McCurdy, letter, in private collection of Alexander McCurdy, son of Flora Greenwood McCurdy.

### CHAPTER 10. HONOR AMONG WOMEN

1. Susan Davis, "Renowned Cellist Elsa Hilger Celebrates her 98th Birthday," *Shelburne (Vermont) News*, April 2002.

2. David Madison, interview by the author, May 1, 1991.

3. Ammer, *Unsung*, 250.

4. Toff, *Monarch of the Flute*, 129.

5. Roger Dettmer, "Eugene Ormandy, An Appreciation," *Fanfare* 9, no. 1 (September–October 1985): 54–69.

6. Herbert Kupferberg, "The Ormandy Era," in Ardoin, *Philadelphia Orchestra*, 72–91.

### CHAPTER 11. A MONTH OUT OF SCHOOL

1. Kupferberg, *Fabulous Philadelphians*, 5.

2. "Philadelphians in Pullmans," *Time*, April 27, 1936, www.Time.com/time/archives, accessed May 7, 2012.

3. Ibid.

4. Philadelphia Orchestra Program, October 1936, Philadelphia Orchestra Association Archives, Academy of Music, Philadelphia.

5. H. Howard Taubman, "Stokowski Finds Us Turning to Music," *New York Times*, June 14, 1936.

6. Ibid.

7. Philadelphia Orchestra Program, October 1936.

8. Ibid.

### CHAPTER 12. ON TO *FANTASIA*

1. Kupferberg, *Fabulous Philadelphians*, 103.

2. Edna Phillips interviewed by Sharon Eisenhauer October 5, 1991, for the Eugene Ormandy Oral History Project conducted by the University of Pennsylvania Library. Transcripts are kept in the Otto E. Albrecht Music Library in Van Pelt-Dietrich Library Center, Philadelphia.

3. "A Little Garlic," *Time*, November 20, 1939, www.Time.com/time/archive, accessed May 8, 2012.

4. *Philadelphia Public Ledger*, July 6, 1937.

5. Quoted in Daniel, *Stokowski*, 350.

6. Martha Kerr, "Garbo Finds Love," *Modern Screen*, June 10, 1938.

7. "Idyl," *Time*, March 14, 1938, www.Time.com/time/archive, accessed May 8, 2012.

8. Leopold Stokowski to Edna Phillips, letter, family collection.

9. *Musical America*, October 1938.

10. Kupferberg, *Fabulous Philadelphians*, 125–26.

11. Daniel, *Stokowski*, 379–80.

12. Ibid., 382.

13. Gabler, *Walt Disney*, 307.

14. Ibid., 308.

15. Lesley Valdes, *Philadelphia Inquirer*, September 16, 1990, Free Library of Philadelphia Newspapers and Microfilm Center.

16. Ibid.

17. Sol Schoenbach, speaking at "Leopold Stokowski: Making Music Matter," a symposium sponsored by the Friends of the Library and the Music Department of the Penn Libraries, University of Pennsylvania, April 15, 1998. A recording of the speakers is in the Scholarly Commons Repository.

18. Gabler, *Walt Disney*, 313–14.

19. Daniel, *Stokowski*, 389–90.

### CHAPTER 13. A SILENT EXIT

1. Chasins, *Leopold Stokowski*, 178–86.

2. "Rival Tours," *Time*, June 10, 1940, www.Time.com/time/archive, accessed May 8, 2012.

3. Ibid.

4. Daniel, *Stokowski*, 399–416.

5. Ibid., 400.

6. Daniel, *Stokowski*, 412–15.

7. Howard Taubman, "Youth Concert at Carnegie Hall; Stokowski Returns," *New York Times*, September 19, 1940, New York Times Archives, www.NYTimes.com/archive, accessed May 8, 2012.

8. Daniel, *Stokowski*, 414.

9. Ibid., 420.

10. Ibid., 419–21.

11. *Philadelphia Evening Bulletin*, December 20, 1940, Free Library of Philadelphia Newspapers and Microfilm Center.

12. Daniel, *Stokowski*, 420.

13. *Philadelphia Evening Bulletin*, December 20, 1940, Free Library of Philadelphia Newspapers and Microfilm Center.

14. Edwin H. Schloss, *Philadelphia Record*, December 7, 1940, Free Library of Philadelphia Newspapers and Microfilm Center.

15. "Philadelphia Bids Stokowski Return; Orchestra Head Empowered to Negotiate Contract; 'Certain Limitations' Set," *New York Times*, December 12, 1940, New York Times Archives, www.NYTimes.com/archive, accessed May 8, 2012.

16. Quoted in *Philadelphia Evening Bulletin*, March 13, 1941, Free Library of Philadelphia, Newspapers and Microfilm Center.

17. Daniel, *Stokowski*, 424.

## CHAPTER 14. CAJOLING AND
## SEDUCING COMPOSERS

1. Robert L. Parker, "Carlos Chavez's Phantom Harp Concerto," *American Music* 10, no. 2 (1992), 203–16.

2. See the appendix for a list of composers and compositions.

3. Samuel L. Laciar, "The Orchestra: Miss Phillips Scores as Soloist," *Philadelphia Public Ledger*, January 20, 1941, Free Library of Philadelphia Newspapers and Microfilm Center.

4. "Philadelphia Orchestra Loses Harpist," *Philadelphia Public Ledger*, March 15, 1941, Free Library of Philadelphia Newspapers and Microfilm Center.

5. *Ibid.*

6. Collins, *America's Women*, 348.

7. J. R. Josephs, "Motherhood and Careers Mix into Success Stories," *Philadelphia Evening Bulletin*, November 23, 1939.

8. Ellen Taussig, "First Harpist's Harp Now Takes Second Place," *Philadelphia Ledger*, June 19, 1941.

9. Jay Nordlinger, "A Point of View Made Loud and Clear," *New York Sun*, January 9, 2007.


## CHAPTER 15. WAR STORIES

1. Marilyn Costello, interview by the author, October 14, 1991.

2. Wright, *Color of Life*.

3. On Habe, see Whiting, *Ghost Front*, 85. On Heym, see Hutchison, *Stefan Heym*, 46.

4. PBS, *Battle of the Bulge*.

5. Hutchison, *Stefan Heym*, 46.

6. Sam Rosenbaum, audiotape, Jan.–Feb. 1945, transcript provided by Joan Rosenbaum Solaun.

7. Résumé of the Season, 1944–45, Philadelphia Orchestra Association Archives, Academy of Music, Philadelphia.

8. Don Fairbairn, "Heart Strings vs. Harp Strings," *Philadelphia Evening Bulletin*, March 26, 1946.


## AFTERWORD

1. "Musicians Select Trustee for Fund," *New York Times*, December 11, 1948, New York Times Archives, www.NYTimes.com, accessed May 8, 2012.

2. Laura Lee, *Philadelphia Evening Bulletin*, May 8, 1930, Free Library of Philadelphia Newspapers and Microfilm Center.

3. For more information about Young Audiences, see www.youngaudiences. org.

4. Robert Capanna, interview by author, January 16, 2012.

5. Ann Hobson Pilot, telephone interview by author, June 16, 2011.

6. Judy Loman, telephone interview by author, August 1, 2011.

7. "In Our Town," Earl Selby, *Philadelphia Evening Bulletin*, February 11, 1954.

8. William J. Lohan, "Thousands Flock to Museum For Start of Art Festival," Philadelphia Evening Bulletin, Feb. 26, 1955.

### APPENDIX

1. The listing of the Edna Phillips Harp Commissions that accompanied "A Tribute to Edna Phillips," written by Jane B. Weidensaul for the *American Harp Journal* 15, no. 4 (winter 1996), provided the starting point for this compilation.

2. See "The Bacarisse Commission: An Exercise in Bibliographic Detection" by Mark Palkovic in the above-cited *American Harp Journal* for further information on the Bacarisse commission.

3. Standard orchestra instrumentation is used throughout the appendix to indicate the instruments used in each of the works listed.

4. "Samuel Rosenbaum, Philadelphia Orchestra Vice President, announced in 1938 his commission to Chávez for a concerto for harp and 'radio orchestra.' Other projects prevented Chávez from writing the piece." See Parker, *Carlos Chávez*.

5. According to Cheryl Cunningham: "Jim Day, our violist, transcribed the parts from the original manuscript score. To our knowledge it was never published. It was probably never played because it is very difficult. The score is now in the Edna Phillips Collection at the University of Illinois." Cheryl Cunningham to Clinton Nieweg, email July 12, 2011.

# BIBLIOGRAPHY

Ammer, Christine. *Unsung: A History of Women in American Music.* Portland, Ore.: Amadeus Press, Century Edition, 2001.

Ardoin, John, ed. *The Philadelphia Orchestra: A Century of Music.* Philadelphia: Philadelphia Orchestra Association and Temple University Press, 1999.

Arian, Edward. *Bach, Beethoven, and Bureaucracy: The Case of the Philadelphia Orchestra.* University of Alabama Press, 1971.

Bernier, Rosamond. *Some of My Lives: A Scrapbook Memoir.* New York: Farrar, Straus and Giroux, 2011.

Biddle, Francis. *A Casual Past.* New York: Doubleday, 1961.

Bitter, Marietta. *Pentacle: The Story of Carlos Salzedo and the Harp.* Salzedo Committee of the American Harp Society, 2010.

Burgwyn, Diana. *Seventy-Five Years of the Curtis Institute of Music: A Narrative Portrait.* Philadelphia: Curtis Institute of Music, 1999.

Burt, Nathaniel. *The Perennial Philadelphians: The Anatomy of an American Aristocracy.* Boston: Little, Brown, 1963.

Chasins, Abram. *Leopold Stokowski: A Profile.* New York: Hawthorn Books, 1979.

Collins, Gail. *America's Women: Four Hundred Years of Dolls, Drudges, Helpmates, and Heroines.* New York: William Morrow, 2003.

Curtis Institute of Music. *Overtones.* 50th Anniversary Issue, vol. 11, no. 1 (October 1, 1974).

Daniel, Oliver. *Stokowski: A Counterpoint of View.* New York: Dodd, Mead, 1982.

Ewen, David. *Men and Women Who Make Music.* New York: Thomas Y. Crowell, 1939.

————. *Music Comes to America.* New York: Allen, Towne & Heath, 1947.

Gabler, Neal. *Walt Disney: The Triumph of the American Imagination.* New York: Knopf, 2006.

Graffman, Gary. *I Really Should Be Practicing.* Garden City, N.Y.: Doubleday, 1981.

Greenfield, Howard. *The Devil and Dr. Barnes: Portrait of an American Art Collector.* New York: Viking Penguin, 1987.

Hall, Ben M. *The Best Remaining Seats: The Golden Age of the Movie Palace.* New York: Da Capo Press, 1988.

Horowitz, Joseph. *Classical Music in America: A History of Its Rise and Fall.* New York: Norton, 2005.

Hutchison, Peter. *Stefan Heym: The Perpetual Dissident.* New York: Cambridge University Press, 1992.

Jímenez, Heather. *But I Wouldn't Want to Live There.* New York: E. P. Dutton, 1958.

Kline, Donna Staley. *An American Virtuoso on the World Stage: Olga Samaroff Stokowski.* College Station: Texas A&M Press, 1996.

Kupferberg, Herbert. *Those Fabulous Philadelphians: The Life and Times of a Great Orchestra.* New York: Charles Scribner's Sons, 1969.

Lawrence, Lucile, and Carlos Salzedo. *Method for the Harp.* New York: G. Shirmer, 1929.

Lebrecht, Norman. *The Maestro Myth: Great Conductors in Pursuit of Power.* New York: Birch Lane Press, 1991.

Locke, Ralph P., and Cyrilla Barr. *Cultivating Music in America.* Berkeley: University of California Press, 1997.

Marion, John Francis. *Within These Walls: A History of the Academy of Music in Philadelphia.* Philadelphia: Academy of Music Restoration Office, 1984.

Mueller, John H. *The American Symphony Orchestra: A Social History of Musical Taste.* Bloomington: Indiana University Press, 1957.

Neuls-Bates, Carol, ed. *Women in Music: An Anthology of Source Readings from the Middle Ages to the Present.* Boston: Northeastern University Press, 1995.

O'Connell, Charles. *The Other Side of the Record.* New York: Alfred A. Knopf, 1948.

Opperby, Preben. *Stokowski.* Tunbridge Wells, England: Midas Books, 1982.

Owens, Dewey. *Carlos Salzedo: From Aeolus to Thunder.* Chicago: Lyon & Healy, 1993.

Parker, Robert L. *Carlos Chávez: A Guide to Research.* New York: Garland Publishing, 1998.

Pendle, Karin, ed. *Women and Music: A History.* 2nd ed. Bloomington: Indiana University Press, 2001.

PBS. *Battle of the Bulge: The Deadliest Battle of World War II.* American Experience, PBS, 1994.

Rensch, Roslyn. *Harps and Harpists.* Bloomington: Indiana University Press, 1989.

Robinson, Paul. *Stokowski: The Art of the Conductor.* Toronto: Lester and Orpen, 1977.

Rodriguez-Peralta, Phyllis W. *Philadelphia Maestros: Ormandy, Muti, Sawallisch.* Philadelphia: Temple University Press, 2006.

Schonberg, Harold C. *The Great Conductors.* New York: Simon and Schuster, 1967.

Seib, Philip. *The Player: Christy Mathewson, Baseball, and the American Century.* New York: Four Walls Eight Windows, 2003.

Shanet, Howard. *Philharmonic: A History of New York's Orchestra.* New York: Doubleday, 1975.

Siegel, Adrian. *Concerto for Camera: A Photographic Portrait of the Philadelphia Orchestra.* Philadelphia: Philadelphia Orchestra Association, 1972.

Smith, William Ander. *The Mystery of Leopold Stokowski.* Rutherford, N.J.: Fairleigh Dickinson University Press, 1990.

Stokowski, Leopold. *Music for All of Us.* New York: Simon and Schuster, 1943.

Storch, Laila. *Marcel Tabuteau: How Do You Expect to Play the Oboe If You Can't Peel a Mushroom?* Bloomington: Indiana University Press, 2008.

Toff, Nancy. *Monarch of the Flute: The Life of Georges Barrère.* New York: Oxford University Press, 2005.

Varèse, Louise. *Varèse: A Looking-Glass Diary.* New York: W. W. Norton, 1972.

Whiting, Charles. *Ghost Front: The Ardennes Before the Battle of the Bulge.* Cambridge, Mass.: Da Capo, 2002.

Wister, Frances Anne. *Twenty-five Years of the Philadelphia Orchestra, 1900–1925.* Philadelphia: Women's Committees for the Philadelphia Orchestra, 1925.

Wright, Catharine Morris. *The Color of Life.* Boston: Houghton Mifflin, 1957.

# INDEX

MARY SUE WELSH is a former executive director of the Bach Festival of Philadelphia, where she worked with its chair Edna Phillips. She lives in Philadelphia.

# MUSIC IN AMERICAN LIFE

The University of Illinois Press
is a founding member of the
Association of American University Presses.

---

Designed by Jim Proefrock
Composed in 10.25/13 Fairfield
with Victorian and Eccentric display
at the University of Illinois Press
Manufactured by Thomson-Shore, Inc.

University of Illinois Press
1325 South Oak Street
Champaign, IL 61820-6903
www.press.uillinois.edu